THE CHILD GAZE

Children's Literature Association Series

THE CHILD GAZE

Narrating Resistance in American Literature

Amanda M. Greenwell

University Press of Mississippi / Jackson

The University Press of Mississippi is the scholarly publishing agency of
the Mississippi Institutions of Higher Learning: Alcorn State University,
Delta State University, Jackson State University, Mississippi State University,
Mississippi University for Women, Mississippi Valley State University,
University of Mississippi, and University of Southern Mississippi.

www.upress.state.ms.us

The University Press of Mississippi is a member
of the Association of University Presses.

Portions of this work have appeared in altered forms in African American Review and Studies in the American Short Story.

Amanda M. Greenwell's "Aesthetic Resistance: Racist Visual Tropes and the Oppositional Gaze in Joel Christian Gill's Tales of the Talented Tenth" first appeared in African American Review, vol. 53, no. 3, Fall 2020, pp. 181–200. Copyright © 2020 Johns Hopkins University Press and St. Louis University.

Amanda M. Greenwell's "The Narrative Dynamics of a Counter-Surveillant Child Gaze in Langston Hughes's 'Red-Headed Baby'" first appeared in Studies in the American Short Story, vol. 1, no. 1, 2020, pp. 86–94. https://doi.org/10.5325/studamershorstor.1.1.0086. Used with permission from Penn State University Press.

Excerpt(s) from ROLL OF THUNDER, HEAR MY CRY by Mildred D. Taylor, text copyright © 1976 by Mildred D. Taylor. Used by permission of Dial Books for Young Readers, an imprint of Penguin Young Readers Group, a division of Penguin Random House LLC. All rights reserved.

Any discriminatory or derogatory language or hate speech regarding race, ethnicity, religion, sex, gender, class, national origin, age, or disability that has been retained or appears in elided form is in no way an endorsement of the use of such language outside a scholarly context.

Copyright © 2024 by University Press of Mississippi
All rights reserved
Manufactured in the United States of America

∞

Library of Congress Cataloging-in-Publication Data to come

Names: Greenwell, Amanda M., author.
Title: The child gaze : narrating resistance in American literature / Amanda M. Greenwell.
Other titles: Children's Literature Association series.
Description: Jackson : University Press of Mississippi, 2024. |
Series: Children's literature association series |
Includes bibliographical references and index.
Identifiers: LCCN 2024026131 (print) | LCCN 2024026132 (ebook) |
ISBN 9781496854544 (hardback) | ISBN 9781496854551 (trade paperback) | ISBN 9781496854568 (epub) | ISBN 9781496854575 (epub) | ISBN 9781496854582 (pdf) | ISBN 9781496854599 (pdf)
Subjects: LCSH: Gaze in literature. | Children in literature. |
American literature—20th century—History and criticism. |
American literature—21st century—History and criticism. |
Visual perception in literature. | Visualization in literature. |
BISAC: LITERARY CRITICISM / Children's & Young Adult Literature |
LITERARY CRITICISM / Semiotics & Theory
Classification: LCC PN56.V543 G74 2024 (print) | LCC PN56.V543 (ebook) |
DDC 813/.5093523—dc23/eng/20240828
LC record available at https://lccn.loc.gov/2024026131
LC ebook record available at https://lccn.loc.gov/2024026132

British Library Cataloging-in-Publication Data available

*For my father,
who taught us the art of observation
and the power of a look*

The world changes according to the way people see it, and if you alter, even by a millimeter, the way a person looks or people look at reality, then you can change it.
—JAMES BALDWIN

CONTENTS

Acknowledgments xi

Introduction: The Power and Possibilities of Centering
Child Sight Lines 3

Chapter One: The Appreciative Child Gaze:
Valuing Visions of Marginalized Childhoods 21

Chapter Two: The Countersurveillant Child Gaze:
Looking Back at Authority 54

Chapter Three: The Transactional Child Gaze:
Wrestling with Ideology in the Visual Surround 97

Chapter Four: Comics Form and Materialization
of the Child Gaze 133

Epilogue: Envisioning Avenues for Further Study 170

Notes 175

Works Cited 183

Index 195

ACKNOWLEDGMENTS

This book came about with the support of many academic and personal communities, and I am forever indebted to them for their generosity. Katharine Capshaw, Victoria Ford Smith, and Anna Mae Duane, your invaluable excitement about this project, engaged feedback on many early chapter drafts, and smart advice for the shape of the book made this volume possible. You anchored my efforts and made them matter, and I am in awe of you. David Cappella and Christine Doyle, you treated me as if I had written a book before I'd even decided to do it. That depth of belief is incredibly motivating. Everyone should be so lucky to have such mentors. I will always pay it forward.

My colleagues at Central Connecticut State University welcomed me in and held space for me while I wrote. Mary Anne Nunn, Mary Collins, and Candace Barrington, you are inimitable. Stephen Ostrowski, Melissa Mentzer, Aimee Pozorski, Leyla Zidani-Eroglu, Brian Folker, Gilbert Gigliotti, Stephen Cohen, Eric Leonidas, Jotham Burrello, Katherine Sugg, Matthew Ciscel, and Elena Koulidobrova, you each had a hand in opening doors to opportunities and closing them against threats of mismanaged time and unreasonable demands. You shared laughter and rants and made sure that I had the encouragement and the savvy to follow this project to completion. The sentiment is worth repeating: Everyone should be so lucky to have such mentors. I will always pay it forward.

Amanda Fields, Julia Blau, and Kimberly Meyer, the faculty writing circle we began is a gift, as is our camaraderie. Cristina Rhodes, Nicole Lawrence, Hayley Stefan, Lakmali Jayasinghe, Julien Strong, Meaghan Davis, Michael Bartone, Candice Wallace, Aimee Loiselle, Thomas Ratliff, Jennifer Cote, Jessyka Scoppetta, and the many, many folks with whom I've shared both the challenges and delights of wrangling ideas into words while handling university life during the necessary pit stops, food, drinks, zooms, or walks along the way, writing alongside all of you has been inspirational.

Shawn Salvant and Kathy Knapp, you were the first readers to respond to the manuscript as a whole in its earliest form, and your keen questions and sincere encouragement propelled me forward.

Kiedra Burston Taylor, your friendship and brilliance helped me keep this project at the forefront of my mind, and your responses to very late chapter drafts buoyed me through. I can't wait for your own book.

Thank you to the conferences of academic organizations at which I presented and received valuable feedback on portions of this work, including the Children's Literature Association, the Modern Language Association, the Society for the Study of Multi-Ethnic Literature of the United States, the Young Adult Literature Association, the Society for the Study of the American Short Story, and the American Literature Association. Thanks to Central Connecticut State University and CSU-AAUP for the reassigned time and travel funds that enabled these endeavors, and thanks to Brian Matzke, digital librarian extraordinaire, for the image scanning assistance.

To the editors at the University Press of Mississippi and the anonymous manuscript readers, thank you for your praise and your insights. Katie Keene, you sent me a letter about my work before this book was ready to exist, and I am so glad it eventually found a home at your press. I also gratefully acknowledge *African American Review* and *Studies in the American Short Story* for publishing earlier versions of portions of the introduction and the second and fourth chapters.

And finally, to my family and family-in-law, you offered me the love, joy, and help that I needed before I even had to ask for it. I treasure your gifts of time, your respect for my focus, and your ever-present comfort. Mom and Dad, your support means the world to me. Rob, Nolan, Sean, and Connel, you are my everything. I love you, and I see you.

THE CHILD GAZE

Introduction

THE POWER AND POSSIBILITIES OF CENTERING CHILD SIGHT LINES

In Mildred D. Taylor's 1976 historical fiction novel for young people, *Roll of Thunder, Hear My Cry*, nine-year-old Cassie Logan watches, frozen, as cars full of powerful white men, visible only as a string of headlights that look "like cat eyes in the night," swoop toward her Black family's farmhouse (67). In Philip Roth's 2004 allohistorical novel for adults, *The Plot against America*, young Philip looks out at monument park in Washington, DC, and feels "expelled" for his Jewishness (66). In Betty Smith's 1943 semiautobiographical novel *A Tree Grows in Brooklyn*, school-aged Francie Nolan refuses to write the "beautiful" stories her teacher requires because they are not true to what she sees—quite literally—as an Irish American girl growing up in the deep poverty of Brooklyn tenements (328). And in Gene Luen Yang's 2006 graphic novel *American Born Chinese*, adolescent Jin repeatedly stares directly out of the page at a reader, as if asking for a nod of understanding as he navigates the white-dominated world of his California high school.

Appearing in texts about childhood experiences in the United States, these ideologically charged acts of looking exhibit the evocative narrative technique that is the subject of this book: the child gaze. By placing the child within a sociopolitical environment laden with visual ideological signals and by narrating the child's sight lines in relation to them, these texts activate their critique of narrow, exclusionary definitions of belonging in the United States. Cassie's racialized fear is evident in her frozen stare, just as the racial hierarchy of her world is evident in the headlights' predatory appearance; narrating her act of looking allows the text to countersurveil agents of racism in 1930s Mississippi. Philip's profound sense of outsiderness is made manifest in the contrast between the "paradise" he sees and the knowledge of how he is seen by its white, Christian members, and his gaze becomes the text's vehicle for laying bare the ethnic exclusion possible in and often built into US government spaces. The clash between Francie's and her teacher's aesthetics arises from their class-based perspectives on the "ugly" and the "beautiful," and Francie's insistence upon what she can see from her vantage point reflects the text's insistence upon the worthiness of her lens as a working-class girl. And Jin's direct gaze emphasizes his lack of connection in a nation that demeans his Chinese appearance and identity, demanding the reader acknowledge the racist attitudes that have implications for the choices of Asian American teens. It is the rhetorical effect of the child gaze that energizes this project: how it mobilizes a text's confrontation of exclusion.

The Child Gaze: Narrating Resistance in American Literature examines how twentieth- and twenty-first century literature in the United States—including but not limited to literature written for young people—employs the child gaze as a powerful narrative tool for social critique, specifically regarding narrow understandings of national belonging. It takes "gaze" literally, focusing on the precise narrative cues enabled by representations of child acts of looking. In doing so, it maps a legacy of children in twentieth- and twenty-first century US literature who look in ways that confront hegemonic ideologies of race, ethnicity, creed, class, and at times their intersections with gender—all categories of critical importance to hierarchies of inclusion and exclusion in the United States. *The Child Gaze* considers how and why children matter when their looking performs this cultural disruption, and it likewise contemplates how, on the level of narrative, such looking both performs and invites critique of privileged narratives of national identity.

In undertaking this examination, *The Child Gaze* weaves together lines of inquiry heretofore largely separate: scholarship on the construction of the American child, visual studies, and narrative theory. It investigates how acts of looking, performed by children in various texts across the better part of a century, function narratologically on diegetic, extradiegetic, and aspirationally extratextual levels, directing the attention of the implied reader and positing the child's sight lines as signals to renegotiate hegemonic understandings of belonging and value. It theorizes those sight lines in three modes over the course of the first three chapters—appreciative, countersurveillant, and transactional—by demonstrating their nuances across several representative texts each. In the fourth and final chapter, it turns to a particularly expressive form for acts of child looking—comics—which implicates the reader in the relay of gazes performed on the page. *The Child Gaze* posits that the modes of the child gaze laid out in this study exhibit methods, both subversive and bold, by which US literature brings into relief ways of looking that disrupt scripts of power and widen the lens through which belonging in the United States can be understood.

The child characters this book analyzes are inheritors of a national history in which rhetorics of childhood performed powerful state-sanctioned and state-defying messaging. Theorists of the child have long understood this figure as a touchstone for changing cultural ideologies and US identity in particular, which has been tied to the child via concepts such as rebellion, infancy, and idealized youthfulness. Anna Mae Duane, Caroline F. Levander, and Karen Sánchez-Eppler have demonstrated the link between the child and the state in the centuries leading up to and following the American revolution, paying attention to the figure's centrality in fraught discourses about nationhood and racialized and class-based social divisions.[1] Robin Bernstein's formulation of "racial innocence" further emphasizes how children and discourses about them highlight and resist dominant narratives in US culture, where innocence is historically "raced white" (*Racial* 4). According to Bernstein, performances of childhood, real or imagined, play a significant part in the American political arena, often "justify[ing] granting or withholding the rights of living adults and children" (3). The child, sutured to American ideologies in various states of flux, is a flashpoint for ideological friction.

That friction manifests in the contradictory valences the child figure encapsulates. Sánchez-Eppler writes about the "mutability" of childhood as a concept, the protean qualities embedded in a stage of life not bound by rigid borders but rather "transitional," and therefore rife with possibilities (xxv). Historically, the child has served as a conduit for both progressive and conservative political movements, and literature has reflected and joined such efforts. Levander and Carol J. Singley note that writers in the United States often employ the figure of the child in order to think through issues of national identity, especially "seiz[ing] upon the image of the child in opposition to that which is constructed or institutionalized [. . . and] promot[ing] the child as force of resistance as well as innocent vulnerability" (4). Scholars such as Julia Mickenberg, Katharine Capshaw, Nazera Sadiq Wright, Lara Saguisag, and Emily A. Murphy have explored how US literature for or about children shapes and maps tensions in conflicts over national belonging, showing us the multivalent, subversive, and slippery ways child figures wield various ideologies on the literary page.[2]

Like many of these scholars, I am interested in the way the literary figure of the child manifests and resists cultural norms. In particular, I am interested in how the ways of looking I set forth here, wielded by the literary figure of the child, perform narrative sleights of hand by conjuring the child's complex ties to national belonging even as they propose the need to rearrange them. I also contend that many of the texts that represent these ideologically powerful ways of looking on the part of the child tend to harness modified notions of the "innocent" or "deserving" child in order to characterize the political undertones of their looking as right and worth emulating. If Levander and Singley claim that "inextricably linked to understanding of the self, the family, and the nation, the concept of childhood offers a unique lens from which to glimpse assumed, neglected, or hidden processes of cultural signification" (11), then this book examines the implications of the *literalization* of the child as lens—the presentation of the child's eye and its sight lines—in texts where the child performs acts of looking that do not just "offer glimpse[s]" but invite extended "viewing" of cultural signification and its potential disruption. *The Child Gaze* looks to and with the child figures who notice—for themselves and for their readers—facets of US culture that arbitrate belonging.

These facets are endemic to the circumstances of the fictional children discussed in this book. Most of them are marked as outsiders to institutional power and national belonging in the United States, whether by race, ethnicity, class, creed, gender, or a combination thereof. Their positions at the margin often result from their not fitting into the white, middle-class, Christian paradigms that have driven racist and classist definitions of "the American people," narrow paradigms that create an illusory and damaging image of what "American" means. This book does not assume a uniform US culture—indeed, the texts I examine rather focus on the subdivisions, gaps, and counterexistences that belie the myth of cohesion, which rests upon those whom it subordinates. And one way to understand the figure of the child as theorized herein is that all of the child characters under discussion—even those who reside relatively further within the parameters of hegemonic standards of national belonging—are marked as outsider to institutional power by their very age category as young people. This quality of age-related exclusion makes any of their political interventions on the literary page particularly compelling, especially given contradictory cultural mandates about looking in relation to children. In her introduction to the spring 2020 issue of *Children's Literature Association Quarterly*, Sara K. Day remarks on some of those mandates as they appear in common parlance:

> [There are] myriad ways that young people are caught up in systems of looking, perhaps best represented by the various prepositions we attach to that verb: children are looked at and looked after; children look to and look for; children remind us of the past we look back on and represent the future we look forward to . . . characters in children's and young adult literature, especially marginalized characters,

are frequently figured as objects that others are invited or feel welcome to stare at and comment on. (1)

Now outdated but nevertheless persistent adages such as "children should be seen, not heard" also attest to the objectification against which these texts write.

That children occupy a particularly visible position in US culture also, however, invests them with a certain type of power: they can focus attention. Lydia Kokkola notes the "primacy of the *adult* gaze" in relation to the embodied child, a gaze biologically and culturally "sanctioned" since it is necessary to child survival and care (11). Surveillance scholars Gary T. Marx and Valerie Steeves track the long-standing practice and continuing rise of the surveillance of children in the United States, not only by parents but also by educational, healthcare, corporate, private, and governmental institutions, who under the aegis of safety tend to observe them in order to "identify and 'manage' genetic or behavioural deviations from the norm" (193). They also point out that when surveilling institutions do allow children to act as observers, such allowance exists to align the child with commercial or state interests (206). Given the ongoing cultural practices that seek to inform and limit children's modes of looking—from the imperatives to "Look!" in early readers and *Where's Waldo*-style search-and-finds to the rise of age-related restrictions in ratings systems for the highly visual modes of television, film, and digital games—the child is a particularly subversive figure for enacting a type of looking that confronts institutional prerogatives about what should be seen and who is allowed to see it, especially when "it" involves failures of national inclusion.

For children who look are fraught cultural conduits who might accept, reject, or revise the conditions into which they have been born. bell hooks, in the opening paragraphs of her chapter "The Oppositional Gaze" in *Black Looks: Race and Representation*, anchors her theory in childhood, and it is thus worth citing her remarks at length.

> When thinking about black female spectatorship, I remember being punished as a child for staring, for those hard intense direct looks children would give grown-ups, looks that were seen as confrontational, as gestures of resistance, challenges to authority. The "gaze" has always been political in my life. Imagine the terror felt by the child who has come to understand through repeated punishments that one's gaze can be dangerous. The child who has learned so well to look the other way when necessary. Yet, when punished, the child is told by parents, "Look at me when I talk to you." Only, the child is afraid to look. Afraid to look, but fascinated by the gaze. There is power in looking.

> ... Since I knew as a child that the dominating power adults exercised over me and over my gaze was never so absolute that I did not dare to look, to sneak a peep, to stare dangerously, I knew that the slaves had looked. That all attempts to repress our/black peoples' right to gaze had produced in us an overwhelming longing to look, a rebellious desire, an oppositional gaze. By courageously looking, we defiantly declared: "Not only will I stare. I want my look to change reality." Even in the worse circumstances of domination, the ability to manipulate one's gaze in the face of structures of domination that would contain it, opens up the possibility of agency. (115–16)

hooks's rumination crystallizes several notions foundational to this project. The gaze is about the affective and often hierarchical relationship between subject and object, and it is inextricable from the often-racialized context in which gazing is permitted and punished. The gaze is itself power-laden, manifested and disputed by contradictory mandates, and it is, therefore, a destabilizing act. The gaze is a right, even if a dangerous one to enact, and that very danger makes it all the more necessary to assert its intervention: to claim one's agency, and to potentially "change reality." And, crucially, the impulse to gaze is strongly tied to the experiences and impulses of childhood.

Duane remarks in her introduction to *The Children's Table: Childhood Studies and the Humanities* that children are "often seen as peripheral to the important work of understanding social, political, national, and ethnic structures," and that studying childhood can reorient our understandings of "what constitutes knowledge and what animates the work of power and resistance" (1). The children in this book are disenfranchised by age and more within their storyworlds, and yet they are also positioned as particularly powerful figures in their texts via the exertion and narrative effect of their gazes. Thus, all of them perform along the spectrum of outsiderness and insiderness, weaving in and out of the very power structures that work to relegate them to the nation's peripheral vision. What—and how—they see from those vantage points carries significant ideological weight.

This study investigates how literature that employs children who look from the margins manages to center the looking child, moving them from periphery to foreground by redrawing the circle of inclusion around the locus of their gaze. It focuses on literal acts of looking performed by embodied children that, in turn, perform as narrative cues to the implied reader, directing their attention and eliciting their complicity. Certainly, "gazes" can be more generally conjured by various elements in a text and, therefore, metaphorically understood, but it is the actual representation of the child's physical acts of looking that form the raw material of this study. I am less interested in assumptions made about age-related fields of vision—which tend to remark (and often in far too general and even erroneous terms) about how children, as a monolithic group, must figuratively and preciously "see" the big wide world—than I am in the literally depicted act of a fictionalized child looking at various elements in their storyworlds. It is in these instances that a text presents the child character as an embodied and mentally agential actor in a specifically rendered ideological environment, thus eschewing generalities that tend to result in pat truisms about children viewing the world differently than adults do.[3]

Those specific ideological environments are carefully constructed by texts that contain a child character who looks evocatively. Visual studies theorist Irit Rogoff has noted that privileged legacies of Western thought "produced a notion of vision in the service of a particular politics or ideology and populated it with a select set of images, viewed through specific apparatuses and serving the needs of distinct subjectivities" (21). Such production of vision constitutes a "gaze," in one particular meaning of the word—what Shawn Michelle Smith defines as "a dominant mode of looking that is culturally sanctioned as well as circumscribed and often contested" ("Guest" 3). Apparatuses tied to government, commerce, textbooks, and media, for instance, promulgate a heavily curated visual culture that upholds white, male, Christian, middle-class ways of seeing and constructions of nation and citizenship. All of the texts this book discusses are written in relation to these constructions; most of the texts represent some facet of those conditions, and those that do not I read as obliquely writing against them, for they inform the historical context of the work's publication.

But looking back at these conditions is possible, as bell hooks asserts in her theory of the Black feminist "oppositional gaze" (*Black*), and as Fatima Tobing Rony makes clear in her theory of the "third eye," an agentic form of resistance enacted by people subjected to negative ethnographic spectacle. hooks and Rony both emphasize the vantage point of "opposition" or "returning the gaze" as repelling and therefore empowering, an act asserting the individual against the paradigms created by the male gaze (Mulvey), the white gaze (Yancy), and the colonial gaze (Said). I am thus indebted to scholars whose work on the gaze has focused on documentation, disruption, or complication of power structures and binaries—especially those involving race and gender.[4] I build on their work most overtly in chapter two's treatment of the countersurveillent child gaze, but it also inspires and informs much of the work in this book, which details gazes enacted with different inflections by a wide cast of characters, all of whom look in ways that push back at the hegemonic US imaginary. Their gazing threatens to invert or collapse its hierarchies and posits the child, in all of its protean power, as a site of resistance.

I also extend their work by considering the ways that several other modes of looking perform disruption of hegemonic visions, including an appreciative gaze that turns away from the powers that be to privilege a milieu often pushed to the periphery (in chapter one), and a transactional gaze that emphasizes subjectivity-in-process (in chapter three). In each case, I demonstrate how these modes of looking draw upon cultural constructions of the child to ignite the power of the child gaze in the text. In all, I theorize the child's gaze as a discursive narrative tool that functions as a strategy of contest in the hegemonic "field of vision" (Rogoff 22).

In examining the discursive quality of the child gaze and the narrative cues it affords, I pay close attention to acts of looking as they are written on the page. A work in any narrative perspective might describe a room into which a character walks with a sentence such as, "There were bookshelves on the wall and a well-worn chair by the window." The sentence makes clear the objects a child might see within that environment, but it omits the child's act of looking as the locus of the narration. The inflection of such a description works quite differently when its disposition includes being directed by a character's gaze. "I noticed the bookshelves" or "She looked at the well-worn chair" energizes a closer relation between character and setting, between child and environment, than does the previous statement. Casting the child as the literal and often grammatical subject of the gazing act draws attention to its performance by the child, weighting the look with meaning because of its relationality.

That relationality undergirds a key understanding of this project, that the child gaze makes an object, event, person, or image *noticeable* not only in relation to its environment but also in relation to the embodied child in the storyworld, the written child on the literary page who sees it, and the text in which it appears. Furthermore, these moments of child gazing elicit reactions from the implied reader, who both notices the character performing the action and participates in the character's looking. In rhetorical narrative theory, the implied reader's imagined reactions are referred to as "readerly dynamics," and they are prompted by "textual dynamics," or the features of the text as it unfolds over the progression of the narrative (Herman et al. 6). I use the terms "implied reader" or "authorial audience" to refer to the "ideal reader" of a text (Phelan 4), though I understand that it is a fraught concept that requires a cultural positioning and espouses an idealism not always met in reality by the flesh-and-blood reader. Still, the implied reader remains a useful concept in the study of textual dynamics, and, indeed, one way I propose we study the child gaze is as a method the text uses to conjure its ideal reader—by directing them not only to look but also to consider a particular way of looking and its implications.

Considering the relationship between textual and readerly dynamics can help us make sense of a text's rhetorical power as it is drawn from what narrative theorist Shlomith Rimmon-Kenan refers to as an event's "disposition in the text" (3). Peter J. Rabinowitz notes how depictions of eyes matter to a reader's understanding of character (88), as well how a character's focused attention calls readerly attention to both that interest and its object (55). That association between character and object I understand to be inherently ideological, following Mikhail Bakhtin's formulation that "the person in a novel may act—but such action is always highlighted by ideology, is always harnessed to the character's discourse (even if that discourse is as yet only a potential discourse), is associated with an ideological motif and occupies a definite ideological position" (334). The phrase "potential discourse" is especially applicable to the situation of some of these literary children, who exist along a spectrum of knowing and not-knowing regarding the ideological valences of their own looking, and who can also be depicted as silent, even in their interior thoughts, about what they have seen. It is the discourse of the gaze—potential or realized—that the texts harness to make their interventions, on the level of narrative, into conceptions of national belonging.

Consider this instance in Jesse Jackson's 1945 novel *Call Me Charley*, which is also discussed in chapter two. Charley, the first Black boy to live in his white neighborhood, meets Tom and George, two white boys, for the first time. After their initial conversation, during which George expresses his racism and targets Charley, George and Tom talk privately. George's earlier dialogue provides a context clue that the conversation is about Charley's unbelonging, but rather than continue to privilege George's words, the text concerns itself with the fact that Charley is too far away from his peers to hear the conversation. That distance, crucially, allows the novel to comment on the fact that he can see it happening: "Charley watched them stand and talk for a while. George seemed excited" (Jackson 9). With these lines, the text withholds the conversation's verbal content (otherwise easily reported through its third-person narration) and instead recounts Charley's act of looking before making a subtle comment about that looking that privileges Charley's perspective: "George seemed excited." The note about Charley's watching is the transition into a very brief focalizing moment with which the text centers his vantage point rather than that of the white boys. His gaze also allows the text to provide extended attention to George's racism—what has made him "excited"—without further indulging its verbal form, and it is also the way the text postures solidarity with Charley in resistance to

George's behavior. It is important to note that while this example employs focalization, the effect of the child gaze is not always due to that narrative technique, nor is it dependent on narrative "person" or point of view. Also in chapter two, for instance, I discuss the remarkable case of Langston Hughes's "Red-Headed Baby," where the titular baby is neither a focalizing agent nor a narrator, but he nevertheless engages in one very powerful act of looking.[5]

Ultimately, the effect of the child gaze as theorized in this book is predicated upon the embodied act of a diegetic character, who may or may not be a focalizing entity in the narrative, whose gaze resonates inside and outside of the storyworld. That is, their gaze constitutes a diegetic (within the storyworld) action and simultaneously enacts an extradiegetic (reaching outside of the storyworld) cue that may have extratextual impact.[6] In this way, the narrative function of the child gaze relies on several narratological dimensions of character. The first is mimetic, where the character seems to be a realistic child within the storyworld; the second is synthetic, where the character is understood to be a crafted, artificial construct within a crafted piece of literature; and the third is thematic, where the character aids in conveying a larger concept with which the text seems concerned.[7] Some dimensions are stronger than others at various points in any story, and I contend that during moments of ideologically charged child gazing, all three are energized to create subtle yet powerful effects. Diegetic resonances of the gaze are a result of the mimetic child performing an act of looking within the storyworld, and extradiegetic and extratextual resonances have to do with the way the synthetic character's actions direct readerly attention and, ultimately, achieve thematic impact.

In addition, the readerly engagement the text constructs, wherein the reader is prompted to watch an act of looking in which they may also vicariously participate, doubly focuses attention on the act of looking, making it a potent narrative tool for the cultural work endemic in the figure of the child. The child who looks has gravity—we are drawn to them—and the child's gaze is an illuminator—we follow its signals. Together, these literary children and their gazes are meaning-makers, active arrangers of that which they perceive in their world. Looking, as an act, implies a certain faculty of mind in the child without necessitating that the child articulate or ruminate on it; the attention that looking implies is, itself, a type of agency. Mimetic child characters notice things, and their synthetic noticing has profound thematic implications for how their texts ask readers to understand the world.

Thus, children who look are well positioned to act as trojan horses for the myriad ways of looking that literature ushers into readerly consciousness. As a figure often sutured to US ideologies, but whose relation to them is complicated by categories of exclusion related to age, race, ethnicity, class, creed, and gender, the child who looks in literary texts like those in this study makes visible to the reader not just the objects of their gaze but also *their modes of looking*, which have the potential to disrupt scripts of power.

There are important affective implications of the child gaze as well. As Jean Paul Sartre suggests in *Being and Nothingness*, when we see one who looks, we understand that they "apprehend" the world in a way specific to their own subjectivity (343). The literary text, in representing looking, invites the implied reader to recognize and, in some cases, inhabit the apprehension of that character. Patrick Colm Hogan points out that facial expressions elicit human reactions due to our innate biological makeup (240), and we react to literature with the same perceptual system as we do to our real world (Blau and Capetta). Susan Keen postulates that readerly empathy arises, in part, from the activity of our mirror neurons—the "possibil[ity] that descriptions of characters' dispositions in space or in imagined locations of prose or verse fictional storyworlds call upon readers' motor mimicry" (128). When the character who looks is a child situated in ideological spaces, that child's looking also engineers readerly attention to those spaces and their relation to the child—as well as, potentially, empathy for that child, thus positioning the child gaze as a powerful rhetorical force. Indeed, Jim Phelan points out that "narratives explicitly or more often implicitly establish their own ethical standards in order to guide their audiences to particular ethical judgments" (10); as is evident in the close readings throughout this book, the child gaze is one method of that guidance.

Combining narrative theory with critical race theory and other approaches that consider texts within a larger sociopolitical conversation is imperative to understanding the resonance of that guidance. Sue J. Kim, Catherine Romagnolo, Jennifer Ann Ho, and other contributors to James J. Donahue, Jennifer Ann Ho, and Shaun Morgan's edited collection *Narrative, Race, and Ethnicity in the United States* point out that critical race studies and narrative theory are compatible in several ways, including their shared interest in how embodied and mental experiences are represented on the literary page (Kim "What") and in the argument that race, nation, and narrative are all constructs worth critiquing (Ho 208).[8] Critical race narratology shares with feminist and queer branches of narrative theory an interest in "decentering a narratological criticism that assumes a white, male heterosexual, Euro-American subject" (Romagnolo 43). Indeed, Shaun Morgan's note about focalization is especially useful to moments of the child gaze that are not necessarily focalized by the child but are nevertheless narrated by what he terms a "culturally-focalized narrator," which "is not embodied in a single perceiving subject" and "illustrates the ways narration can convey the psychological and social significance of race as an identity and the ways the control of information made possible by narration can affect the interpretation of raced narratives" (150–51). In *Call Me Charley*, for instance, that dip into Charley's perception ("George seemed excited") is rare, but the text otherwise postures in line with Black sensitivities of the 1940s when it uses Charley's gaze to point to noticeable visual markers of the environment, even without his comment thereon. That pointing, to use Morgan's words, highlights the "structural, social conditions" (161) of his lived experience as a Black boy.[9]

Situating texts in their respective historical moments, therefore, is paramount to considerations of the child gaze. Romagnolo calls for overcoming the division between race and ethnic studies and narrative theory by examining the "complex interplay between the formal and contextual elements" of literature (58), and the contextual elements under study in this book are many: constructions of the child in the West and in particular the United States (discussed at further length in chapter one), the era and lived experiences of the authors of the texts, the sociopolitical moments attendant upon the publication of the literature and in some cases its form, and more. This book is not aiming to contribute to a narrative theory that pretends to be "transcendent, universal, ahistorical" (Kim, "Introduction" 237) but rather sets forth a theory of the child gaze as enacted in this select yet representative set of narratives. The formulations are not so much abstract as phenomenological, and narrative theory provides a vocabulary for parsing their nuances, especially as we attend to their contexts.

Narratological attention to the child figure is much needed. In the volume referenced above, only Roy Pérez directs attention to a young character, the queer Latino child. While Pérez's work does not engage questions of the gaze, the premise of studying "how narrative acts, theorized as performances in their world making capacity, can approximate something other than the familiar, rote, and even deadening affects of racial and sexual normativity" (194) finds resonance in *The Child Gaze*. Meanwhile, scholars of children's literature such as Sara K. Day and Mike Cadden have exhibited that narrative theory is a useful lens to apply to children's literature but have not yet focused on child characters whose gaze confronts the ideologies that attempt to subjugate them.[10] *The Child Gaze* argues that narratological attention to representations of the figure of the child—which is itself a construct on the page and in the national imagination—in US literature for children and adults provides a much needed contribution to the ways we consider narrated figures in relation to age, race, ethnicity, class, creed, gender, and the various categories upon which the nation builds exclusionary notions of belonging. Because children are liminal figures in relation to institutional power and personal agency within national mandates—supposedly both protected and disciplined, for instance, by institutions such as compulsory schooling—they open up productive avenues for examining alternate perspectives from positions of subordination. Centering these children's sight lines postures us to consider the power latent in such peripheral visions.

A handful of scholars in the field of children's literature have examined the looking child in article-length pieces. Eric L. Tribunella has authored two pieces that link the child to the figure of the flâneur in children's literature of the modern city, arguing that the gaze of the child flâneur allays fears about the effects of modernity. Emma Hayes reads gendered gazing as a socializing process in *The Secret Garden*, and Robin Bernstein reads the negative reception of Louise Fitzhugh's *Harriet the Spy* in terms of adult perceptions of threat in the queer gaze of the child and its provocation to partake in looking that questions heterosexual norms. Janet Wondra, meanwhile, theorizes child looking in the film *Days of Heaven* as curious and "gathering." *The Child Gaze* builds on these pieces in that it considers the literal child gaze as a complex act situated in relation to the embodied fictional child, the depicted fictional world, the implied reader, and their sociopolitical contexts.

This project departs from earlier considerations of the child gaze in that it asks how this technique has been employed over a large body of texts in the United States. It surveys texts aimed at both child and adult audiences throughout the majority of the twentieth and the opening decades of the twenty-first century, and it focuses on texts that employ the child gaze as a tool to confront exclusionary notions of national belonging. It also brings to bear on this examination discussions from fields such as childhood studies, children's literature, critical race theory, narrative theory, visual culture studies, and ecological perception theory, as well as historical and critical contexts for each of the texts under discussion. It pays attention to the historical trajectories that contextualize the phenomenon of each mode of looking, thus rooting its analysis in US conditions that made way for the resonance of this narrative technique.

Each chapter also offers attention to the literary genres and forms (e.g., historical fiction, realistic fiction, children's and young adult literature, allohistory, biography and autobiography, comics) and literary techniques (e.g., first-, second-, and third-person points of view, dual narration, free indirect discourse) that produce the child gaze in each of the representative texts. Such contextualization is not meant to be comprehensive, as this is the first book-length examination of the child gaze as a narrative technique. Attention to the child gaze could and should extend beyond this project, which chooses as a starting place literature in the United States from 1930–2018 and focuses on texts that represent challenges to exclusionary ideologies predicated upon race, ethnicity, creed, class, and at times their intersections with gender. Locating the child gaze in a textual archive that begins in the 1930s allows me to examine child figures written in a country that in the early twentieth century recognized childhood—and was well on its way to asserting adolescence—as a distinct stage of life characterized by significant cognitive and emotional development and sacralized by mainstream culture (Zelinzer). These texts were all written in a post-Freudian world that had already firmly rooted human subjectivity in the child (Steedman) and in a nation increasingly dedicated to the propagation of culture via visual means, such as advertising and film, wherein observation and spectatorship became and remain key markers of cultural participation.

The United States also provides a complex setting in which to locate the looking child, especially given the ideologically fraught conditions that mark its engagement with race, ethnicity, class, creed, and gender. From the Great Depression to de jure and de facto segregation, through the propagation of and challenges to state-sanctioned racism during World War II and the Cold War, from the civil rights, Chicanx, and Black Arts movements to present day, twenty-first century opposition to police brutality via Black Lives Matter as well as heated debates over immigration, ICE, and the inhumane treatment of detainees, the United States has been and continues to be a crucible for contests over power, opportunity, and civil and human rights. Each text in this study contains a nod to the specific political and social circumstances of the child, whether that be, for example, via the child character's interaction with American institutions such as the public school or the city library, as in the case of Jesse Jackson's *Call Me Charley* and Sydney Taylor's *All-of-a-Kind Family*, or via overt engagement with questions of national belonging, as in Philip Roth's *The Plot against America* and Jason Reynolds and Brendan Kiely's *All American Boys*. The book also includes texts exhibiting deployments of the child gaze that, while liberatory in some senses, uphold exclusionary principles in others.

This project also reads children's literature and literature written for adults together across the American literary landscape in order to exhibit how these modes of the child gaze function within and across different types of implied readers. Indeed, several of the texts I include tend to waver, historically, among audiences, as is the case for Betty Smith's *A Tree Grows in Brooklyn* and Sandra Cisneros's *The House on Mango Street*: neither were originally published for children but have since been claimed for young readers. Furthermore, James Baldwin's only picture book, *Little Man, Little Man: A Story of Childhood*, is a crossover text in both audience and in form and was intended as such from the start. My archive suggests that overall, the child who looks in the evocative ways I theorize is a figure that crosses readership boundaries. While I discuss each mode of looking in ways that make room for various, nuanced iterations—and I choose texts that allow me to exhibit them—I am interested in those variations more in relation to the narrative techniques and textual silences each literary work employs to construct its looking child than in regard to the supposed age of its implied audience, though I do make some remarks to that effect at times. Indeed, I find that the ways of looking theorized in this book tend to dissolve the often-assumed binary between children's and adult literature, which speaks to the power embedded in a child figure deployed to manipulate ways of looking at the nation and its possibilities.

The first chapter theorizes the *appreciative child gaze*, which situates the child as the arbiter of value for childhoods and their contexts that are often located outside of the "quintessential" white, Christian, middle-class suburban milieu. It begins with a discussion of the historical trends that cast the child as a figure of value and valuing in US culture. Weaving together scholarship such as Viviana Zelinzer's work on the changing cultural valence of the child, Diana Selig's historical analysis of the cultural gifts movement, and Julia Mickenberg's assessment of progressive ideologies in mid-twentieth-century children's literature, it demonstrates how the twentieth-century child acts as conduit for appreciation. The chapter then examines the "appreciative" gaze mode for its many levels of meaning by analyzing its narrative nuances in three texts. Appreciative gazing can range from the joyful and reverent looking upon Jewish custom and cuisine in Manhattan's Lower East Side in Sydney Taylor's *All-of-a-Kind Family* (1951), to Francie's pensive and hopeful—though sometimes discriminatory—gazing in her tenement section of Brooklyn in Smith's *A Tree Grows in Brooklyn* (1943), to the ruminating but rarely judgmental looking enacted by TJ in the Harlem neighborhood of James Baldwin's *Little Man, Little Man* (1976). Wielded by children within marginalized communities, the appreciative child gaze combats denigration and erasure of such communities by demanding celebration of or ethical, attentive interest in them. It also takes child noticing and perspective-taking seriously, positing agency in the child's attention.

The second chapter examines the *countersurveillant child gaze*, which documents institutionalized oppression and its inequitable dogma. In this mode, the child gaze insists on the child's youthfulness even as it confronts exclusionary practices at work in the United States by exposing the dangerous surveillance trained upon bodies falling outside of accepted parameters of normativity. Considering scholarship on surveillance, oppositional looking, and visual studies, it employs work by Michel Foucault, George Yancy, Simone Browne, W. E. B. Du Bois, Fatima Tobing Rony, bell hooks, and Irit Rogoff to emphasize the power of the child's countersurveillant gaze. It then reads its instantiation across disparate texts, where it is effectively wielded by characters on a spectrum from subversively silent—as in Jesse Jackson's *Call Me Charley* (1945)—to overtly insistent—as in Mildred Taylor's Cassie Logan of *Roll of Thunder, Hear My Cry* (1979); from electrically aware—as in Philip Roth's *The Plot against America* (2004)—to obliviously unaware—as in Langston Hughes's short story "The Red-Headed Baby" from *The Ways of White Folk* (1934). I argue that the countersurveillant child gaze is a flexible narrative technique that resonates on the level of narrative even when it fails to defeat oppression within the diegetic world of the text. Furthermore, the countersurveillant gaze, insistent as it is on the child as truth-seer, rejects the notion of such seeing as transcendent in the ways associated with Romantic childhood vision; it, rather, enmeshes the child in the real sociopolitical unrest perpetrated by the surveillance of those oppressed by authority. That is, this gaze is not a goal or ideal longed for with nostalgia or spiritual desire, but rather a means of intervening in real and often violently exclusive narratives of nationhood in the United States.

In chapter three I turn to a mode of looking without the stark contrast that separates the appreciative and countersurveillant modes discussed in chapters one and two: the *transactional child gaze*, which might coexist with appreciation, countersurveillance, both, or neither. Literature that employs a transactional child gaze lays bare the alchemy between viewer and environment, requiring a child character who is aware—or slowly coming to be aware—that they are looking at the visual markers of an ideological space. The literary children examined in this chapter are reflective about what they view and how they view it, and their heavily narrated looking invites readerly attention to the processes of signification and levels of agency wrapped up in the gaze. Deployed as a way to trace the character arc of the child—already assumed by generic and cultural expectations to grow or develop over the course of a text—the transactional child gaze makes accessible to the reader the subjectivity of the child as it is formed and reformulated in relation to the ideologies of their environment. Thus, the transactional child gaze allows for an examination of how visual markers of exclusionary ideology work upon the child, as well as the extent to which the child's agency is shaped—and to what end—by their transactions with them. In theorizing this gaze, the chapter employs Louise Rosenblatt's term "transactional" (borrowed from John Dewey) to name the feedback loop between viewer and visual text; it also draws on scholarship from visual theorists James Elkins, Irit Rogoff, and Roland Barthes, as well as findings from ecological perception theory in the field of psychology to position looking as a dynamic, liminal space between personal agency and the cultural demands that the child must negotiate.

Bringing these discourses to bear upon representations of literary youth, the chapter reads the implications of the transactional child gaze in Sandra Cisneros's *The House on Mango Street* (1983), which visualizes a Chicana girl's contentious relationship with gender discrimination in her Chicago barrio; Toni Morrison's *The Bluest Eye* (1970), in which two young Black girls' alchemical reactions to the visual ideologies permeating their environment document the devastating effects of racist standards of beauty and belonging; and Jason Reynolds and Brendan Kiely's *All American Boys* (2015), which offers the dual narration of a white teen and a Black teen coming to activist sensibilities via their racially inflected processes of looking. In each text, those processes are key ways the protagonists initiate and wrestle with difficult decisions about how to position the self within the machine of culture.

The fourth chapter turns away from what has largely been an examination of prose narrative (with the exception of Baldwin's illustrated book) to the form of comics, which provides a particularly provocative site for mobilization of the child gaze. Comics as a form is historically linked to the child, and its verbal-visual form physically directs the readerly gaze, quite literally teaching us how to look. Comics thus materializes the gaze and positions the reader more fully as its student. Examining graphic novels that disempower racist visuals with a long and persistent history in the United States, the chapter discusses how three different texts engage in pedagogies of the gaze that match with the three previously theorized modes of child looking: appreciative, in John Lewis, Andrew Aydin, and Nathan Powell's *March: Book 1* (2013); countersurveillant, in Joel Christian Gill's *Bass Reeves: Tales of the Talented Tenth* (2014); and transactional, in Gene Luen Yang's *American Born Chinese* (2006). Drawing on comics scholarship in relation to race, cultural criticism, and narrative theory, the chapter exhibits how graphic narratives employ the child gaze to engage readers in the role of the looking child who notices their ideological surround (itself made material for the character and the reader on the comics page) and reflect on their attitudes toward it. Ultimately, each text leads its implied reader through a process of looking that recruits them to reject oppression.

Finally, a brief conclusion gestures toward avenues for further study. It highlights that while *The Child Gaze* puts forth several modes of child gazing that resonate widely in US literature, it is not—nor is it meant to be—an exhaustive categorization and investigation of this narrative technique. It gestures to the potential for study by scholars of areas outside of the scope of this project, including, for example, queer theory, disability studies, genres aside from the realistic fiction and nonfiction on which the book's archive heavily relies, and forms such as drama and film. Other national and literary landscapes also provide opportunities rife for examining the child as a potent wielder of the gaze.

The Child Gaze: Narrating Resistance in American Literature provides a necessary intervention into the discussion of how national belonging is narrated in literature of the United States, and it does so by centering the child and the child's acts of looking as they posture within and against hegemonic ideologies of Americanness. It demonstrates how the child gaze is a subtle and versatile narrative strategy, operating on many literary registers; it is flexible across first-, second-, and third-person points of view, various focalizations and polyvocality, and audience and form. Furthermore, it mobilizes childhood as a site of resistance, achieved through the ways child characters can produce the poignant, nonvocal discourse of an evocative gaze that compels readers to look at and with them. Centering the child's sight lines as cues to reinvent attitudes about national belonging, *The Child Gaze* supplies a useful paradigm through which to consider the roles children play in literary narratives' constructions of the US national imaginary.

Chapter One

THE APPRECIATIVE CHILD GAZE

Valuing Visions of Marginalized Childhoods

In the image below, TJ, the main character in James Baldwin and Yoran Cazac's picture book *Little Man, Little Man: A Story of Childhood*, eats Sunday breakfast with his parents (figure 1.1). The scene is happy. The warm yellow watercolor infuses the kitchen with fresh morning light, a hearty breakfast spread is in progress, and the family's faces are turned to each other. Their sight lines produce a network of gazes that tie parents to child to reader, especially since the composition of the portrait seems to position that reader as approaching the family table. There is also a dynamism to the image, each character poised in action: the mother with her pan of eggs in transit and her face turned with interest to her husband and son, the father and TJ with their hands lifted in conversational gestures, and TJ with his smiling eyes turned to the reader, as if inviting them to share the exchange. Outside the window are the tall buildings of Harlem underneath a soft blue sky, and the same blue is picked up in the mother's dress as well as the coffee pot, cups, and saucers, which help create the appealing spread on the table. This image is celebratory and inviting. It places the reader in this warm kitchen with this nice family, at a time when TJ "real happy" (56).

Little Man, Little Man is written in the third person, but TJ's gaze, concretized and thematized in this image as he meets the reader's eyes, is the controlling feature of the text. Looking at the people and places in his Harlem neighborhood, TJ takes an appreciative stance, one that considers at length many aspects of his community, including this happy moment in his own kitchen as well as a series of lonely, playful, exciting, and frightening moments outside of it. TJ's life includes the many facets and people of Harlem

Figure 1.1. "**TJ real happy on Sunday mornings**" (Baldwin and Cazac 54–55). The bold text corresponds with a bolding of the text in the original document, from which the caption is procured and which I note as part of my analysis. Used with the permission of Beatrice Cazac.

with whom he shares his world—a world too often painted as unworthy in dominant American media representations of Black urban life, and a world recast in this picture book as valuable, via TJ's careful gaze. Indeed, TJ's kitchen, a bastion of family life, only appears in this image, which suggests that Baldwin and Cazac's project is less one of contrast between TJ's family and those around him than one of continuity between TJ and his surroundings. Baldwin and Cazac's work argues for the value of looking appreciatively at the complexities of Harlem from a vantage point like TJ's, one that refuses to demean and instead seeks to consider.

I term this type of child gaze on the literary page "appreciative," as it enacts a way of looking that performs and elicits impulses along the spectrum of celebration, care, and weighty consideration. Denotatively, the term has several meanings, including (1) celebratory or grateful ("I appreciate you!"); (2) perceptive of the worth, quality, or significance of ("I appreciate your point about. . . ."); (3) aware of the complexities of ("I appreciate the situation you're describing"); and (4) lending value to (in contrast to depreciation; "the sum will appreciate over time"). Connotatively, it relates to concepts such as warmth, welcome, awareness, and worth. Tying perception to value across all of these meanings, the appreciative child gaze suffuses scenes and often whole texts with a sense of careful and caring attention to child characters and their surroundings. In doing so, it works to elicit readerly appreciation for that upon which the child looks as well as readerly affinity for the child as bestower of value.

By positing the looking child as creator of alternate structures of worth, texts that employ an appreciative child gaze set the child within and against dominant paradigms of value that structure US social understandings. Wielding this gaze to represent with care American children or childhoods that are often disparaged, underrepresented, or dismissed from its conventional connotations, these texts suture the "othered" child firmly to both the category of valued and the act of valuing. Thus, the appreciative child gaze imbues the child with a social dynamism that recasts their subjectivities, experiences, and communities as important. In performing as well as inviting such looking, the appreciative child gaze widens a too narrow lens that circumscribes the boundaries of American childhoods in white, Christian, middle-class paradigms. This version of the child gaze, while nonconfrontational within the mimetic world of the text, functions thematically and synthetically—and therefore subversively—to renegotiate gated notions of national belonging.

It is this nonconfrontational quality through which the appreciative child gaze produces its quiet activism, imbuing texts not with the overt opposition that explicitly confronts exclusionary regimes (as with the countersurveillant gaze, discussed in the next chapter) but with gentle (though not unproblematic) inclusion achieved by turning eyes toward people, places, and experiences too often made invisible by such exclusion. This is not to say that the appreciative child gaze always comes with a smile. Appreciation can attend to the gravity of a situation or event, to intensity, and even to trauma. As will be discussed at more length in the close readings that follow, the appreciative gaze is not solely celebratory, and it can open up questions and critique.

This narrative strategy is at once "safe" and risky. Because children who look appreciatively tend not to connote aggression within the diegetic world of the story, readers are more likely to accept such looking as an appropriate rather than deviant standard of behavior; thus, texts that employ this gaze are less likely to be impugned by gatekeepers of hegemonic social understandings than if they confronted them overtly. Some of the power of this gaze, therefore, arises from the quiet ways in which it advocates for wider inclusion, eluding censorial impulses by aligning with characteristics such as wonder, affection, and curiosity, which are often associated with and valued in the figure of the child. However, a child's appreciative gaze runs the risk of making that which remains unseen even more invisible: not only, for instance, discriminatory powers that be but also people, places, and facets of life often erased from or unjustly vilified in hegemonic notions of belonging. Those in this last category, when left out of the range of this gaze, become doubly excluded by their invisibility even to the careful, appreciative child who otherwise highlights that which deserves to be valued. At its most inclusive, the appreciative child gaze generates a curiosity to witness, to experience, and to know without inflections of hierarchy or mastery and often with inflections of joy. It provokes a desire to consider and to care; it invites a being-with, an acknowledging, a respectful witnessing, and, in some cases, a celebration. However, the appreciative gaze can also perpetuate exclusion, as the child might look appreciatively on one milieu while degrading or ignoring another. Indeed, the appreciative child gaze emerges from a legacy of liberal thinking that works within and against nativist, exclusionary rhetorics in the United States—a cultural genealogy taken up at more length below.

The texts under examination in this chapter each function to expose the registers in which US authors have employed this relatively "safe" narrative technique—diegetically innocuous, but extratextually radical—to widen conceptions of childhood in the United States that have excluded people based on identity markers such as race, ethnicity, faith, and class. They also exhibit the range of genres, forms, and audiences across which such a gaze is employed: a children's chapter book, Sydney Taylor's *All-of-a-Kind Family* (1951); a semiautobiographical novel published for a general audience, Betty Smith's *A Tree Grows in Brooklyn* (1943); and a crossover picture book aimed at both adult and child audiences, James Baldwin and Yoran Cazac's *Little Man, Little Man: A Story of Childhood* (1976). Each of them is a community-oriented text, taking as its subject a group of people living at a particular time and in a particular place, a group of people whose real-life counterparts experienced erasure or rejection by mainstream US political sensitivities. Each is also set in a different neighborhood and time period in New York City, itself a site of tremendous diversity. *All-of-a-Kind Family* takes place in the turn-of-the-century Jewish enclave of the Lower East Side, *A Tree Grows in Brooklyn* depicts the early twentieth-century ethnically divided tenement sections of Brooklyn, and the titular character in *Little Man, Little Man* goes about a day in the life in his 1970s Harlem neighborhood. Taken together, they demonstrate the features as well as the limits of the appreciative child gaze; taken separately, they exhibit the nuances with which individual texts have employed this gaze to perform cultural work within their particular milieus.

Sydney Taylor's children's novel *All-of-a-Kind Family* spotlights the celebratory capabilities of the appreciative gaze, which postures against degrading stereotypes of Jewish life in the tenements of Manhattan's Lower East Side at the turn of the twentieth century by staking a claim for the joy and value in the family's community. The patterns of looking in this text afford insight into the appreciative gaze as a narrative technique that provokes the reader, through subtle affective signals originating in the child, to value and celebrate that upon which the child looks. Through child gazing that asserts the significance of Jewish American citizens to US national belonging, *All-of-a-Kind Family* quietly engages and rejects stereotypes tied to the Jewish populace without erasing the ethnic and religious practices that hegemonic narratives tend to marginalize or exclude.

Betty Smith's semiautobiographical novel *A Tree Grows in Brooklyn* exhibits the appreciative gaze as one concerned with noticing and making sense of the complexities of the child's environment. However, it also brings into relief the exclusionary possibilities of this gaze, as it others and erases lives that do not fall into the parameters of mattering the text draws around and through its central child character. Francie Nolan's white, Christian milieu dominates her field of vision; her nuanced attention to the dirt, struggles, delights, and beauty of Brooklyn tenement life also keeps at a rejecting distance those who do not share her race or faith.

James Baldwin and Yoran Cazac's picture book *Little Man, Little Man: A Story of Childhood* demonstrates how combining the responsive noticing of the child with the ineffable mode of the visual develops a gaze that performs appreciation by withholding or wrestling with judgment. Through TJ's inquisitive lingering over the visual dimensions of his Harlem neighborhood, evoked in the narration and made manifest by illustrator Yoran Cazac's watercolors and sketches, Baldwin and Cazac evoke a sympathetic, curious witnessing that directs the reader to appreciate the complexity and the value of both TJ and his neighbors. Evading overt or simple conclusions about what TJ sees, the picture book asserts the Black child's gaze as an alternative mode of knowing that eschews dominant US value structures that demean inhabitants of Baldwin's Harlem.

These texts' publication dates span the middle decades of the twentieth century, a time period that hosts widespread use of this narrative technique in US literature, but one that certainly does not lay exclusive claim to it. The child as a figure capable of wielding this evocative gaze emerges from the changing value of the American child through the nineteenth century as well as the cultural gifts movement and liberal education and publishing trends for children in the early twentieth. The legacies of these historical phenomena persist today, evident in late twentieth- and early twenty-first-century texts that continue to employ the appreciative child gaze.

I turn now to these historical trajectories that make possible the appreciative child gaze's power and provide a shared context uniting the literary works the chapter goes on to examine. Ultimately, in harnessing the power of the child as constructed in relation to appreciation, all of these texts write within and against mid-twentieth-century narratives about race, class, faith, and ethnicity in the United States.

APPRECIATION AND THE CHILD: INHERITED LEGACIES OF VISION AND VALUE

The historical circumstances that empower an appreciative child gaze arise from several contexts converging in the twentieth century. Viviana Zelinzer's work has demonstrated how the nineteenth-century paradigm of the "useful child" gave way to the "economically useless but emotionally priceless child" (209) of the twentieth. This "'sacralization' of children's lives" posited the value of the child in the affective, emotional realm (11), resulting in a notion of the child that "has created an essential condition of contemporary childhood" (3): the child as a distinct individual who requires and deserves care and protection. By the middle of the twentieth century, as Elaine Tyler May shows, raising such children also became a recognized way to enact citizenship in the postwar patriotism of US ascendency (160). Children were cast as the future of a strong nation and the nuclear family as a stronghold for the development of ideal "Americans." Twentieth-century American children and childhood functioned in body and in image as a conduit for national rhetorics with ostensibly positive connotations of US life.

However, while the "priceless child" phenomenon spread from the middle class to the working class and reached across racial categories—evidence of its permeation of US culture and its status-oriented nature—it did not do so without disparity. Childhood as a concept was and still is often tethered to a white suburban milieu (Bernstein; May 166; Mintz 41) and thus participates in the continued exclusion of children of color and children living in economically depressed communities. This disparity is an essential context for the power of the othered child's appreciative gaze, which harnesses and exploits the potential of these competing twentieth-century narratives about the child figure. On the one hand, the child who wields this gaze obtains legitimized power via the culture of sacralization that centers their value as child. On the other hand, their marginal position outside of the white, middle-class paradigm manifests their subversive act of directing value-making, which intervenes in US structural hierarchies that otherwise render their experiences important or invisible.

Indeed, a rich and fraught history of the promotion of inclusive social values centers on the figure of the child. It has roots in what Diana Selig has termed the "cultural gifts movement" of the interwar years and branches through and beyond the Cold War era via literary, psychological, and educational conduits. Selig documents the efforts of socially minded activists and educators of the 1920s, '30s, and early '40s to create projects that "celebrated the cultural contributions of immigrant and minority groups to American life" (1). Positing the compatibility of many ethnic cultural traditions with dominant "American" practices and patriotism, the cultural gifts movement endeavored to replace the "melting pot" model of assimilation with one that purported to uphold ethnic traditions as a way to fortify and invigorate the stability of the United States. Key to this movement's legacy is that the target audience for most of these efforts was children, who could be taught to "appreciate America's cultural diversity" (1). Newly deemed by psychosocial interests in child development to be susceptible to the racial attitudes of their environment and in need of specialized, age-appropriate care and support, the child became the site of interventions imbued with "hope for a future of racial understanding" (5–7). Within a period known for its nativist rhetoric, schools, religious organizations, youth-focused community organizations, and parenting educators created curriculum, programs, activities, and seminars that targeted discrimination as harmful to the child and to the nation, touting tolerance as the way forward.

The movement itself did not survive much beyond World War II, in large part due to its underdeveloped notions of ethnic identity and considerable inconsistencies, and these very same problematic contours shaped the racial liberalism of the twentieth century, which still has significant hold over discourses about prejudice today. For instance, Selig exhibits how the cultural gifts movement involved very limited or discriminatory attention to African Americans and Indigenous peoples and how it also reified whiteness. It tended to elevate European ethnicities over others, to select only those cultural qualities that seemed easily assimilable into hegemonic American values, and to isolate characteristics and rituals out of context. Most of its early twentieth-century efforts replaced stereotypes with other stereotypes, treated ethnic groups as monolithic, and paid little attention to the complexities of being part of a distinct ethnic group in the United States, let alone being part of several. It also maintained a fairly narrow focus on the personal rather than the institutional and systemic. But the abstract figure of the child nevertheless survived the dissolution of the movement, continuing on as a fulcrum for later instantiations of liberal work: as Selig points out, along with these persistent legacies of 1920s and '30s educational and social efforts, midcentury racial liberalism in the United States took up the cultural gift movement's model of casting the child as a central figure in rhetorics of progress and inclusivity.

Thus, children retained a privileged position for liberally minded activists even in the midst of the particularly robust rhetorics of isolationism and suspicion that characterized the Cold War. When education and educational materials fell under intense scrutiny during the Red Scare of the late 1940s and '50s, which resulted in widespread firing of teachers suspected to be linked to the Communist Party, liberal educators often turned to trade book authorship for children as an alternate venue for teaching their value systems to youth. Julia Mickenberg traces the subversive role that children's literature played in sustaining liberal values during this era, particularly in relation to editors, writers, librarians, and progressive parents following practices popularized by child development experts such as Dr. Spock.[1] Texts written, promoted, and read by this segment of the population feature characters, often children, who enact a value system that works against Cold War anxieties about containment, isolation, and narrowly defined patriotism and Americanness. Like the cultural gifts movement, this tradition contributed to the construction of children as "the nation's most open-minded citizens" (Mickenberg 8), capable of "imagination, free expression, cooperation, and commitment to social justice" (16). It leveraged the child to construct patriotism as "inclusive, democratic, and egalitarian" (17). The success of these efforts is evident in the fact that exposure to and ostensible endorsement of these values became "hallmarks of American childhood" (16) and, though not without considerable contention, continues to infuse much school curricula.[2] Viewing the world appreciatively is one approved way of seeing for children in the United States.

It is important to note that Selig and Mickenberg, respectively, demonstrate that neither the cultural gifts movement nor the majority of the "leftist" children's publishing tradition of the Cold War were overtly political in nature; furthermore, neither was directly linked to the Communist Party.[3] Rather, each supported values of community, social inclusion, and interpersonal kindness: values difficult to call "un-American," given that a discourse of racial inclusion was state mandated (even if hypocritically so) after World War II, and messages of unity and neighborliness were employed to strengthen American patriotic sentiment throughout the majority of the twentieth century. These practices and the literature they produced benefited from a course of political activism that did not perform overtly as radical or resistant and thus was not targeted seriously by proponents of exclusionary national narratives. However, they also "encouraged [the child reader] to trust their own instincts, imaginations, and critical capacities" (7), gesturing outside of the text to the possibilities for the agential child in the real world. Mickenberg's work points to the fact that children's literature, by way of its very position as a marginalized and therefore underscrutinized subdivision in the politics of publishing, provides a lively venue for resistant ideas packaged in innocuous forms.

The appreciative child gaze, in literature written for young people or adults, can itself be called innocuous because it refrains from overt political posturing but nevertheless smuggles resistance. Its performance involves diegetic attention to the people and places it makes matter through the figure of the child, which rehearses the virtues esteemed by twentieth-century shifts toward progressive parenting and education. As a narrative technique cuing responses in the implied reader, this gaze visualizes a corrective to the narrow hegemonic lens that distorts or occludes ways of being an American child or experiencing American childhood that are underrepresented, underappreciated, dismissed, or erased from its conventional connotations. That is, while the appreciative child gaze allows the texts in and of themselves to perform appreciation, it also allows the texts as artifacts of material culture produced within their geohistorical contexts to perform subtle opposition to exclusionary narratives that dominate those contexts. And those contexts include acts of looking. Consider, for instance, demands to gaze suspiciously as part of World War II and Cold War era civil defense initiatives, such as the Aircraft Warning Service and the Ground Observer Corps,[4] as well as the fevered hypervigilance aimed at neighbors, co-workers, and friends during the McCarthy era—a vigilance that resurrects repeatedly over time, as in the "If you see something, say something" campaign after 9/11. Looking appreciatively at that which is not characterized by the powers that be as quintessentially and safely "American" rejects these demands, even as it surveys a scene with careful attention to detail. An appreciative child gaze can thus perform benignly within and defiantly against state-sanctioned imperatives.

But when a narrative strategy works within acceptable paradigms in order to make a gentle intervention, it can also prove slippery. The appreciative child gaze's subtle and disarming visual directives can function in alignment with narratives of exclusion, since any child who wields it occupies a space in US hierarchies built on characteristics such as class, race, ethnicity, and creed. Jodi Melamed asserts that racialization in particular, retaining its hold via Cold War practices, "code[s] human beings into regimes of social value" (14) and continues to cause those regimes to appear part of a "normative system" (11). Though representations of children are linked to their own value category by age—a category Zelinzer reads as eliciting impulses to care (5)—their identities are also linked to other markers subjected to manufactured levels of social value. Thus, texts that employ the child as value-maker can both intervene in and uphold normative systems that propagate the oppression of those ranked at lower social worth. Like the contradictions of the cultural gifts movement and the shortcomings of racial liberalism, both of which contribute to the sociopolitical context for the appreciative child gaze's power in

US literature, this gaze does not create perfect visions of inclusive harmony. As the following close readings detail, considering the appreciative child gaze at work as a narrative strategy in children's and adult literature requires close attention to the various levels of highlighting and erasure that it accomplishes.

WARM-EYED CELEBRATION: SYDNEY TAYLOR'S *ALL-OF-A-KIND FAMILY*

Sydney Taylor's *All-of-a-Kind Family* employs the appreciative child gaze to document and celebrate a Jewish American family living in a tenement community in the Lower East Side of New York City at the turn of the twentieth century. This text thus provides a platform to demonstrate how the affective resonance of this gaze celebrates—and invites the reader to celebrate—a marginalized and sometimes vilified community's practices. *All-of-a-Kind Family* also exhibits how such a gaze energizes an implicit critique of hegemonic narratives, which in this case are those that maintain white, Christian, middle-class dominance in the United States. However, the celebratory aspect of this appreciative gaze also elides the poverty-related dangers of tenement section life, refraining from reference to systemic inequities that perpetuate dangerous living conditions, and even from depicting those conditions themselves. This type of looking, in the act of making invisible the circumstances that might otherwise connote stereotype or victimhood, also makes invisible, in this case, the urgency of the plight that inhabitants of the American Jewish ghettos faced.

June Cummins points out that correspondence between Taylor and her editor at W. W. Follett reveals that Cold War anxieties about American identity were at stake in the production of this text. Isolationist responses to Communism as well as events such as the execution of the Rosenbergs required Taylor to strike a balance between her project—to combat stereotypes and celebrate Jewish American life—and editorial pressures for her characters to perform Americanness overtly ("Becoming").[5] Taylor, in acquiescing to as well as resisting this mandate, employs the rather quiet strategy of the child's appreciative gaze to subtly negotiate Jewish life into American sensitivities. As the text turns this nonconfrontational gaze onto sites and institutions specific to US and Jewish life in the Lower East Side, the text refuses to subordinate the Jewish experience to the American, even as it postures Jewish citizens as a valuable part of the country.

First calling subtle attention to the precarity of its main characters in relation to state-sanctioned institutions, *All-of-a-Kind Family* begins with concerned child gazes when the five all-of-a-kind sisters become anxious about their patronage of the New York Public Library. "The children all looked at each other in dismay" (Taylor 13), as sister Sarah cannot find the library book she borrowed, and they expect that means "we can't go to the library, ever again" (13). As Meghan Sweeney has pointed out, libraries were a key site for cultural assimilation in the early and mid-twentieth century (58). Since library offerings and regulations afford "opportunities . . . to mold the perfect library patron—and the perfect American citizen" (41), the "anxious" looking for and about Sarah's book (Taylor 14) reflects anxieties about losing citizen-related privileges. Furthermore, Sarah's sisters' gazing back at her with "brown eyes large in sympathy" (15) signals to the reader the appropriate affective response to the possible exclusion of the Jewish child: shared concern.

This concern works in tandem with the appreciative mode. It casts exclusion as a problem, which is made further clear as the girls find reason to enact their first appreciative gazes: a new library lady, who engages in the concern those sympathetic eyes elicit and recruits the children back into a paradigm of belonging. The eye imagery and gaze-related visual detail in the scene positions appreciative looking as the conduit for positive interactions. Sister Henny notices the lady and alerts her sisters with a directive to "Look" (Taylor 17)—an invitation often repeated throughout the text. Sarah then "studie[s]" her clothes, hair, and "kind face" (17), reorienting the mood from anxiety to hope. In contrast to her predecessor, who was perhaps less accepting of the children's patronage (and likely contributed to their anxiety), this lady "look[s] up" and "smile[s]" when she sees "five little girls dressed exactly alike" (17). Gathering from the children's "sad-looking faces" that they are trepidatious and so she should treat them with care (19), her careful gaze casts the children as worthy and welcome patrons to the library. Furthermore, the narration makes clear that she is aware of the fiscal plight and personal pride of the population she serves in her East Side branch (20–21), and she uses this awareness to suggest a payment plan for the children. Miss Allen's actively sympathetic understanding of their situation prompts the children's "eyes" to go "wide in unbelief" at the accommodation (22), signaling that they apparently had no reason to expect their situation to be validated.

It is important to note that the children command Miss Allen's appreciative gaze, which is indicative of the way the text continually recenters its visuality—even when gazes are enacted by adults—on the embodied child who both looks and is looked at. Miss Allen does not just watch the girls, but "f[i]nd[s] herself watching" them (23). The text makes clear they must be seen, rather than ignored. The free indirect discourse of the next line— "How quaint they were in their stiffly starched white aprons over dark woolen dresses . . . like wide-open umbrellas" (23)—signals rather than erases the ethnic origins of their visual difference, as "quaint" connotes "old world" in

Miss Allen's perspective. And lest the gentle fun of the umbrella image be understood as mockery, the narration takes the occasion of Miss Allen's gaze upon the children's clothing to provide detail that highlights their mother's care and work ethic without eliding their social class: "Had she been able to peek under those dresses, she would have understood why they billowed out in such a manner. Underneath were three petticoats . . . topped by a fancy muslin garment . . . starched to a scratchy crispness. In order to save money, Mama made those petticoats herself. . . . Mama . . . always reknit the holes" (23). Thus, the looks the girls elicit from the librarian suggest the text-approved careful and appreciative gazing that should underpin US institutional interaction with its economically disadvantaged Jewish populace.

The text continues its appreciative project by introducing several key facets of the Jewish faith through the child's visual entry point. As the children look upon their world and its happenings, the reader is invited to see that world with appreciation as well. For instance, the children arrive home from the library "just in time to see Mama saying the prayer over the candles" for Sabbath (Taylor 78). "Just in time" connotes anticipatory pleasure, and it is followed by a paragraph break that asks the reader to pause over the luck of this initial seeing before being invited to witness the ritual: "The children stood around the table watching her. A lovely feeling of peace and contentment seemed to flow out from Mama to them. First she put a napkin on her head; then placing four white candles in the brass candlesticks, she lit them. She extended her arms" (78), and so on, the passage dilating the moment as it details the observance carefully and makes the reader privy to that "lovely feeling of peace" as they look vicariously through the children's eyes. The organic imagery of looking and feeling works to transfer that appreciation to the reader, drawn close by the visual attention turned to the sacred rite and to the family who partakes in it.

Likewise, when the children first approach the synagogue, the narrative explicitly ties their gaze to the appreciation it should create, foregrounding feeling before looking to conjure a sense of pleasurable expectancy: "The children loved coming here. Always they would gaze with reverent awe at the red velvet curtains richly embroidered in gold, which hung before the place where the five books of the Torah were kept. The Torah are large parchment scrolls made of goatskin and sewed together with goat-gut. They tell in Hebrew writing done by hand the history, the laws, and religious customs of the Jewish people" (94). The "love" the children feel due to the "reverent awe" that attends their gaze infuses pathos into the scene, which documents the child's reaction as endemic to the aesthetics of ceremony: the "red velvet curtains richly embroidered" and the presence of the Torah, carefully created and preserved. Furthermore, this is one of many moments in the text where the narration gestures toward an implied audience of outsiders to the Jewish faith, here indicated by the brief definition of the Torah. While passages like these can be read as decentering the potential Jewish child reader and privileging a "default audience" of their white, Christian peers, this one also demonstrates how the appreciative child gaze of the all-of-a-kind sisters can redirect the white gaze that would presumably come with such readership. The honoring that this gaze constitutes works in tension with the othering of Jewish faith and practice prevalent in white Christian narratives that dominate American social and political discourses.

Taylor also details daily domestic undertakings through this gaze, such as visits to the Jewish marketplace, thereby positioning the child and the reader to perform appreciation of the buying and selling in the tenement section that stereotypes otherwise marked as miserly and dirty. With Sarah's excited cry to her sisters as well as to the reader—"Just *look* at all the pushcarts!" (67; emphasis added)—the scene turns into a celebration of marketplace life and of the children's joy therein. Here the children view displays and signs in Yiddish that are translated for a wider audience by the English-speaking narrator, and they admire the skill of the vendors, such as the chickpea seller: "Everyone watched as he fished out the peas. First he took a small square of white paper from a little compartment on one side of the oven. He twirled the paper about his fingers to form the shape of a cone and then skillfully twisted the pointed end so that the container would not fall apart" (76). The child gaze marks the vendor and his work as worthy of interest and appreciation and characterizes the children as delighted patrons thereof, denying stereotypes that cast any life lived in the Lower East Side as one of squalor.

Indeed, by calling attention to the "foreign" nature of the Lower East Side, Taylor also manages to engage in a sleight-of-hand that bolsters the power of the child gaze as part of the text's political project to combat prejudice. "Only one tongue was spoken here—Yiddish. It was like a foreign land right in the midst of America. In this foreign land, it was Mama's children who were the foreigners since they alone conversed in an alien tongue—English" (72). Casting the children's use of English as "alien" to this "foreign" area both allows the child characters to perform the Americanness Taylor's editor required *and* destabilizes hegemonic understandings of included and excluded. "Quaint" in the library but "America[n]" here, the children reconcile—or at least confound—competing notions of belonging that shift from perspective to perspective. Furthermore, deputizing the child as embodying American identity in this scene suggests that the appreciative child gaze here stands for appropriate ways Americans should gaze upon Jewish marketplaces largely disparaged in popular media. In this way, the children in the market function like Miss Allen in the library, noticing the differences between themselves and "old world" inhabitants of the Lower East Side, and turning to appreciation, rather than rejection, in response.

The scene that demonstrates particularly how the appreciative gaze can be celebratory even while it negotiates a quiet critique of national mandates for social belonging is the one that most explicitly performs Americanness: a Fourth of July celebration. It does so by casting the celebration of America as a novel spectacle rather than as the normal material of the children's lives. Taylor wrote the scene at the insistence of her editor, and Cummins details Taylor's drawn-out resistance to its inclusion as well as her refusal to follow her editor's repeated suggestion to use a quintessentially midcentury American "picnic" scene to commemorate it ("Becoming" 334ff). Instead, Taylor locates the celebration on the streets of the Lower East Side, positioning the American holiday in the milieu of her characters, rather than removing them from their milieu to endorse it. Furthermore, by way of its contrasts with the Passover account of the previous chapter, the scene resists normalizing this American ritual in the lives of her characters above the practices that mark their faith and ethnicity. These contrasts are effected via the appreciative child gaze.

The strategy is subtle, as the chapter opens with Papa "carefully" displaying a flag that he knows should not touch the floor and older siblings teasing and teaching Gertie, the youngest, about what day it is (Taylor 132–33). Such details posture the family as repeatedly celebrating the holiday in proper American form. But while Gertie's lack of knowledge might make sense for her age, it contrasts with her knowing appreciative gaze in the previous chapter, which details how she "*always* found pleasure in looking through" the "droll pictures" of the Haggadahs her family uses each year on Passover (124–25; emphasis added). That chapter is steeped in carefully described ritual well known to all the children, and Gertie has rehearsed her role in preparation for it. If spectacle, positively connoted, is associated with Passover, it is that of the familiarly sacred.

The Independence Day celebration, however, stands out as "different" within the text's episodic organization, and while Cummins argues that its exceptionality underscores its relation to a budding assimilation narrative that becomes more robust in the text's sequels ("Becoming" 331), its exceptionality also and again destabilizes the categories of familiar and foreign in this novel. In the Fourth of July scene, Gertie mistakes firecrackers for "red candles" (Taylor 135), and her older sister joins her to look out the window, where they both "noticed that almost all the neighbors, up and down the street, had hung out flags also" (133). It is the "noticed" and the "also" (rather than a "saw" or the use of a "their" to modify "flags") that casts the event as a novelty in the children's eyes, unlike the familiarity of Passover. The Fourth of July is a festive lark, Passover is a beloved observance, and the narrative employs the appreciative child gaze with careful inflections to mark the difference.

To be clear, American and Jewish traditions do not compete in this text so much as fill out its contours. The child eye oscillates, from American library to Jewish market, from Passover rituals to a Fourth of July celebration. And yet the appreciative eye of the child lingers most happily and comfortably over those that signal Jewish identity. The implications of that lingering enable the celebratory intervention of the novel's appreciative child gaze: it invites the reader to enjoy that upon which it looks, drawing the reader close as it positions the Jewish child as director of affective response to the Jewish community. For readers who identify as part of the real-life counterpart of a text's depicted community, the representation of this insider vantage point can be affirming and empowering. For readers who identify as outsiders to this community, the child's eyes become the lens through which the reader must look in order to perceive and enjoy the pleasures of the people, places, and practices within it.

The appreciative child gaze also, however, entices the reader to ignore that which it does not bring into its visual field—in this case, the racial, ethnic, and socioeconomic hierarchies and attitudes toward immigrants that led to ghettoized tenement living in New York and other major US cities. Omission of the urgency of these forces and their consequences is both an advantage and disadvantage of this narrative strategy for social inclusion. On one hand, their removal metaphorically wipes clean of discrimination a lens that might otherwise cloud the ability to see value and joy in the life of Jewish immigrants and their families. Turning its readers' eyes away from hegemonic looking practices that reject the lives of those they survey, this instantiation of the appreciative child gaze instead invites readers to see a community on its own terms, through the eyes of a child raised within its cultural milieu. On the other hand, such turning away can also perpetuate ignorance of—and even complicit support for—forces of oppression that are often already invisible on the national stage, thwarting opportunities to incite systemic change. The celebratory register of the appreciative child gaze thus trades the urgency of social critique for positive representation that eschews overt reference to stereotype, ultimately inviting, through its affective signals, celebration of that upon which it looks. It also invests heavily in not only the value but also the agentic pleasure of the looking child, elevating their eager joy over that which threatens it.

CONFLICTING VISIONS OF CLASS, CREED, AND RACE IN BETTY SMITH'S *A TREE GROWS IN BROOKLYN*

Betty Smith's *A Tree Grows in Brooklyn* demonstrates how the appreciative child gaze can energize a text's renegotiation of and complicity with paradigms of belonging and value in the United States—specifically by exhibiting the degree to which investment in the elevation of one marginalized identity perpetuates the erasure of others. Via narrative attention to the looking that Francie Nolan, the daughter of Irish and Austrian immigrants, performs in an early twentieth-century Brooklyn tenement community, the text lends serious weight to the sights she beholds. Rather than omitting details that reflect the poverty, indignities, and struggles endemic to her existence, her visual field includes them, making them worthy of pondering alongside those that mark beauty, enjoyment, and hope. Engaging appreciation on the level of joy as well as inquisitive and measured consideration, this text registers as celebratory as well as contemplative. Yet the text's keen engagement with Francie's perspective also distances, subordinates, and sometimes erases people other than white Brooklyn residents, thereby demonstrating how the appreciative child gaze can reinforce some aspects of hegemonic narratives even as it reenvisions others. Indeed, a key way by which *A Tree Grows in Brooklyn* engages the ideological slipperiness of the appreciative gaze is the deference the third-person text pays to Francie's acts of looking—which it does not treat with the ironic distance some adult audience texts cultivate regarding their child (read: naive) characters. In Smith's case, Francie's gaze impresses upon the reader the weighty value of her experience as a child living in an economically depressed community, but it also codifies such value in the Christian whiteness it elevates above representations of people of color and of other faiths. In this way, the appreciation of the white, Christian first- and second-generation working-class immigrant population that is performed by Francie's careful looking is an intervention into US hierarchies of value, but one that erects boundaries denying the worth of those outside her field of vision.

The publication and reception circumstances of Smith's text illuminate the double-sided cultural work her text accomplishes in 1940s America and beyond. Her work declined early on by multiple editors who told her that "Nobody was interested in Brooklyn," "the poor we always have with us," and "People want to get away from the poor" (qtd. in J. Smith 47), Smith went on to publish a novel that was one of the first to represent without demeaning stereotype a childhood like Francie Nolan's—a childhood based on Smith's own upbringing in Williamsburg. Response to her novel was effusive, and Judith Smith documents extensively the letters Betty Smith received from people across the country thanking her for a story about working-class life that resonated with their own. According to J. Smith, the popularity of her work "helped to establish a public narrative in which [white] ethnic looking back expanded the idea of American citizenship" (74). Storying the early twentieth-century European immigrant on the midcentury US literary page reinforced a belonging that had been in question only a generation earlier but was now touted by libraries, book clubs, schools, and church groups promoting the book. Published as a special military edition for US troops overseas during World War II—which was so popular it earned a second printing for that audience as well (41)—the memoiresque novel stirred a kind of patriotism that privileged the plight and possibilities of the white child of European immigrants. In doing so, it "popularized a vision of postwar citizenship in which a nostalgic version of an 'ethnic past' became a universal American past" (74).

But, as J. Smith also points out, because this narrative of an Irish-Austrian-American girl in the early twentieth century posited that "Americanization took place in mixed ethnic but white neighborhoods" (74), it also "circumvented racial and economic tensions of wartime working-class neighborhoods in which Blacks and whites jostled for housing and employment" and aligns with white flight practices that maintained racial segregation (56). Betty Smith herself found such jostling repulsive, which she makes clear in racist comments about midcentury Brooklyn's Black residents (qtd. in J. Smith 57ff). Smith's use of the appreciative child gaze enables these cultural resonances, building on the US-sanctioned value of whiteness as a platform for elevating the worth of the European Christian population living in deep poverty over that of other races and creeds. Francie's contemplative mode of appreciation lends narrative weight to her experience that further distances the devalued experiences of others; that is, the very serious nature of her seeing and its attendant intervention into representations of working-class communities strengthens the paradigm of whiteness it upholds as the basis for such value negotiation. In my examination of this text, I turn specifically to moments that engage the primacy of Francie's appreciative gaze to combat narratives that cast aside the human worth of communities like hers, as well as those that employ that same gaze to distance characters of other faiths and races, thereby naturalizing their subordination within white Christian paradigms of belonging.

Francie's appreciative observing is a controlling feature of the third-person text. Often engaging free indirect discourse, the looking-back narrative voice defers to Francie's reactions as a child even when they are couched in the language of an older narrator. Indeed, the collapsing of their perspectives and even language is limned in the first scene. The text introduces Francie to the reader by positioning her looking as a crucial, ongoing act, one that sparks her emotions and cognition: "Looking at the shafted sun, Francie had that same fine feeling that came when she recalled the poem they recited in school" (5). The mythical and pastoral poem, with its linguistically lush references to "forest primeval" and trees like "Druids of eld" (5), demonstrates the appreciation Francie feels for the view from her backyard, where only one "Tree of Heaven" grows (6). Known for growing "in boarded-up lots and out of neglected rubbish heaps . . . out of cement . . . in the tenements districts" (6), the Tree of Heaven contrasts the "pines" and "hemlocks" (5–6) of the poem, but not to signal failings in Francie's perspective. Rather, the juxtaposition of both scenes calls attention to the primacy of her subjectivity, which sees them in continuity. The poetic language of the narrative takes root in the experience of her Brooklyn childhood, and her point of view, quite literally, directs the narrative development.

Evoking the virtue of her gaze via the Romantic child's tie to nature and intensifying its vigor by tethering it to a tree that survives urban landscapes otherwise harsh to vegetation, this opening scene imbues Francie's perspective with tremendous value and strength. As she witnesses her neighborhood through the leaves of this tree, she suffuses the scene with affective appreciation for the beauty of daily life. "She looked into the open uncurtained windows and saw growlers being rushed out and returned overflowing with cool foaming beer" and "young girls making preparations to go out with their fellers. Since none of the flats had bathrooms, the girls stood before the kitchen sinks in their camisoles and petticoats, and the line the arm made, curved over the head while they washed under the arm, was very beautiful. There were so many girls in so many windows washing this way that it seemed a kind of hushed and expectant ritual" (26). The lack of curtains and private bathrooms is mentioned but not maligned; rather, their lack enables kitchen sink windows to be portals that invite Francie's appreciative looking. The adjectives "overflowing," "cool," "curved," and "beautiful" render the looking as pleasing without overtones of voyeurism, and Francie's visual focalization of the "hushed and expectant ritual" casts the scene as not only lovely, but holy.

But Francie also turns her eyes upon the danger and neglect in her community, which speaks to Smith's use of an appreciative gaze as not purely celebratory. As a young girl, she "walked home slowly from school with her eyes in the gutter looking for tin foil from cigarette packages or chewing gum" (7) to trade to the neighborhood junkie, who runs his business out of a "tumble-down stable." Inside, it is so dark that Francie has to blink, "adjusting her eyes to the darkness" where he pays a girl an extra penny if she lets him pinch her cheek (8). Her apartment has an airshaft running through it that Francie, who "once . . . looked down into" it, connects to purgatory (130).

At one point, Francie teases her brother that God must not see them: "If He went around looking into people's windows like you say, He'd see how things were here; He'd see that it was cold and that there was no food in the house; He'd see that Mama isn't strong enough to work so hard. And He'd see how Papa was and He'd do something about Papa" (276). Francie's matter-of-fact tone here speaks to the practical importance of looking, and slyly replacing God's gaze with her own demands that the shortcomings of her living conditions be part of the portrait of Brooklyn worth considering at length.

Indeed, the text makes clear that observing is itself an act to be valued; from her window at night, Francie "feel[s] like a spectator in a theater box," casting the neighborhood in the realm of high art and her gaze as that of a patron. Such a metacommentary on the worth of looking exists in direct contrast to the sentiments of one of her teachers, who, later in the novel, tells Francie that stories she has written about her late father are about "poverty, starvation and drunkenness . . . ugly subjects to choose. We all admit these things exist. But one doesn't write about them" (321). Echoing the sentiments of the editors who rejected Smith's manuscript, the teacher provokes Francie's anger. When she tells Francie to look up the word "sordid," the text registers that anger visually with "the page turned red under her eyes" (324). After the teacher tells her to burn her stories while chanting "I am burning ugliness" (324), Francie ultimately overturns the paradigm, burning instead her stories that did earn As because they performed her teacher's ideal of "beautiful." She burns them specifically because they are not representative of the reality of her own, literal gaze: "I never *saw* a poplar . . . and I never *saw* those flowers except in a seed catalogue" (328; emphasis added). This material is burned with a chant for *its* "ugliness" (328), and the next image she considers appreciatively is a pathos-laden visual of her pregnant, tired mother coming home from a long day of housecleaning: "She saw her mother's face in the trolley car when Mama sat with her head back and her eyes closed. She remembered how white and tired Mama had looked. Mama *did* love her" (329). Refocusing her gaze upon the value of her life in the very "poverty" that repulses her teacher, Francie reads the beauty of love in the commitment and work ethic of her mother and her undernourished, tired body. That which the teacher calls ugly matters—in and of itself and because it indexes humanity deserving of appreciation.

But while the text's insistence on the primacy of child's appreciative gaze seems to signify the value of early twentieth-century Brooklyn tenement communities, it does not extend its project of social inclusivity beyond Francie's white, Christian paradigm and thus perpetuates exclusion. When Francie's eyes fall on characters different from her by way of religion, ethnicity, and race, her gaze devalues them through discriminatory distancing. Often her eyes turn away altogether, leaving such characters invisible. For example, in her white experience of Brooklyn, "the mystery of mysteries to Francie was the Chinaman's one-windowed store" (137), her entrance into which launches a brief passage abounding with descriptions that steep the scene in Orientalism. Variations of the word "mystery" appear at least six times in a page and a half, marking the Chinese owner of the store and his merchandise as unknowable, "wonderful" oddities that are there for her pleasure, rather than people and things to be honored in their own right. While she is here "appreciating" the store's effect on her, the focus is on her vantage point as a visiting, tourist-like white girl rather than on the inherent value in what she is seeing.

In addition, her gaze also becomes a "stare" when she applies stereotypical descriptives to Jewish persons: "She stared at the bearded men in their alpaca skull caps and silkolene coats and wondered what made their eyes so small and fierce" (11). She also witnesses her brother and his friends harass several young Jewish boys and does not intervene (18–19). Tellingly, in this moment of witness, the text pulls back from her commentary about what she sees and reports only the actions. Unlike the effect of Charley's gaze in Jesse Jackson's *Call Me Charley*, discussed in this book's introduction and later in chapter two, when Francie's moment of looking dilates in a weighty narrative silence, *A Tree Grows in Brooklyn* distances her from the object of her gaze, the non-Francie-focalized narration marking the scene of harassment as inconsequential to her otherwise appreciative contemplation of her world.

There is at least one moment, however, when Francie's appreciative gaze overtly struggles with the possibility of resisting such deeply entrenched stereotypes, and the resolution of this moment reflects the possibilities for an appreciative child gaze even as it forecloses them. Consider her thoughts upon seeing a Jewish woman "big with child . . . watching the life on the street and guarding within herself, her own mystery of life" (11):

> Francie remembered her surprise that time when Mama told her that Jesus was a Jew. . . . Mama said that the Jews had never looked on Jesus as anything but a troublesome Yiddish boy. . . . And the Jews believed that their Messiah was yet to come. Thinking of this, Francie stared at the Pregnant Jewess.
>
> "I guess that's why the Jews have so many babies. . . . And why they sit so quiet . . . waiting. And why they aren't ashamed the way they are fat. Each one thinks that she might be making the real little Jesus. That's why they walk so proud when they're that way. Now the Irish women always look so ashamed. They know that they can never make

a Jesus. It will be just another Mick. When I grow up and know that I am going to have a baby, I will remember to walk proud and slow even though I am not a Jew." (12)

Mama as remembered interlocutor prompts but does not control Francie's thoughtful gazing here. By recalibrating stories she has been fed about Jewish people's attitudes toward Jesus, their large families, and their habits when pregnant, Francie makes sense of their pride in a way that somewhat honors the woman as well as the unborn child—so much so that she decides to align herself and her future child with them. But her use of "Mick" and the derogatory intonation in her use of "fat" suggest an underdeveloped critique of the attitudes toward pregnant Irish women she has witnessed in her own community, and the use and capitalization of "Pregnant Jewess" also posits the lady as a type rather than as a person. The narration delivers Francie's visual rendering as portrait-like and from a distance. She has renegotiated her view of the Jewish woman with child but ultimately in order to attend to her own trajectory as an Irish girl—and the text's deference to her perspective condones the act.

There is also a glaring omission of Black characters in an area where they would surely have lived (J. Smith 56). Their very absence from Francie's sight lines upholds their erasure from national scripts of belonging, during both the time period in which the novel is set and that in which it was written. Furthermore, given the popularity of Smith's text and its role in propagating the nostalgic white ethnocentrism that still underpins notions of America as an "immigrant nation," the text's support of such erasure persists into the present day. Francie's gaze does not highlight but nevertheless reinforces the limits of her perspective. Complicit in perpetuating the practice of othering, her thoughtful contemplation—her careful appreciation—thus makes that very complicity seem a part of the seemingly thorough looking that is the text's controlling paradigm.

Given that the appreciative child gaze achieves a careful and sometimes celebratory examination of that which falls into its purview, that which it distances or leaves out can be made to seem by the narrative as *rightfully* left out—as if by a beautifully textured curtain dropped against that which does not "fit" the intended lens. While Sydney Taylor's use of the appreciative child gaze in *All-of-a-Kind Family* excludes aspects of tenement life that do not support her warmly celebratory project, Betty Smith's use of the child gaze in *A Tree Grows in Brooklyn*, even as it seems to argue for an inclusive understanding of working-class Brooklyn life, exclusively focuses on whiteness as the controlling paradigm for appreciating the working class. In doing so, it reproduces racial hierarchies that align with discriminatory notions of belonging in the United States. Indeed, the emotionally and cognitively inflected dynamism of the contemplative mode of the appreciative gaze renders the stereotypes it promulgates and the boundaries it erects as static in comparison to the dynamism elsewhere perceived. Furthermore, the lack of engagement achieved by simply averting the gaze—as is the case with Black inhabitants of early twentieth-century Williamsburg—erases even the act of marginalization. Not made visible within the storyworld of the text, such erasures can mobilize the discriminatory efficacy of an appreciative gaze wielded by a child who fits into one or more nationally "preferred" identity categories.

APPRECIATING COMPLEXITY IN JAMES BALDWIN AND YORAN CAZAC'S *LITTLE MAN, LITTLE MAN: A STORY OF CHILDHOOD*

The picture book collaboration between writer James Baldwin and illustrator Yoran Cazac, *Little Man, Little Man: A Story of Childhood*, also participates in the contemplative dimension of the appreciative child gaze, but it does so by manifesting alternate ways of seeing that topple exclusionary and stereotypical narratives. Baldwin and Cazac turn the appreciative child gaze on the spectrum of experience in main character TJ's life, including the celebratory moment with family with which I began this chapter, as well as that which is not necessarily to be celebrated but is nevertheless not to be erased. Thus, Baldwin and Cazac emphasize the dimension of the appreciative gaze having to do with perceptive awareness of complexities. Employing a combination of verbal (through the text's prose) and visual (through the text's illustrations) cues to follow TJ's gaze, *Little Man, Little Man* postures TJ and his life in 1970s Harlem as worth careful consideration rather than the anti-Black condemnation aimed at his milieu in hegemonic popular media of the time. Melamed argues that race-radical "literary texts make meanings [beyond the boundaries of permissible representation policed by official antiracisms] by creating repertoires of value, difference, analogy, and comparison that . . . replace liberal antiracist epistemes with experiential-analytical ways of knowing race" (xvii). Baldwin and Cazac's race-radical project is enacted via their use of an appreciative child gaze, a narrative strategy that proposes a "repertoire of value" centered on the experiences and contemplations of the urban Black child. Evading overt or simple conclusions about that which falls into TJ's field of vision, the picture book asserts the Black child's gaze as an alternative mode of knowing that resists US hegemonic value structures that demean the inhabitants of Baldwin's Harlem.

In his piece "A Talk to Teachers," Baldwin himself puts forth a brief theory of child looking:

> Children, not yet aware that it is dangerous to look too deeply at anything, look at everything, look at each other, and draw their own conclusions. They don't have the vocabulary to express what they see, and we, their elders, know how to intimidate them very easily and very soon. But a black child, looking at the world around him, though he cannot know quite what to make of it, is aware [of his oppression] . . . and it isn't long—in fact it begins when he is in school—before he discovers [it]. (124–25)

Twice the book points out that TJ will begin to attend school next year (Baldwin, *Little* 49, 66), which positions TJ as one of these children who does not "yet have the vocabulary to express what they see" but who can nonetheless look "deeply." It is fitting, then, that in order to consider 1970s Harlem through the eyes of a young Black boy, Baldwin chose the picture book—his only publication in this form—as his medium. In this form, which can contain a host of varying relations between verbal text and visual illustration, Baldwin and Cazac engage with the vocabulary and impulses of the child in order to preserve TJ's point of view both as a narrative positionality and as a literal lens that captures an appreciative portrait of the residents and community it depicts.[6] Combining ekphrastic description with watercolor and sketched artwork allows the text to refrain from providing the precise, analytical language Baldwin uses to convey overt social and political insights in his writing for adults. As *Little Man, Little Man* enacts Baldwin's sense of child vision, it dwells upon, though does not fully articulate, the meaning of what TJ sees, which is nevertheless evoked in Yoran Cazac's watercolor depictions of Harlem and its people. The appreciative child gaze in this text is thus both manifest and ineffable. It legitimizes a way of looking that makes visible complexities so profound that they elude straightforward or simple understanding. TJ's gaze is appreciative specifically because it highlights those complexities without reducing them to foregone conclusions.

This is not to say that TJ does not think or reason; on the contrary, the extent to which he can articulate his impressions of and reactions to his sensory world are crucial to the narration and thus attach to his gaze a process of observing, considering, and weighing that mark it as fundamentally appreciative of the complexities he witnesses. TJ is the sole focalizer indulged by the third-person narration, and the collapsing of the narration into the focalizing child, a narration couched in the immediacy of the present tense, demands the reader honor the perceptions of TJ on his own terms and in his own time.[7]

TJ's acts of looking comprise a series of narrative moves that linger and mull over the complexities of a situation while maintaining a focus on the image that prompts them. This manifestation of the appreciative child gaze casts the reader as unable to rely on the looking child *or* the third-person narrator for direct, overt conclusions, thus eschewing closed circuits of meaning. And yet, the reader remains beholden to the details and connections the child perceives as crucial—as *valuable* to the very conclusions the text withholds. In this way, the text performs appreciation while resisting judgment, opening through the present immediacy of an interested, lingering child gaze possibilities for considerate perception of Harlem life. The text supplies what Nicholas Boggs terms an "important counter-narrative to the dominant representations of Black childhood that Black children of the time encountered on a day-to-day basis in Harlem and beyond" ("Baldwin" 119), and it is important to note that this counternarrative is not directive but invitational.[8] Its appreciative child gaze is agential, tethered to the thinking and exploring Black child; the text requires, through its appreciative child gaze, a witnessing act of its reader, who is deterred by the narrative dynamics from ascribing a specifically articulated meaning to what they see that dishonors the subjectivity of the child. I turn to several moments in the text that exemplify this way of witnessing the features of TJ's Harlem life and bring to the fore the complexity and the worth of his neighbors.

The opening pages of the text exhibit TJ's careful concern for those whom he sees in his neighborhood, those who look back at him, and the emotional and cognitive dynamics such seeing prompts. Noticing Mr. Man, the building superintendent, collecting garbage cans, TJ's loose association of thoughts leads him from the way "Mr. Man always try to act like he mean" to his "old" age of "thirty-seven" to his "color of chocolate cake without no icing on it," which is amended by "except when he grin." That, in turn, becomes a meditation on the fact that "he don't hardly never grin, except at TJ," though "sometime he act like he don't see him. But TJ know he see him" (7). The string of contrast words throughout the passage—"but," "except," "though," and so on—signal the many adjustments TJ makes to his ideas as he watches Mr. Man, who is sometimes, but not always, a "**real, real nice man**" (9; bold in original).[9] TJ understands that people are legible, even in their complexities and ambiguities; he appreciates the multifaceted image

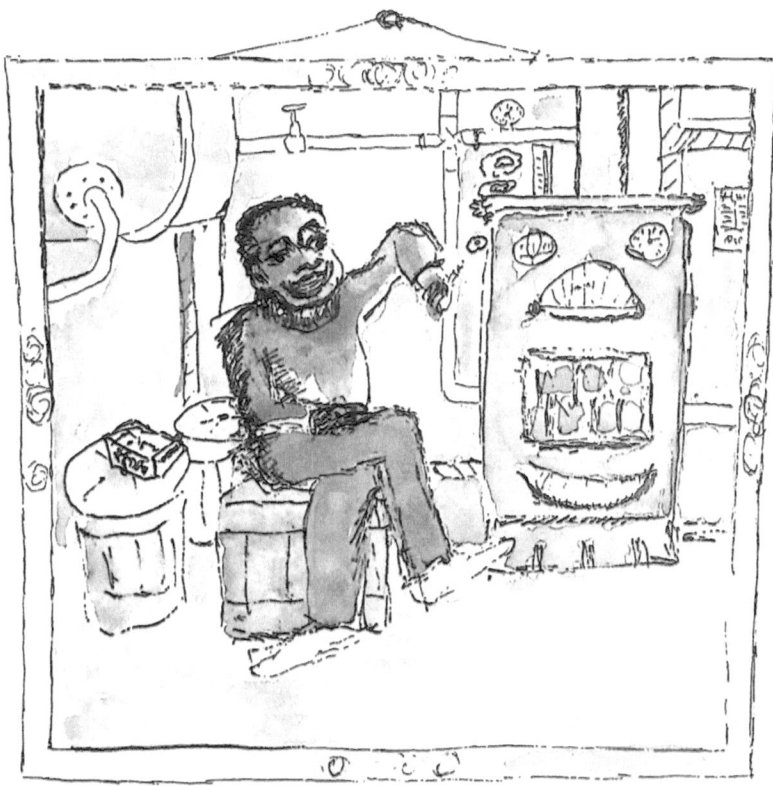

Figure 1.2. "he a real, real real nice man" (Baldwin and Cazac 8). Used with the permission of Beatrice Cazac.

they present to him, contradictory as it may be. Yet there is an emotional inflection here, key to Baldwin and Cazac's project. The bold "**real, real nice man**" is part of a pattern of bolded lettering that functions as captions connecting the verbal narration to Cazac's illustrations, and here it gestures to the portrait of Mr. Man sitting and smiling by his basement furnace, which itself seems to be smiling (figure 1.2). That the image is bordered by a drawn frame that appears to hang on the page asks the reader to consider this facet of Mr. Man's personality most prominently—and appreciatively, in the celebratory sense. TJ's articulation of his gaze leading up to this moment, however, weighs the celebratory against the puzzling, refusing a portrait of Mr. Man that rests on oversimplified characterization.

The worth of those upon whom TJ gazes is clear from the very fact that he considers them at length, even if he questions or does not understand exactly how to think about them. TJ's reasoning process about his friend Blinky, for instance, who wears "**them eye-glasses blinking just like the sun was hitting**

Figure 1.3. "**Them eye-glasses blinking just like the sun was hitting you in the eye**" (Baldwin and Cazac 11). The bold text corresponds with a bolding of the text in the original document from which the caption is procured and that I note as part of my analysis. Used with the permission of Beatrice Cazac.

you in the eye" (10), exhibits his interest in her as well as his struggle to form and articulate conclusive ideas about her and the way she sees the world:

> She say she can't see without [her glasses]. Maybe that true, if she say so. But TJ put them on one time and he couldn't see nothing with them on. He couldn't see across the street. Everything looked like it was rained on. So TJ ain't too sure about Blinky. It was some white folks at school bought her them glasses. If *he* can't see out them how *she* going to see out them? And she older than he is. She eight years old. She ought to know better. But she a girl. (10)

TJ applies different lenses to explore his confusion about her lenses (Blinky's words, his vision, her teachers' race, their age and gender difference), engaging

Figure 1.4. "**They didn't think so, neither**" (Baldwin and Cazac 24–25). The bold text corresponds with a bolding of the text in the original document from which the caption is procured and that I note as part of my analysis. Used with the permission of Beatrice Cazac.

the perspective-taking the text requires and embodying the unsettledness of the narrative's conclusions.[10] His bolded statement, with a "you" both conversational and imperative, functions as a narratively integrated caption for a striking full-page watercolor of Blinky, which sutures his free indirect discourse to the visual (figure 1.3). Placing the reader in the perspective of TJ, mesmerized by the radiating sunbeams glinting off her glasses as she meets the reader's gaze, Blinky's image manifests a figure at once commanding, complicated, and warmly rendered in the oranges and yellows of a sunburst. Furthermore, the slight angle of concern in the lines of her eyelids mimics and elicits the appreciative gaze constituted by the text: a concentrated, considered care. Blinky is often tasked with keeping an eye on TJ, and so this appreciative gazing is somewhat mutual; she, along with their friend WT, Mr. Man, and other characters in the text, legitimate TJ as a seen and cared about child—a valuable child.[11]

Cazac's multiple illustrations of the same figures or scenes in the text often employ contrasting rhetorics of color, line, and composition, following TJ's verbally delivered, ambivalent consideration of that upon which he gazes, thus marking his attention as appreciative rather than rejecting. For example, there are four very different visual/verbal renderings of the people struggling with drug addiction who populate TJ's neighborhood. TJ's initial visual sense of them, that they "look like they gone to sleep" and "don't look like they never bother nobody" (24–25), contrasts with his friend WT's assessment, that he needs to "look out for TJ, so TJ won't never get to be like that" (25). In the accompanying illustration, hurried, chaotic lines contour the faces of the people sketched across the bottom of the double spread, limning the rough subject matter (figure 1.4). The figures seem immobilized, as in TJ's assessment, and yet worthy of attention due to their representation in the form of busts. Indeed, more to the point, they are sketched studies thereof, which gestures toward the unfinished, the nondefinitive. TJ sets himself apart from them, not "see[ing] how he ever going to be like that," but WT's response—"**They didn't think so, neither**" (25)—is the bolded statement on this page, suggesting that TJ's vision of the figures is affected by WT's contribution. Many figures have their eyes closed or cast aside from the viewer, signaling TJ's view of them as "asleep" but perhaps also gesturing to defeat, shame, loss of vision, or loss of interest—a state none of them, according to WT, could anticipate.

Their numbers also emphasize the vulnerability to addiction of all folks in this neighborhood. In his "Talk to Teachers," Baldwin mentions "junkies" as a key feature of the housing projects in which Black "street boy[s]" live (125–26), calling them the "results of a criminal conspiracy to destroy [the Black child]" (130). In these pages of *Little Man, Little Man*, Baldwin and Cazac are rewriting US narratives about "the criminalization of urban communities" (Melamed 39) by casting the figures as victims of circumstance rather than perpetrators. By doing so, the book works against what Melamed terms the "dematerializ[ation]" that can make such people and their communities "illegible" (Melamed 39).

The next pages both confirm and complicate this portrait by their inclusion of two different renderings of WT's older brother, who "**sit on the stoop like that a whole lot of times**" (26). Immediately above the bold statement about WT's brother, a warm, watercolor image depicts an older boy, sitting with his elbows on his knees and his hands on his cheeks, staring through open, emotive eyes into the middle distance off the right margin (figure 1.5). Captured at a three-quarter view and framed by an arched border that implies his centrality in TJ's visual exploration of Harlem, the boy appears melancholy, and poignantly so. His eyes as well as the bright hues of his blue T-shirt, his orange pants, and the warm yellow steps upon which he sits invite rather than deter the reader's gaze—a gaze that aligns with TJ's vantage point. Even the trash can lids in the background seem to form a sad cluster of ironic halos around the troubled boy's head, whose skin picks up traces of their bright green to suggest his sickness. This is one image TJ has of his friend's brother: a sympathetic figure who deserves consideration.

The complexity of such consideration, however, is made clear in the next image, rendered in jagged black lines (which recall the busts on the previous

Figure 1.5. "**WT got a brother older than him and he sit on the stoop like that a whole lot of times**" (Baldwin and Cazac 26). The bold text corresponds with a bolding of the text in the original document from which the caption is procured and that I note as part of my analysis. Used with the permission of Beatrice Cazac.

page), of a scene TJ has witnessed (figure 1.6). "One time TJ watch WT while he beat on his brother . . . , slap him all over his face . . . , curse his brother . . . , and his brother just make sounds and spit coming out his mouth and running down his chin and his eyes roll up" (27). The contorted bodies of the sketched figures exude trauma. No bold statement calls attention to this drawing, which perhaps suggests the primacy of the previous watercolor. However, the image's composition of harsh, dark strokes emphasizes the physical violence and emotional distress it depicts, and it is positioned at the top of the page to assert its importance to TJ's ruminations. This is a moment that demands the depth of consideration the text calls for regarding WT and his brother's situation and demonstrates that the text's appreciative mode encompasses more than the celebratory connotations it has in the kitchen scene. The beating here is not to be enjoyed, but rather understood as an important part of the situation to which Baldwin and Cazac call attention: TJ's witnessing WT's experience as a younger sibling, devastated and angry that his brother is overpowered by an inert hopelessness he self-medicates to numbness.

Figure 1.6. "One time TJ watch WT while he beat on his brother" (Baldwin and Cazac 27). Used with the permission of Beatrice Cazac.

The final rendering of WT's brother moves into the realm of TJ's visual imagination, signaling that he seeks an alternate way to make sense of what he witnesses. He likens the brother's swaying to "them plants TJ saw under the water, just back and forth and back and forth like that, just like them plants TJ saw way at the bottom of the water that time when they went to Jones Beach and his Daddy carried TJ out in the water on his back" (28). Above the ekphrastic passage is a watercolor, in much darker tones compared to the warmth of the three-quarter portrait, that depicts an underwater plant in the shape of a boy (figure 1.7). Bubbles float up from his face, implying that he is alive and breathing in his plant body, but he is also rooted to the ocean floor, unable to move and subject to the power of the current. The stray anchor dug into the silt to his right is thus both poignant and whimsical, and the ocean life swimming and growing around the plant boy manifests a vibrant dynamism in both the image and the child mind that visualizes it, even as the strangeness of the scene refuses a simple interpretive stance.

These juxtaposed images, all connected by TJ's rumination on the drug-addled young men on the stoop, are evoked—but not made sense of—in

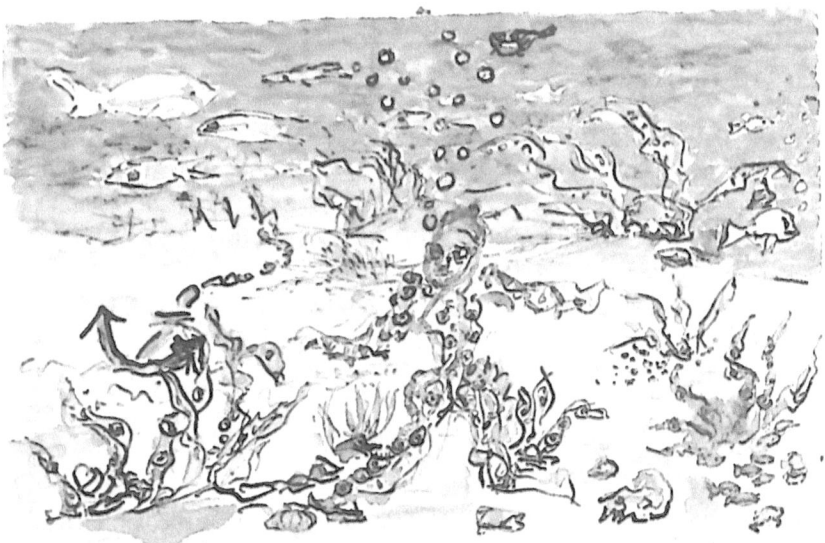

Figure 1.7. "Just like them plants" (Baldwin and Cazac 28). Used with the permission of Beatrice Cazac.

the verbal narration. Rather, after witnessing WT beat his brother, TJ feels "scared" and "don't know what to say" (29). Refusing verbal explanation, the picture book, rather, retains its focus on TJ's gaze via the drawn-out visual attention to its complexities, which arise as much from the scene TJ witnesses as from TJ himself. The dimensions of these complexities are signaled, too, in the differences in composition among all four images. TJ's gaze carries the weight of his ineffable appreciation of WT's and his brother's plight. That he sees them in multiple dimensions emphasizes the depth of consideration that characterizes his gaze and the confrontation of reductive understandings that it subtly performs.[12]

In Baldwin and Cazac's text, representation of Harlem life is so bound up in child vision that it is both concrete and esoteric; even the watercolor medium reflects a desire to capture a particular perspective while limning the fluidity of perspective-taking made possible by the appreciative child gaze. In David Leeming's biography of Baldwin, he offers only one brief remark about *Little Man, Little Man*: that it exhibits Baldwin's "concern with the whole question of black self-esteem" (330). I posit that the appreciative gaze is the vehicle of Baldwin's concern. Seeing appreciatively—that is, carefully, allowing for complexities and ambiguities otherwise elided by stereotype or dismissal—is the way the text makes clear that what a child witnesses matters and that their witnessing itself matters. Indeed, when texts assert such a gaze through the figure of the child, they subvert scripts that, to use Melamed's indictment of "official" antiracisms, limit "which social representations of difference have appeared reasonable, possible, or desirable" (xvi). The appreciative child gaze in texts such as Baldwin and Cazac's rejects such limited representations, opting instead for a range of representation that resists a unified, simplistic, and dangerously reductive understanding. The insistence on the appreciative gaze in the picture book positions the reader to look at the complexities of TJ's world *with* the child. The textual dynamics honor some readers' similar experiences and contemplations while deterring other readers from drawing simple and potentially discriminatory conclusions that ignore or devalue the child's perspective.

CONCLUSION

The appreciative child gaze in US literature, pivoting on the connections historically and socially established between the figure of the child and value, allows texts to recast children, childhoods, and communities that have been ignored or vilified in a discriminatory national imagination as worthy of considerate attention, and sometimes celebration. Works that employ this narrative strategy center the source of value-making in marginalized children as opposed to the hegemonic narratives that often reject or erase them, and therefore posit a radical revision of US hierarchies of value and belonging. All of the registers on which the appreciative child gaze can function, from celebratory to contemplative to comprehensively aware, connote the worth of that upon which the child gazes as well as the worth of the child who performs such looking. Yet, as texts such as *A Tree Grows in Brooklyn* and *All-of-a-Kind Family* show, its subtle power also runs the risk of upholding problematic hierarchies, especially when it distances or turns away from those who remain in oppressed positions or those who enforce that oppression.

The appreciative child gaze is a quiet strategy, one that manifests as non-confrontational in the diegetic world of the text—and may thus elude or disarm critics opposed to its aims—but also one that makes the bold move of naturalizing through a child figure radical calls for revaluing. While the texts featured in this chapter were published between 1943 and 1976, the appreciative gaze persists as a narrative technique beyond the middle decades of the twentieth century, sometimes employed as a controlling perspective through which a story is told and other times deployed in brief but pointed moments to signal worth. Texts such as Louise Erdrich's *The Birchbark House* (2002), Matt de la Peña and Christian Robinson's *Last Stop on Market Street* (2015), and David Levithan's *Boy Meets Boy* (2003), for instance, all employ scenes or extended engagement with appreciative gazing, where a young person's acts of looking work against hegemonic practices and narratives that have marginalized groups of people—in these cases, Ojibwe people, individuals from economically depressed communities, and LGBTQ persons, respectively.

As a narrative strategy, the appreciative child gaze's literal and unironic engagement with the sight lines of the child imbues texts with attitudes that honor the child as purveyor and conveyor of value, thus insisting that the narration be received by the implied reader on the child's own terms. It also takes child noticing and perspective-taking seriously, positing agency in the child's attention. Chapter three's work on the process of signification wrapped up in what I term the "transactional child gaze" will take up this notion of agency in relation to child looking with more rigor, but here it is worth noting that appreciative looking requires a child character who is alert and alive to the world around them. Even in the case of the more celebratory register of the appreciative child gaze, which need not be attended by profound depth of thinking and weighty consideration (here examined in relation to *All-of-a-Kind Family*), the strategy conjures child agency in the child's experience of pleasure in their sight lines. Texts that employ the appreciative child gaze on any register thus imply a dynamism in the children's interiorities and in their responses to their worlds. These children and their looking constitute the locus of each text's—or in the case of texts with more sparsely employed appreciative gazing, each scene's—attitudes. The children are the mimetic originator of a gaze that, as thematic and synthetic narrative device on the literary page, rewrites the troubling narratives that otherwise relegate their real-life counterparts and communities to the periphery.

Chapter Two

THE COUNTERSURVEILLANT CHILD GAZE

Looking Back at Authority

In October 2015, South Carolina high school resource officer Ben Fields, an adult white man, body slammed, dragged over the floor, and arrested a fourteen-year-old student, an African American girl, because she did not respond to a summons to the "discipline office" (Stelloh and Connor). The footage of the scene is alarming, not the least due to the disparities in age, gender, and race that position the officer's assault as part of a discriminatory and violent history involving grown white men and young Black girls in the United States. Seeing that legacy acted out with physical violence in a classroom—a state-sanctioned space—puts even more emphasis on the dangers of political realities for the country's most marginalized children. Monique Morris's work highlights how Black girls are subject to criminalization in American public schools, and this moment, repulsive and uniquely violent as it may have seemed to many news watchers, is representative of the widespread derogation, abuse, and exclusion aimed at young people who do not fit the persistent image of the ideal American child—suburban, white, and "innocent."

But the footage that prompted circulation of the story was captured by several of the girl's classmates on their cell phones in acts that upset hierarchies of power and surveillance (Sorkin). Run by news outlet after news outlet, the videos appeared in network newscasts, online publications, and social media. Non-state-sanctioned acts of documentation, the videos capture not only the scene but also the verbal and facial expressions of other classmates as they reacted in shock and anger at the officer's treatment of the girl. These cell phone videos fall under the category of sousveillance, a term coined by

Steve Mann to refer to a countersurveillant measure achieved by the use of wearable or cell phone cameras by individuals below (i.e., *sous*: below, rather than *sur*: above) the controlling surveillant hierarchy (Monahan, *Surveillance* 158). The young people in this classroom, from a position of subordination surrounded by the authority of teacher, officer, school system, and state, took up countersurveillance as a strategy to document the discriminatory and violent practices that take place there. This type of resistant witnessing and documentation is a key way children can achieve agency and political potency within the modern surveillance state. It is a way to look back at the performers of top-down surveillance, flipping the subject/object paradigm assumed by those in the privileged position of surveillant.

The texts examined in this chapter exhibit the ways writers for children and adults have constructed children who gaze countersurveillantly to imbue their texts with such child-centered resistance. Representing children looking countersurveillantly is a rhetorical move that turns attention in the opposite direction from the appreciative child gaze discussed in chapter one. While an appreciative gaze works nonconfrontationally by focusing on bringing value to that which has been marginalized or erased by systemic exclusion from national belonging, a countersurveillant child gaze focuses directly upon the agents of such systemic exclusion, targeting them within the child's sight lines in order to confront and reject the surveillance-dependent ideologies that uphold their power. Children who gaze countersurveillantly in these texts are marginalized by race or ethnicity, thus enabling a pointed exposure of and refusal to adhere to discriminatory mandates about "approved" ways of seeing. These are children who look back at the systems of oppression that surveil their bodies, deny their freedoms, and perform violence in the name of maintaining whitewashed images of US childhood and nationhood.

Furthermore, texts that employ the countersurveillant child gaze evoke but refrain from embracing the Romantic concept of an innocent child with purity or "truth" of vision; they ask readers to see the oppression of authority clearly even as they eschew the accompanying notion of the child as transcendent. These children do not transcend. Rather, they are mired in the sociopolitical milieu into which they have been born. Given that innocence has long been "raced white" (Bernstein, *Racial* 4), it matters that the countersurveillant child gaze relies on narrative rhetorics that reclaim children of color as part of the innocence paradigm—even as they impugn authority with their sight lines. In doing so, the countersurveillant child gaze refuses the phenomenon of adultification, whereby marginalized children, especially Black children, are apt to be discriminatorily perceived as "not child."[1] Roy Pérez theorizes a narrative strategy he terms "approximation," whereby a "strategic falling short of the normal" allows a text to posture with "measured imprecision, contingency, unpredictability, and the refusal of repetition and resolution in relation to the normal" (194). Ascribing the act of countersurveillance to such children participates in this strategy, evocatively combining the power attached to looking back at authority with culturally ascribed notions of child innocence and therefore both refusing hegemonic conceptions of innocence that exclude certain children and positioning the implied reader to perceive the child's gaze as an ethical imperative. In addition, such children inherit the legacy of value and worth discussed in the previous chapter. Thus, the countersurveillant child gaze energizes competing constructions of the child, rearranging them in an alchemy of resistance, worth, and vulnerability. Rather than diffusing the power of the gaze, this rearrangement propels its arresting magnetism on the literary page.

This chapter begins with a discussion of the relationships among surveillance, countersurveillance, and the literary child before moving to close readings of four twentieth-century US texts that construct a countersurveillant child gaze. In order to exhibit the flexibility of this narrative strategy across time periods, I begin that examination with two novels for young readers, one written near the beginning and one written near the end of what Jacqueline Dowd Hall terms the long civil rights movement: a historical understanding that civil rights movement work for the Black population in the United States spanned from the liberal 1930s through the 1970s in a dialectic of protest and backlash. Each features scenes in which communities deny the value of the Black child in ways that are visible to that child, who in turn functions as literal witness to systematic methods of exclusion and discrimination. Jesse Jackson's *Call Me Charley* (1945) performs the countersurveillant child gaze quietly, employing it as a narrative technique that subverts the text's otherwise apparent focus on interracial friendship. Mildred Taylor's historical fiction novel *Roll of Thunder, Hear My Cry* (1976) provides Cassie Logan's more assertive countersurveillant gaze, one that sharpens her character's power diegetically and extradiagetically. Taken together, these texts demonstrate the ways literature written for young people uses the countersurveillant child gaze as a narrative strategy that works as a subversive call to action in stories that might otherwise couch their critiques in forms considered "safe" for broad child audiences. Both also evoke even as they blur the innocence of the child in order to document and evaluate, through the child's gaze, the mechanisms that deny the marginalized child entrance into narratives of US belonging.

From this pair of texts, I turn to two pieces written for presumably adult audiences: Philip Roth's allohistory *The Plot against America* (2004) and Langston Hughes's short story "The Red-Headed Baby" from his collection *The Ways of White Folks* (1934). Roth's child character, young Philip, navigates an alternate 1940s United States where a newly elected president targets the Jewish population as unwanted and un-American; he watches closely while his country turns on him and his family. His gaze, recounted by his adult self, engages overlays of past and present, allohistorical and contemporary, child and adult—all of which position the child as a serious, knowing, and pathos-laden lens through which to view political shifts that restrict the definitions and protections of citizenship. Hughes's "Red-Headed Baby," on the other hand, provides an interesting counterpoint to the other texts in this chapter, in that the titular child does not wield his countersurveillant gaze consciously, but the narrative dynamics of the text emphasize its power both diegetically and extradiegetically. Though the text is focalized through a racist white man, the Black child's gaze operates mimetically, thematically, and synthetically to indict the racism levied at Black Americans by the white communities who assume authority over them, even as it provides a conduit for the hope to defeat it. The opacity of the child in this story, as well as the free indirect discursive narration that exhibits its focalizing character's attempts to objectify him, highlights the flexibility of the child gaze as a narrative tool for radical social critique.

Functioning across texts written for children and adults, the countersurveillant child gaze does not trade in the binary of innocence/experience so much as it collapses it, rooting moments of looking in the lived experience of being a child in the United States—and signaling to child and adult readers alike that childhood is a stance from which social critique can emanate. It is true that the child characters in these texts take on the countersurveillant mode with varying degrees of awareness, from Mildred Taylor's explicitly purposeful Cassie Logan to Langston Hughes's narratively opaque yet effective red-headed baby. These degrees of awareness can be partially attributed to the eras in which and audiences for whom these texts were created, contexts that tie the carefully crafted countersurveillant gaze of the literary child to political and social orientations. Indeed, understanding these pieces of literature in their unique contexts across the better part of the twentieth century, even as we understand them as sharing the countersurveillant child gaze, serves to highlight this gaze as an effective and versatile narrative strategy for making visible the racial ideologies that undergird the mechanisms of exclusion on which US nationhood is built.

SURVEILLANCE, COUNTERSURVEILLANCE, AND THE LITERARY CHILD GAZE

The countersurveillant child gaze in these texts is steeped in a culture of surveillance. Michel Foucault's often cited theories of "hierarchical observation"—manifest in, among other overlapping models, Bentham's panopticon, military camps, hospitals, and schools—posit surveillance as a key disciplinary mode of the state, and it is limned in each of the texts under discussion here. Objectifying and controlling the actions of individuals, state-sanctioned surveillance operates less by grand show than by quiet infiltration. Fortified by the assumption of surveillance as a foundational truth of social existence, observation aligned with the order of the state becomes personal impulse, as individuals surveil fellow members of the social order and understand themselves to be surveilled in turn (*Discipline* 170ff). In this way, surveillance is not enacted by one locus of power but is rather diffused over the multitudes, and, starting in childhood, social forces urge us to look in ways that support the power of the state.

Contemporary surveillance studies scholars argue that surveillance has become a quotidian way of life as we continue to organize communities via information infrastructures (Lyon 17), and many modes of surveillance tend to recapitulate the notion that individuals belonging to certain groups are more guilty or undesirable than others (Marx, *Undercover*).[2] Lyon points out that surveillance continues to depend on "social sorting," that is, "sorting the population into categories so that different groups may be treated differently" (19), and Torin Monahan notes that surveillance as a method of social control—think gated communities and privatized parks—often "naturalize[s] the exclusion of economically or culturally marginalized groups through architecture or infrastructure" ("Counter" 516). Surveillance is thus "never neutral" (Lyon 19). If child figures in texts like those I discuss in this chapter expose state-sanctioned surveillance by using a countersurveillant gaze to confront its concrete manifestation in their daily lives, the tenor of that exposure energizes anti-discriminatory critiques of their social contexts.

The dynamics that Marx, Lyon, Monahan and other surveillance scholars understand as crucial to the study of surveillance—and which the texts in this chapter represent—engineer what visual culture theorist Irit Rogoff refers to as "the visual codes by which some are allowed to look, others to hazard a peek, and still others are forbidden to look altogether" (16). Those codes are significantly inflected by identity markers such as race, class, gender, ethnicity, and creed, the foundation of much "social sorting" in the United States. People of color, for instance, are subject to an institutionalized white gaze in the United States with which all of the child characters discussed below contend. In *Dark Matters: On the Surveillance of Blackness*, Simone Browne draws on the work and experience of Frantz Fanon to demonstrate that US government surveillance—evident, for instance, in the CIA and FBI tracking of Black writers and thinkers such as Fanon, W. E. B. Du Bois, Ralph Ellison, James Baldwin, Claudia Jones, Lorraine Hansberry, and Angela Davis (3)—is irrefutably racialized. Since such "enactments of surveillance reify boundaries along racial lines, thereby reifying race," they often result in "discriminatory and violent treatment" (8). Her analysis of items ranging from slave ships to lighted surveillance of urban spaces, from information technology to film and modern airport practices, testifies to the ubiquity of racializing surveillance in US law and practice.

In *Black Bodies, White Gazes*, George Yancy also takes inspiration from Frantz Fanon and analyzes everyday lived experiences of blackness as well as literary representations thereof in relation to the white gaze. Focusing on the cultural and individual impact of white surveillance, he argues that "the current and historical epistemic . . . sustain[s] the white gaze and function[s] to objectify the Black body as an entity to be feared, disciplined, and relegated to . . . spaces that restrict Black bodies from 'disturbing' the tranquility of white life, white comfort, white embodiment, and white being" (xvi). In the legacy of thinkers like W. E. B. Du Bois and his formulation of "double consciousness"—himself an "early *visual* theorist of race" according to Shawn Michelle Smith (*Photography* 25)—Yancy argues that white surveillance "foreclose[s] any possibility of [his] being other than that dictated by the white imaginary" (55). Such surveillance privileges the literal and figurative eyes of those in power who control the types of images and ways of looking that relentlessly work to assert a dominant cultural gaze, one that excludes, disempowers, and fundamentally undermines the personhood of those not authorized to wield it. Given that those in control tend to be both white and adult, the child marginalized by US racial ideologies is a potent vehicle to assert opposition to that dominant gaze, for such a figure is doubly subject to both the social powerlessness and the perception of social threat that promulgate hierarchy.

According to Yancy, the spatialization of race also has a corollary in the internal figuration of the self. Those targeted by the oppressive gaze are "attacked at the level of one's personhood; it involves the invasion of the ontological integrity of one's sense of self, one's self-conceptualization" (Yancy 55). Given how the figure of the child has been associated with concepts of the self since at least the late 1800s via the work of Sigmund Freud, the countersurveillant child gaze can be understood as a primal rejection of such ontological attacks.

The possibilities of agency in the countersurveillant child gaze might be understood via exploration of Rogoff's key question: "In what political discourses can we understand looking and returning the gaze as an act of political resistance?" (Rogoff 16). Du Bois locates his first moment of double consciousness in the childhood experience of seeing a white classmate look askance at a card he offers her, which speaks to childhood as a viable site for noticing discriminatory social cues. Such noticing is the seed of empowerment, according to film scholar Fatimah Tobing Rony: "the racially charged glance can also induce one to see the very process which creates the internal splitting, to witness the conditions which give rise to the double consciousness" (4). The act of witnessing such conditions can catalyze agency, for "the Other perceives . . . the process of being visualized as an object, but returns the glance. The gesture of being frozen into a picturesque is deflected" (213). Black feminist scholar bell hooks, who like Du Bois locates the genesis of oppositional looking in childhood, refers to a similar politics of looking with her concept of "the oppositional gaze," wherein "subordinates in relations of power learn experientially that there is a critical gaze, one that 'looks' to document, one that is oppositional" (*Black* 116). Furthermore, Gillian M. E. Alban notes how women who look back at the patriarchy are figurative Medusas whose power lies in a gaze that paralyzes the men who attempt to capture them. This chapter examines what literary texts accomplish when that "subordinate" who looks back is also a child, one whose gaze serves to "capture" and, if even for a moment, freeze "the face of structures of domination" (hooks 116) for the reader, reversing the direction of surveillance and aligning the reader with a countersurveillant gaze that impugns discriminatory authority.

Rogoff, Rony, hooks, Yancy, Alban, and like-minded theorists all posit the act of looking by those who are oppressed as a point of tension and potential agency within the would-be controlling dominant visual field. That a child, already subjugated by age, might attain such agency only emphasizes the potency of looking back from a supposedly disempowered position. Foucault's rendering of panoptic power suggests that pervasive surveillance is successful precisely because it remains invisible to those it affects (187). However, these children point us toward a resistant looking that reverses the invisibility of authority by casting it as the seen object of a countersurveillant gaze from the figure least suspected by those in authority as capable of wielding it. The juxtaposition is arresting. It posits an implied or precocious agency in child subjectivity because it privileges child perception against hegemonic practices and directives.

Such acts of looking, of course, can be dangerous to the bodies who perform them, specifically because they occur within a system designed not just to deny agency but destroy it. In the case of Black bodies in the United States, returning the gaze is a historically dangerous practice. Enslaved people, for instance, "could be brutally punished for looking, for appearing to observe the whites they were serving as only a subject can observe" (hooks, "Representing" 168). The legacy of such punishment continued in "reckless eyeballing," a charge levied by many members of the Jim Crow era white community at a Black person who, they alleged, had committed a crime simply by looking at a white person—a crime recognized by the legal system that drew arrests and precipitated death sentences (Berry 8). We need only look at children such as Emmett Till to understand that the child is not removed from the risks of looking.[3] Yancy points out that today, such acts of looking are still deemed "transgression[s]" (45).[4] By looking back, objectified persons take on agency that is dangerous and powerful precisely because of its perceived connotations of threat and freedom; as such, this looking amounts not just to a documentation of the oppressor but also to a radical assertion of the self in the face of an oppressive hierarchy. Representing such looking as enacted by a young person emphasizes the vulnerability of this subject position—a vulnerability that becomes ethically powerful under the aegis of the child, whom these texts figure as deserving protection rather than punishment.

The literary children in this chapter—doubly subordinated by markers such as race, ethnicity, gender *and* age—perform a radical, countersurveillant gaze that documents and opposes the practices of local, state and federal institutions specifically wrought to manage the child's "place" in the US social structure. Respecting that bell hooks's formulation of the oppositional gaze is specific to her understanding of Black women spectators, and given that surveillance studies offers the term "countersurveillance," one that is both broad and flexible in its applicability to this project, I name the gaze at work in the texts I examine in this chapter the countersurveillant child gaze.

The term "countersurveillant" does not have a universal definition within surveillance studies, as it might refer to moves that disrupt surveillance as well as surveillance of the surveillant. Marx narrows it to the latter: a practice that "turn[s] the tables and surveil[s] those who are doing the surveillance" ("Tack" 384), including the action of sousveillance with which I began this chapter. Indeed, child characters are often considered to be "below" those who shape their world, whether that hierarchy or its agents are represented in the text or not. Their youth is generally understood to divide them from and subordinate them to the adult (and often white and male) world that is assumed to control the ideologies and institutions that act upon them. And given the rise in surveillance on children over the course of the twentieth and into the twenty-first century (Marx and Steeves), countersurveillance seems a particularly apt mode for a study of the child gaze in twentieth- and twenty-first century American literature.

Monahan uses the term countersurveillance more broadly, to "indicate intentional, tactical uses, or disruptions of surveillance technologies to challenge institutional power asymmetries." Those who engage in countersurveillance may do so by varied means, but they are "unified in the mission of safeguarding—or creating—the necessary spaces for meaningful participation in determining the social, environmental, and economic conditions of life" ("Counter" 516). This definition, in its inclusion of disruptions of surveillance as well as its mention of surveillance tools, is useful in that it allows me to orient literature as one of those technologies that can be recruited to expose discriminatory systems. As Monahan points out, real-world practitioners of countersurveillance "are foremost engaged in acts of symbolic resistance with the intention of raising public awareness about modern surveillance regimes" (516–17), a description that might well characterize the texts discussed below. Indeed, in Marx's formulation, countersurveillance can "uncover questionable practices" which, if "publicized . . . may lead to their moderation or cessation." Pointing to the case of a Jewish Defense League informant who captured on audio recording threats from his police handler, Marx notes that countersurveillance can have the effect of incriminating the surveillant (Marx, "Tack" 384). I posit that all of the texts in this chapter, by way of their representation of a child's gaze as countersurveillant, become countersurveillant themselves, their symbolic representation of child characters and their sight lines constituting an especially potent narrative technique that illuminates and impugns exclusionary tactics that historically and continually uphold discriminatory practices in the United States. The countersurveillant literary child raises awareness in a way that lobbies for the cessation of such tactics and the initiation of deep changes in the institutions they uphold.

Furthermore, I appreciate the linguistic similarity of "countersurveillance" to Critical Race Theory's term "counterstory," used to name narratives of lived experience from the perspectives of people from underrepresented groups (Delgado). Such stories can, like the texts in the previous chapter, conjure appreciation for a particular cultural group, or they can, like those in this chapter, expose the discriminatory practices of those in power. By way of the child who looks in countersurveillant ways, these texts join a tradition of counter-storytelling that resists and pushes back against the "stock stories" (Delgado) that naturalize exclusionary hegemonic practices.

This legacy of surveillance, countersurveillance, and the racialization of the two informs the following close readings of texts that represent children as agents of visual countersurveillance. In them, I focus on the narrative dynamics that construct the gaze, its object, and its wielder. I pay particular attention to the way the gaze operates diegetically—in the world of the story—as well as extradiegetically—on the level of narrative, especially in terms of its relation to the implied reader. In doing so, I sketch the potency of the child who looks back at authority in texts it imbues with a countersurveillant call for awareness and resistance. I also consider the ways these texts invoke and disrupt the innocence/experience binary (and its counterparts, such as child/adult, ignorant/knowing, powerless/powerful, protected/protecting) in order to position the marginalized child as a conduit for ethical critique of US racial ideologies. That each does so with differing narrative strategies speaks to the flexibility of the countersurveillant child gaze as a literary tool, one that functions on a sliding scale of subversive to overt and which is, even within each individual text, as protean and potent as the very child who wields it.

SILENT OPPOSITION: JESSE JACKSON'S *CALL ME CHARLEY*

In 1945, Jesse Jackson joined the ranks of the first African American writers to contract with major publishing houses in the United States. In the race for liberal national messaging of the early Cold War, which left little room for pointed sociopolitical critique (Dudziak 13), Jackson was faced with representing the struggles of a Black child without transgressing the limits of white tolerance for acknowledging ongoing and systemic racism—limits policed by the white editors who dominated the field.[5] Jackson's first novel, *Call Me Charley*, was marketed and received as a narrative that touted the way interracial friendship can ease race relations. However, Jackson also employs Charley's countersurveillant gaze to subvert this easing and stage a quiet critique of state-sanctioned anti-Black practices that target Black children in the US North.

By closely reading the complex narrative formulations that allow Charley's gaze to resonate both diegetically and extradiegetically, I find that Charley's gaze allows the narrative to "speak" during many of Charley's quiet moments of looking by rendering what I term a "museum silence" on the page. With this narrative cue, the text focuses its reader on visual manifestations of institutional racism that repel Charley's attempts at belonging. By orchestrating a quiet pause over Charley's pointed looking, the novel creates a moment of stillness, like those we might experience when witnessing a particularly evocative piece in a museum, in which the visual discourse of Charley's object is confronted by his gaze. This museum silence, partnered with a nonintrusive third-person narrative voice, creates the subversive conditions that allow the countersurveillant child gaze to perform Jackson's social critique amid Cold War demands to downplay and ignore exclusionary racial ideologies at work in the United States.

From the start, the text foregrounds the gaze as a tool for social navigation. Charley enters the novel under the gaze of two white boys, Tom and George, as they look at their new paperboy, newly moved to their previously all white suburban Ohio town because his parents have taken jobs as live-in servants for a doctor. Tom, the son of liberal parents, looks on with curiosity and even envy, as he wishes to work as a paperboy. George, the son of a bigoted father, "measure[s] the boy coolly" before dismissing him with a racial slur (8), which prompts the reader to understand George as the proxy for a surveilling community of white agents of exclusion. George's surveillant gaze is inflected violently, as his "gray eyes [become] slits" when he threatens Charley with a stick (8). Charley's looking is immediately oppositional—"Charley and George stared at one another like Bantam roosters" (8)—but he lowers his eyes as soon as George claims, "We don't allow n*****s around here" (8).[6] Charley's backing off signals his hurt as well as his powerlessness in the face of George's racialized surveillance, which allows the text to mitigate Charley's resistance by casting him as victim rather than rebel, a position aligned with midcentury race liberal sensibilities.

The novel, however, does not drop his countersurveillant gaze; rather it returns to it to mediate indictments of racism with careful subtlety. For instance, in this same scene, Tom joins George across the street, and "Charley watched them stand and talk for a while. George seemed excited" (9). In a narrative sleight-of-hand, the child gaze rendered on the page conjures a museum silence that emphasizes the content of an unnarrated conversation. Thus, the seemingly uneven third-person narration here—which oscillates among ventriloquizing bigotry through George, documenting Charley's knowing attempt at opposition, and pulling back to the ambiguously focalized "George seemed excited" as we view him out of earshot from across the street—exemplifies the way the text treads carefully; it withholds narrative commentary while privileging a countersurveillant child gaze that focuses the implied reader on the racist behavior of an antagonist without continuing to employ his language.

George's behavior is a way white children policed narratives of belonging related to middle-class childhood in the United States. Historian Steve Mintz recounts classic Cold War boyhood features such as homosocial play in large numbers, model airplanes, sports, lack of adult supervision, and patriotic displays in forms of parades and events (42), all of which Jackson mirrors in his text. Tom's basement workshop as well as the child-run "boys' club" in town represent the interests and groupings that characterized quintessential midcentury childhood for American boys. Tom's interest in Charley as a friend is constantly surveilled by George, who peers into windows and through screen doors whenever Tom invites Charley into his home.[7] When George is present with them in Tom's midcentury boyhood "workshop and hideout" (11), he makes comments such as "watch he [Charley] doesn't swipe" anything (50). Charley's response, however—"Better watch yourself" (50)—disrupts and redirects the intended implication of George's surveillance. Here, Charley asserts his belonging in this space of American childhood and questions George's.[8]

The interplay that characterizes George's hypersurveillance and Charley's documentation and confrontation thereof appears in school- and community-sanctioned practices and events as well, where gazes become enmeshed with the dynamics of institutional apparatuses. When the principal hands Charley an envelope on his first day of school, it contains a letter for his parents, and while Charley does not read the contents of the letter, the text constructs Charley's response to its envelope in ways that signal its function as a tool of surveillance. It does so through the boy's countersurveillant gaze:

> Charley looked at the envelope containing the message to his parents.
>
> Carefully he held it in one hand as he left the school building through the front door. His throat was dry and he went to the drinking fountain beside the front walk. He looked at the envelope again as he bent to drink. (37)

This is a quiet moment for Charley as well as for the text. The paragraph break after the first line dilates the duration of the moment, conveying its narrative weight. Charley's bodily reaction of a dry throat as well as his second gaze while he is drinking uses organic imagery not just to convey but to transfer his wary reaction to the reader, who is asked to share Charley's silent appraisal. Note that Jackson withholds recounting the print on the envelope until after these lines, which positions the letter as an aesthetic object rather than simply a written missive; the reader is asked to examine it closely.

When Jackson does reproduce the print on the envelope, he does so by way of particular fonts, creating an "image-text" that casts this moment as an act of detailed observing. Another paragraph break again dilates the narration over the moment of looking: "Printed on it was: *To the Parents of Charles Moss*. Over this was: PRINCIPAL'S OFFICE. ARLINGTON HEIGHTS JUNIOR HIGH SCHOOL. MR. PERCY WINTER. RETURN IN FIVE DAYS" (37). The italicized script signals the personal target of the missive, especially because the capitalized block letters, in both style and placement (above the addressee), connote authority. Charley's gaze, which is constructed as lingering and hesitating over the letter, directs the reader to the institutional force of its mode of delivery as well as its still unseen contents. There is also pointed irony in the fact that Charley uses a school drinking fountain while looking at the letter, which impugns de facto segregation in the US North alongside its de jure Southern counterpart. He may be able to use the general drinking fountain, but he is not otherwise accorded the same status as white students in the school.

His countersurveillant gaze on the letter also speaks to Charley's position as child, which bolsters the narrative power of his looking. Charley himself is not the addressee; adults in his world, themselves already arranged in a racial hierarchy, will govern the processes by which he must negotiate belonging. This is a moment when the text uses the child gaze as part of its race liberal posturing for white and Black audiences. Most school-attending child readers (and once school-attending adults), regardless of race, can align with the feeling of exclusion from the principal-parent exchange, so this moment of looking mobilizes readerly sympathies with Charley by invoking the vulnerability of any child in these circumstances. But given Mr. Winter's earlier hesitation over accepting Charley's enrollment due to his race, the novel, through Charley's gaze, asks those readers to view the envelope as a mechanism of anti-Black exclusive institutional practices and the child as an undeserving victim thereof.

Indeed, two chapters later it isn't Charley who reads the letter but Charley's mother, who *summarizes* its contents for Charley and the reader: "Mr. Winter says here in this letter that you will only be allowed to attend their school for a three months' trial.... They'll have their eyes on you. First trouble you get into, Mr. Winter will say: 'See, I knew we shouldn't have let that colored boy come here'" (54). Charley consents to "watch his manners" under those "eyes," agreeing to take part in the very surveillance that has targeted him. He is eventually grudgingly accepted—though not without reservation—by the school. But the work of the countersurveillant gaze has been done. Even if Charley does not voice opposition or think in oppositional ways on the mimetic level of character, the narrative has used the thematic and synthetic function of his gaze to signal its politics. Without revealing the actual words of the principal's official letter, this early civil rights, pre–*Brown v. Board of Education* era novel employs the child's countersurveillant gaze to highlight the insidious ways that US racial ideologies engineer and prohibit access to education for young people, specifically by excluding Black children from schooling purported to support—though also to surveil—children growing into "their place" in the US social structure. Privileging Charley's gaze on the envelope of a letter he never sees gestures to both the hidden mechanisms of exclusion at work in federal and state institutions that serve children and the ways of noticing—signaled by the narrative attention to Charley's gaze, if not by Charley himself—that are necessary to expose those mechanisms.

It is important to note that Jackson portrays Tom, the white boy who befriends Charley, as unable to understand the implications of the principal's actions. Just as earlier Tom expresses confusion about why a racial epithet bothers Charley (36), he also misses the point of the letter, waiving away the principal's continual pointed targeting of Charley with a generalized "That's him all over" (56). The boys have two very different lived experiences, and so one way to consider Tom's lack of understanding juxtaposed with Charley's countersurveillant gaze is through psychology's ecological theories of perception. James J. Gibson uses the term "affordances" to refer to the ways people perceive their abilities within specific environments, and visual perception is one key arbiter of those affordances. The field has focused primarily on physical affordances, but recent work by Alexandra Paxton, Julia J. C. Blau, and Mikayla L. Weston calls for further attention to the way people's intersectional identities influence how they perceive social affordances. For example, they suggest that whether a person sees a chair as "sit-on-able" may be "altered by a chair's context—either situated at a table filled with people who match the participant's intersectional identity or people who might be hostile to it."[9] Tom's experience as a white boy in a white neighborhood in the US 1940s has never afforded him reason to look askance at racial motivations for his principal's actions; Charley's experience as a Black boy—and Jackson's own experience—has. Thus, while Charley's countersurveillant gaze is not legible to Tom within the world of the story, the attention Jackson gives it on the level of narrative both affirms the potential personal experiences of child readers of color and seeks to correct ignorance about and perpetuation of systemic racism by white readers with supposedly race liberal values. By juxtaposing Charley's perception with Tom's, the novel also manages to reflect and call for critical assessment of the racialized experiences of both white and Black children in white neighborhoods of the United States.

Perception of social affordances is also apparent in town spaces other than school. The novel directs Charley's countersurveillant gaze at the Arlington Heights swimming pool. When he and Tom are waiting in line to enter, "Charley noticed a big sign over the front of the pool" that reads "Arlington Heights Swimming Pool. The Management reserves the right to exclude applicants for membership. Joining fee Ten Dollars a year" (Jackson 112). The use of title case in the first phrase, in the word "Management" and in the monetary amount, as well as the nod to the location of the sign posits it, like the envelope, as an aesthetic object. An image-text situated visually and spatially, the sign is conjured before its reader's eyes through Charley's.

That Charley is "reading it a second time" while Tom "pull[s] him past the ticket window" (112) suggests that while the sign is noteworthy to Charley, Tom's affordances deny the sign's noticeability. However, Charley's drawn-out moment of gazing—achieved, just as in the case of the letter, by that second look plus a paragraph break to dilate the narrative in the stillness—foreshadows that the policy will be invoked when his Black body is perceived in the white space of the community pool.[10]

While the narrative's withholding any commentary that might accompany Charley's gaze allows the novel to posture safely within the narrow parameters Cold War politics drew around representation of racial conflict, Charley's looking also works to cast the child gaze into high relief, juxtaposing its countersurveillance with the surveillant efforts of the sign. Charley's gaze and the museum silence the narrative conjures to highlight it require the reader to pause over a sign where "exclusion" is claimed as a "right." The narrative performs its callout of the sign as a mechanism of a racist system via its rendering of the countersurveillant child gaze.

That system is run, of course, by agents that perpetuate it, and the narrative implies that the surveillance Charley encounters in the pool area is approved by the state and nation. Charley and Tom are there because they have entered a contest together, and they are announced the winners. When they come up to the podium to be recognized, the other children in attendance cheered, but "Charley watched as [the judges] whispered among themselves and looked at the names of the winners" (Jackson 114). On the facing page is a full-page illustration of a smiling Tom and Charley accepting their prize—pool passes—while on the left side of the podium, and depicted as tallest in the scene, two judges whisper quietly, their heads just below the backdrop of an American flag (115). Their whispering is aligned with national authority. The narrative silence about Charley's thoughts when he notices the judges both superficially tempers the novel's indictment of their racism and highlights its methodology. Indeed, the manager revokes the pool pass Charley was awarded in exchange for ten dollars only *after* the ceremony is over and no one is there to witness it (117–18). Confronted by an institutional authority who dismisses him with a matter-of-factly delivered racial slur, Charley uses his gaze to signal his distress: "Charley swallowed hard and stared at the money in his hand. Then he saw the pool and the way the water showed the clouds overhead. He couldn't say anything" (117–18). His swallow and his gaze on the pool contain the implication of his feelings, and the narrative voice articulates the fact of his silence.

Since, by the end of the novel, Charley does not regain access to the pool, the countersurveillant gaze can be read as ineffectual within the diegetic world of the story, and that lack of power allows Cold War imperatives about silencing racial unrest to be maintained. But in these moments of looking, Charley's gaze is also a narrative gesture that conveys the tension between community practices and his response to them, providing a way for the novel to perform its critique. The museum silence of the story is also a narrative strategy that asserts Charley's belonging in the innocence paradigm, a crucial strategy for children of color whom, as Robin Bernstein has pointed out, are historically excluded from it. The third-person narration keeps Charley from giving voice to his perceptions at these moments of looking, and it refrains from recounting his thoughts, as well. As narratologist Shlimoth Rimmon-Kenan points out, the "external focalizer (or narrator-focalizer) knows everything about the represented world, and when he restricts his knowledge, he does so out of rhetorical considerations" (80). Charley's mimetic gaze signals his noticing, but the narrative lingering over it converts that noticing to thematic and synthetic functions, signaling the text's quiet confrontation. Essentially, the narration protects the mimetic Black child from being the impugner even as it calls attention to the synthetic character's eye movements. Indeed, it is often unclear whether Charley understands why he is noticing what he notices; it is only his gaze that can be understood to imply it. Elsewhere in the novel, of course, Charley's voice is made overt, whether through dialogue in the world of the story or through internalized thoughts reported in the narrative. But in these more pointed moments of gazing, the text retreats from Charley's interiority in order to keep Charley "safe" from being perceived as a threat to the white race liberal systems that surround him and the material book in which he appears.

Such moments also invest in the reader's ability to see with Charley. Given that each moment of careful looking in the novel foreshadows a more overt statement of racial discrimination in the text—such as Charley's mother's recounting of the letter or the pool manager's revocation of Charley's pass—the text makes way for the reader's alignment with Charley through these subtle signals, the reward for which is interpretation on the side of ethical assessment.[11] For by rewarding careful readers who have spent the museum silence noticing the discriminatory mechanisms Charley and the narrator refrain from discussing overtly, the text encourages them to equate their own savvy with Charley's point of view.

Charley is also a sympathetic character in general; the children he knows tend to express their interest in befriending him, and even George (rather inexplicably) comes around by the end of the novel. Charley's role as a paper-delivering, smart, social child who is well mannered at school and around adults recommends him, in the didactic undercurrents of midcentury children's literature, as a child worth including. Charley is depicted as deserving the opportunities Arlington Heights withholds from him, and thus he is a good candidate for Cold War rhetorics of inclusion. The positive readerly reaction his character calls forth contributes to the extradiegetic energy of his gaze through conduits of pathos and sympathy. But crucial to the text's subversive intervention is that the gaze Charley wields does not so much focus on Charley's individual worthiness or woes as it pans outward at his environment. It exposes the agents and mechanisms of exclusion that prevent Black children in the United States from being considered worthy of American childhood and national belonging.

BOLD LOOKS: MILDRED TAYLOR'S *ROLL OF THUNDER, HEAR MY CRY*

The countersurveillant child gaze in Mildred Taylor's *Roll of Thunder, Hear My Cry* is far more aggressively constructed than Charley's, making Taylor's novel, written almost three decades later, a fitting descendant of Jackson's. *Roll of Thunder, Hear My Cry* demonstrates how the child can function as an overt, knowing agent of the countersurveillant gaze, which enables the text not only to point out discriminatory practices but also to unequivocally indict them by way of the righteous anger of a child.[12] While Charley's gaze substitutes for any resistant impulses he may feel, Cassie's gaze supports and enables hers; Taylor's narrative constructs her as ready to think about, talk about, and act upon what she sees, and thus Cassie's looking is far more actively engaged in her storyworld than Charley's. Its liveliness infuses her first-person narration with a countersurveillant mood that sustains itself for the entirety of the novel. Nevertheless, though the text cannot, as in the case of Charley, ease out of Cassie's resistant stance, it does rely heavily upon her position as child to filter that gaze as nonthreatening within the world of the story. Engaging questions of innocence and knowledge in relation to danger and protection, *Roll of Thunder, Hear My Cry* positions the countersurveillant gaze as a necessary tool of survival for Black children and an ethical call to action for the implied child reader of any race.[13]

Writing after the 1954 *Brown v. Board of Education* decision and the Civil Rights Act of 1964—though certainly for a publication market long dominated by white editors, writers, and a presumed-to-be white, middle-class consumer base—Taylor was beholden to fewer restrictions than Jackson regarding the agency with which she might imbue a Black child confronting racist practices. And those to which she was beholden in 1976 were perhaps sidestepped by the fact that she was writing a historical novel, one that represents Jim Crow era surveillance practices that had come to be "officially" condemned under the national narrative of racial progress—despite their persistence in different forms throughout and beyond the latter half of the twentieth century. But though the text's historical interest might mark its overt critique as "safe," several of the practices highlighted by the child gaze within its pages speak to concerns of Taylor's era. While school was desegregated de jure in the United States, it had (and has) yet to become so de facto, and the busing crisis took center stage in racialized school debates in the 1970s.[14] Furthermore, curricular initiatives enjoyed attention throughout the Black Power movement of the 1960s and '70s, which lobbied for schools to teach Black studies and often created alternate schools to do so.[15] Nine-year-old Cassie Logan's countersurveillant gaze on incidents involving school buses, school books, and Black history in the classroom, as well as upon hateful and violent racial practices in her own community that reflect the white retaliatory violence often plaguing advancements in civil rights for people of color, positions this historical fiction novel for children as a powerful exposure and rejection of the racial ideologies of the US past that echo into its contemporary US milieu.

Early on in *Roll of Thunder, Hear My Cry*, the narration establishes the gaze as a key mode of communication and perception for Cassie and her siblings, children in a family of Black landowners in Depression era rural Mississippi. Recounting a sibling interaction, Cassie tells the reader that older brother "Stacey cut me a wicked look and I grew silent," and young brother Christopher-John "glanced uneasily at both of us but did not interfere" with the bickering (4). Certain acts of looking also bind the Logan family together across generations. Cassie's father, for instance, directs her gaze to their land in order to help her understand how important it is that he work to maintain their finances: "Look out there, Cassie girl. All that belongs to you. You ain't never had to live on nobody's place but your own and long as I live and the family survives, you'll never have to" (7). Mr. Logan also has a tendency to narrow his eyes in a way that suggests a keen oppositional mental stance, a gesture shared by the rest of the Logan family and taken up by Cassie, who eventually names it the "Logan gaze" (173). In this narrative heavily imbued with eyes that warm, cut, steel, confront, and much more, acts of looking take on many valences. But it is the child's countersurveillant gaze that enables the novel to examine the relationship between Cassie's interiority and her exterior world—a link that exposes the mechanisms of violent exclusion she witnesses as a child in a nation built to deny her worth and that also lays bare the type of seeing necessary to maintain the self within such a system.

One feature of that system is underfunded education and transportation for Black children, which the novel illustrates via Cassie's pointed looking.

The first scene of the novel depicts the Logan siblings, who must walk quite a ways to their school, nearly being mowed down by a school bus carrying white children whose "laughing white faces" are "pressed up against the windows" to witness the scene (13). The occurrence is frequent enough that Stacey explains it thus: "cause they like to see us run and it ain't our bus" (13). His commentary demonstrates his understanding of Yancy's formulation, that the white gaze turns the Black body into "a site of white racist pleasure, masochism, and dominance" (Yancy xvii), and his insight into the types of surveillance that maintain white control in any public space, including roads.

In this case, the bus incident happens at a crossroads at which the white students will head toward their school, which is also represented by way of the excluded child's sight lines. Cassie recognizes it as a "long white wooden building looming in the distance" (15), and as Cassie's gaze lingers on the destination of the bus, the narrative takes the time to detail its advantages, including sports fields, bleachers (which are so unusual to Cassie that she can only describe them as "scattered rows of tiered gray-looking benches"), a second bus for students who live in the other direction, and an "expansive front lawn" with a large flagpole. Named for the president of the Confederacy, Jefferson Davis County School flies its flags "transposed" (15), the Mississippi flag, "red, white, and blue with the emblem of the Confederacy emblazoned on its upper left-hand corner," above the American flag and so, as Cassie notices, contrary to flag code (15).[16] It is on this image of privileged Confederate sympathies that Cassie's gaze lingers longest in her description, dilating the reader's eye with hers and with the narrative itself, her countersurveillant attention making visible the racial hierarchy, endorsed by the state and nation, made manifest in the education available to its young people.

The main conflict of the first chapter continues the use of the child gaze to countersurveil racial inequities in school. It centers on the "new" books the local superintendent has given to the Logans' school, each of which has a chart stamped inside of it detailing dates of issuance to students—a chart that is reproduced in the text (and is, indeed, the text's only inclusion of an illustration), so the reader is made to see it along with the characters (figure 2.1). The charts are a regulating tool of control. They mark ownership by the board of education, catalog the chronology of use, and track that use by way of the condition of the text as well as the race of the student (depicted with a "genteel" racial slur) in parallel columns that progress in proportion to each other.[17] The chart is a visible rendering of surveillance, a signal to the reader inside and outside of the text that the school is tracking its property in ways that are linked to racial inequity—here

PROPERTY OF THE BOARD OF EDUCATION
Spokane County, Mississippi
September, 1922

CHRONOLOGICAL ISSUANCE	DATE OF ISSUANCE	CONDITION OF BOOK	RACE OF STUDENT
1	September 1922	New	White
2	September 1923	Excellent	White
3	September 1924	Excellent	White
4	September 1925	Very Good	White
5	September 1926	Good	White
6	September 1927	Good	White
7	September 1928	Average	White
8	September 1929	Average	White
9	September 1930	Average	White
10	September 1931	Poor	White
11	September 1932	Poor	White
12	September 1933	Very Poor	nigra
13			
14			
15			

Figure 2.1. The chart inside Little Man's book (Taylor 25). Excerpt(s) from ROLL OF THUNDER, HEAR MY CRY by Mildred D. Taylor, text copyright © 1976 by Mildred D. Taylor. Used by permission of Dial Books for Young Readers, an imprint of Penguin Young Readers Group, a division of Penguin Random House LLC. All rights reserved.

emphasized by the use of the racial slur and even by the way that slur is scripted, the lowercase *n* contrasting with the uppercase *W*'s.

Crucially, this chart is discovered and presented within the narrative by way of the Black child's countersurveillant gaze, a gaze that is carefully detailed through a climactic lead-up modulated by layers of looking. Not all such looking is countersurveillant in nature, but it does, through its repetition in the narrative, call the reader's attention to eyes and directional gazes and is thus worth detailing. Cassie, after hearing her teacher give a speech about how lucky they are to have these books, "could see that the covers of the books . . . were badly worn and that the gray edges of the pages had been marred by pencils, crayons, and ink," a sight that leads to her "sinking disappointment" (21–22). "Glanc[ing] across at [her younger brother] Little Man," she sees "his face lit in eager excitement," which tells her "he could not see the soiled covers" (22). Furthermore, she "did not like to think of his disappointment when he saw the books as they really were" (22). Cassie's gaze directs the reader's attention to Little Man, who, when standing in front of the teacher to receive his book, rejects it on account of its being "dirty" (23). He does so without "tak[ing] his eyes from Miss Crocker"; indeed, even when she stands to "gaz[e] down" at him during her reprimand, he "raised his head and continued to look in her eyes" until he is forced to take the volume back to his desk (23).

These assertive looks serve as prologue to the climax, when Little Man sits at his desk and opens the front cover of the book: "As he stared at the book's inside cover, his face clouded. . . . His brows furrowed. Then his eyes grew wide, and suddenly he sucked in his breath and sprang from his chair like a wounded animal, flinging the book onto the floor and stomping madly upon it" (24). Cassie's reaction to Little Man's embodied physical response is to align her gaze with his: "Rapidly, I turned to the inside cover of my own book and saw immediately what had made Little Man so furious" (24). That sequence ends with a colon, which introduces the chart as a visual artifact for the reader's consumption—an introduction that, by way of its aesthetic interruption of the prose narrative and the relay of gazes that point to it, demands the reader to pause over it and join in the children's countersurveillant gaze.

As with Charley, this gaze is not necessarily crafted as triumphant within the world of the text, but it is marked by persistence. When Cassie attempts to transfer her and her brother's gaze to her teacher by pointing out the racial slur that links the text's condition to their station in US sociopolitical structures—which she does by way of attempts like "See what's in the last row" and "Please look, Miz Crocker," followed by a faltering "S-see what they called us" (26)—Miss Crocker refuses to acknowledge their perspective and punishes them when they stalwartly refuse to take the books. Cassie's conclusion, that the teacher "had looked at the page and had understood nothing" (27), privileges Cassie's interpretation of what she sees over that of her teacher, and it emphasizes Cassie's aggressive assertion of the value of her version of seeing.

The novel upholds that privileging when, later that day, Cassie "peep[s]" into a classroom to witness a scene where Miss Crocker complains about the situation to Cassie's mother, also a teacher at the school. Cassie hears Mrs. Logan verbally agree with Miss Crocker's choice to punish Cassie and Little Man for disrespecting her authority, but at the same time, she sees her quietly paste blank cards over the charts so that her children will not be continually subjected to the offense. Then, when she hears her mother disregard Miss Crocker's warnings about surveillance—"if somebody from the superintendent's office ever comes down here and sees that book, you'll be in real trouble" (30)—she sees her begin pasting cards inside the books for her own students, an act that both keeps her students from the harm the record can cause and thwarts this particular method of surveilling them. These observations make possible Cassie's ending the scene with this decision: "I would wait until the evening to talk to her; there was no rush now. She understood" (31). Cassie's watching her mother's actions in the face of authority-by-proxy allows the text to confirm her own countersurveillance as an authority in its own right.

Indeed, Cassie and her siblings' "peer[ing]" (54) is often the mechanism through which the narrative celebrates attempts to disrupt the surveillance that targets them. Stacey masterminds a plan to create the illusion of a water hazard for the bus that ran Christopher-John off the road, a visual trick that, aided by some afternoon rain, causes one wheel of the bus to become stuck and lurch to a halt. Thus, the spectacle is reversed for both the Logans and the reader. The Logans avoid becoming the object of a racialized gaze, for rather than watching with their former malevolent mirth as their bus splashes the Logans with mud, the driver and children bicker about how to fix the problem and then slip and slide into muddy water—all as the Logans get to watch in "everlasting delight" (55). The readerly gaze, aligned with Cassie's as she and her brothers "peered through the low bushes" (55) at the spectacle, participates in this countersurveillant coup. And even though later that day the children's mother and grandmother do not know the reason for the bus's troubles, they "smile" and are "rather glad it happened" (57) as the children celebrate the fact that the townsmen cannot lift the bus out of the ditch until the rains cease and the land dries. The public space of the road is reclaimed, if only temporarily, in a giddy triumph of countersurveillance that reverses the hierarchy of subject and object.

These early incidents, and Cassie's gaze upon them, ease the reader into a text that does not hesitate to represent the serious physical violence that attends white surveillance of Black bodies and the necessity of countersurveillance under such conditions. Cassie (as well as an inexperienced reader) may not understand the initial warning "they's ridin' t'night" (60) that her family receives from a neighbor, but when Cassie, pretending to be asleep, opens her eyes to see her grandmother "outlined in the doorway, a rifle in her hands" (65), the narrative attention to her gaze reveals the possibility of real danger and the urgency of vigilance. It is questionable whether a real girl in Cassie's geohistorical circumstances would not understand the verbal warning, but introducing a young reader to this concept via Cassie's own discovery thereof enables both the assertion of Cassie's youth—her "innocence" of knowledge of night riders—and the pathos that invites the contemporary reader to align emotionally with the point of view of a child newly initiated into a physically dangerous reality.

Indeed, it is Cassie's childness that makes her next countersurveillant moment resonate on several levels. After creeping out to find her brothers and instead being licked all over by her muddy dog—a very familiar situation to young persons with a dog—Cassie's gaze confronts this scene:

> I started to climb back up onto the porch but froze as a caravan of headlights appeared suddenly in the east, coming fast along the rain-soaked road like cat eyes in the night. . . .
>
> The lead car swung into the muddy driveway and a shadowy figure outlined by the headlights of the car behind him stepped out. The man walked slowly up the drive.
>
> I stopped breathing.
>
> The driver of the next car got out, waiting. The first man stopped and stared at the house for several long moments as if uncertain whether it was the correct destination. Then he shook his head, and without a word returned to his car . . . , then the caravan sped away as swiftly as it had come, its seven pairs of rear lights glowing like distant red embers until they were swallowed from view by the Granger forest. (67)

Cassie's gaze upon the string of predatory "cat eyes" headlights, the coming and going of which draw out her moment of looking and frame the action she sees in between, poignantly emphasizes the imminent threat her family faces and corresponds to Browne's work on the surveillance of blackness. Furthermore, her countersurveillant gaze on the "shadowy" men arriving in the dead of night in large numbers impugns their actions as unlawful and yet communally sanctioned. Her later bodily response when she creeps back to bed before her mother finds her—"the vision of ghostly headlights soaked into my mind and an uncontrollable trembling racked my body" (68)—links their actions to the fear and trauma of a child horribly aware of the way the world victimizes her and her race. The reader is directed not only to look with Cassie, but, by way of this shared gaze, to feel with her as well.

The aftermath of this moment lingers in the text, emphasizing the extent to which her youth matters to the effect of her gaze. Cassie overhears her mother, who has noticed her subsequent loss of appetite and restless sleep, ask her grandmother, "Mama, you think she could've seen—," and Big Ma's interrupting answer, "Oh, Lord, no, child. . . . I checked in there right after they passed and she was sound asleep. She could't've seen them ole devils" (71). Mama and Big Ma's conversation creates a moment of dramatic irony, for the reader is aware that Cassie did, indeed, see and is also aware, based on the adults' exchange, that children are supposed to be protected from such sights. This urge toward protection signals the value and responsibilities adults attach to innocence. But the dramatic irony also makes clear that protecting Cassie—and the reader—from seeing and knowing is not a viable option.

The text never sacrifices Cassie's deserving protection in exchange for the power of her gaze. It is, rather, the deserving that amplifies its narrative power. Cassie's seeing magnifies her childness, asking the implied reader to grapple with the child *as* child rather than one cast out of this category by premature knowing. Furthermore, child audiences—and adult audiences, as well—are urged by the narrative not to patronize Cassie but to honor, empathize with, and join in her well-founded fear. Being invited to share Cassie's countersurveillant gaze means the implied reader is positioned to take an ethical stance against those who produce this fear; being invited to wish for protection for Cassie is less about sheltering her from knowingness—an impossibility—than about exposing and dismantling the systems that target her.

Indeed, her mother actually begins to direct Cassie and her siblings' countersurveillant gazes in ways that demonstrate how crucial child knowingness can be to child protection. She brings them to see Mr. Berry, who with other members of his family has been horrifically burned by the Wallaces, a powerful white family in the community.[18] Afterward, she asks them to consider the sight of his body with compassion (96) but also with awareness of the danger the Wallaces pose, the need to avoid them, and the importance of boycotting their business: "The Wallaces did that. . . . Everyone knows they did it, and the Wallaces even laugh about it, but nothing was ever done. . . . That's why I don't want you to ever go to their store again" (98). By conflating the sight not only with the harsh reality of victimhood but also with pointed knowledge of the perpetrator, Mrs. Logan urges her children to respond to racial injustice by being geographically careful with their own safety and avoiding complicity with the financial gains of that perpetrator—twin efforts of self-preservation and activism. Furthermore, the narrative attention to this moment and to the looking Mrs. Logan encourages enacts its own countersurveillance of folks like the Wallaces, past and present.

The nuance with which Taylor employs Cassie's acts of looking reveals the narrative and thematic weight that rests on it. For instance, after the Logans have successfully organized the boycott of the Wallace store, Cassie happens to be lining a drafty window of her schoolhouse—which recalls the schooling inequities noted in the first chapter of the novel—when she sees powerful men from their town head into her mother's classroom (182). Excusing herself from class to run outside and "peek cautiously" (183) through (yet another) broken window, Cassie observes the observers, documenting through her first-person narration what she sees: white men entering a Black woman's classroom to intimidate her. Cassie knows the men have come because of the boycott, and so through Cassie's gaze the reader witnesses the devastating intersection of discriminatory politics, educational mandates, and economic opportunities.

Nothing in the classroom scene speaks to the boycott, but it has spurred the surveillance that targets Mrs. Logan and results in her punishment on two grounds: first, that she has been teaching a version of history not located in the board-approved textbook and, second, that she has covered the board's surveillance chart in the front cover of her students' books. The latter recalls Cassie's gaze in the first chapter; the former speaks to the fictional Mrs. Logan's activist mindset as well as initiatives for Black studies spearheaded by the Black Power movement during the time of the text's writing. Mrs. Logan is known for teaching Black history, including the accomplishments of Black kings in ancient Egypt (79) as well as historically accurate explanations of the complex material and financial conditions supporting slavery. Mrs. Logan speaks "on the cruelty of it; of the rich economic cycle it generated as slaves produced the raw products for the factories of the North and Europe; how the country profited and grew from the free labor of a people still not free" (183). Cassie's narration from her perch at the window is knowing. She has learned her mother's version of history, and the "people still not free" might refer to enslaved people of the past as well as the students and teachers in her present school. That the men confront her mother about this lesson with "I don't see all them things you're teaching in here [the textbook]" (184) reflects the exclusive and ethnocentric curriculum mandated by US schools; that Mrs. Logan claims she cannot teach from the textbook "because all that's in that book isn't true" (184) reflects the layers of lies and half-truths that sustain that version of history—which itself sustains exclusive racial ideologies.[19] While Cassie overtly countersurveils the upholding of racist national narratives in the storyworld, her narration might be understood to obliquely countersurveil its continuation into the contemporary moment in Taylor's world.

Cassie surveilling the surveillant, however, does not provide a solution to racial injustice within the world of the story, which speaks to the limitations of her power even as it bolsters the narrative effect of her gaze. The observation visit from the townsmen culminates in a mandate to fire Mrs. Logan, which does occur and which creates considerable economic hardship for the family—an effect that highlights the insidious methods by which communities and institutions subjugate Black children and adults as well as other folks of color and thwart their access to education and empowered positions in the social hierarchy. On the level of narrative, however, the text does not emphasize the event in a way that suggests the futility of fighting. Rather, it makes clear the admiration Cassie has for her mother, who answers a challenge about the use of the assigned textbook with "her back straight and her eyes fixed on the men" (184). Taylor herself, of course, is telling a story that does not often end up in history books, and we might understand the stance of this novel to mimic that of Mrs. Logan, while the child reader is positioned to mimic Cassie's gaze through the window.[20] Here the historical novel relies on the "safety" of its pre–civil rights movement setting to suggest that Taylor is writing as part of the legacy of Black women like Mrs. Logan, whose actions contribute to a movement founded on breaking barriers to civil rights and national belonging. The real-life analogues of the children Mrs. Logan teaches would come of age during the dawning civil rights movement proper, which was itself joined by countless children. The might of the scene on the narrative level, then, is carried by the energy of Cassie's countersurveillant gaze: it documents the crushing weight of the power upholding those barriers even as it positions attempts to break them as honorable, righteous, crucial, and eventually *effective*. Ongoing demands for national belonging course through the text even as it relates past moments of national exclusion.

AN INTERLUDE: CHILDREN'S LITERATURE, ADULT LITERATURE, AND THE YOUNG COUNTERSURVEILLANT

Taking *Roll of Thunder* and *Call Me Charley* as a pair offers some insight into the flexibility of the countersurveillant child gaze as a narrative technique in literature written for children. In *Roll of Thunder, Hear My Cry*,

Taylor often accompanies Cassie's gaze with her emotions, which signal to the implied reader how to feel. Jackson's representation of Charley's gaze in *Call Me Charley*, however, is much more subtle, often unaccompanied by such emotional directives. His novel—or perhaps his editor—seems careful to neutralize a young Black boy, at least diegetically, as a potential agent of change. In Jackson's 1945 market publication for children, all activism is carried out on the part of white adults in Charley's new community. Indeed, even Cassie remains inactive during the largest conflict of her novel, relegated to the role of a child too young to take part in a dangerous, racially charged altercation and fire-fighting scenario. The preservation of Charley and Cassie as obedient or young is itself a resistant strategy that casts the Black child as deserving of the attributions of innocence and protection that, as Robin Bernstein has argued, are so often withheld from them in order to maintain the social sacredness of the white child. This move roots the power of the pointed countersurveillant gaze in the pathos energized by the supposedly "innocent" child figures whose vulnerable-to-denigration marginalized status is subverted by the way the text postures to protect them.

It also, of course, makes these texts "safe" in terms of the publishing, parenting, and educating gatekeepers that manage the literature that falls into the hands of young people. Cassie is rebellious, but her rebellion is often approved by or aligned with the behavior of the adults in her family and community. Charley can be quick to chide a friend, but he is polite and often silent in the presence of adult authority, even when that authority discriminates against him. These are children who model ways to act within rather than violate the boundaries of acceptable childhood behavior.

On the other hand, the countersurveillant child gaze provides a narrative strategy that allows literature for young people to represent the fact that marginalized children have no choice but to be confronted with the inequities of their sociopolitical existence in the United States. Such a gaze also invites the reader to confront those inequities through the perspective of that child and wrestle with their implications. Whether the texts make those implications overt in the moment, as is often the case with Cassie, or suggestive in the moment, as is often the case with Charley, they operate by conjuring a field of vision concentrated on the perpetrators of exclusionary practices. Because of the countersurveillant child gaze, these texts look outward to the world, pivoting on the ability of the child figure to enact that looking. In doing so, they signal to child readers that noticing the exclusionary mechanisms of their world is crucial to the self-preservation of marginalized young people as well as to the potential activism that could dismantle those mechanisms.

As this chapter turns to literature written for adult audiences, it further mines the flexibility of the countersurveillant child gaze, which does not appear with any drastic difference in these texts. Each presents a child signaled to be, to a certain extent, innocent, and each of these children looks in ways that allow the texts to document racially and ethnically motivated exclusionary practices in the United States. That they are adult-facing works matters only in the sense that there is an assumption about the arcane knowledge of adulthood their readers possess that actually erects more quickly the notion of the child as a pathos-laden or symbolic construct. But rather than work to other these young children from their adult readers and treat children and childhood patronizingly, these texts figure the child's countersurveillant gaze as an aligning mechanism, a way to command the adult reader to pay serious attention to the child and the child's sight lines and a way for the adult reader to look with fresh eyes upon the exclusionary narratives and mechanisms at work in the United States.

Philip Roth's *The Plot against America* and Langston Hughes's "Red-Headed Baby" are vastly different in their narrative strategies and genres. The former is an allohistorical novel narrated in the first person by the author's adult alter ego working through memories of his childhood as he navigated a crisis of national identity with tragic effects; the latter is a short story of realistic fiction in a collection titled *The Ways of White Folks* told largely in free indirect discourse focalized through a white man who finds himself confronted by the gaze of his just-discovered mixed-race son. One text compounds the interiority of the child, imbricating the adult narrator's commentary into the child's subjectivity; one avoids it altogether, rendering the child as an opaque character whose gaze nevertheless arrests the narrative. Taken together and in concert with the texts for young people discussed above, these distinctly different narrative stratagems demonstrate the litheness of the countersurveillant child gaze for documenting and denouncing agents and systems of exclusion in the United States.

GROWN-UP NARRATION OF THE COUNTERSURVEILLING CHILD SELF: PHILIP ROTH'S *THE PLOT AGAINST AMERICA*

Philip Roth's *The Plot against America* mobilizes questions of vulnerability and resilience similar to those of *Roll of Thunder, Hear My Cry*, again by focusing on the figure of the child living in the past. Roth's past, however, is an allohistorical one, one that never happened but could have. It begins in 1940 with the presidential election of Charles Lindbergh, which precipitates the infusion of overt state-sanctioned anti-Semitism into the American social fabric. The adult Jewish narrator, Philip, focalizes much of the story through his younger child self even as he comments on it from his adult perspective, all the while wrestling with the clash between his pre-Lindbergh and post-Lindbergh visions of America. Representing national identity in crisis—itself an issue of past clashing with present—the novel negotiates citizenship in turmoil through the nuances of a countersurveillant child gaze.

Roth's narrator is an adult version of himself who lives in a present almost identical (aside from the crucial deviation in US history) to that of the contemporary present in which he writes. He may as well live in the world of his implied adult reader and is in both a mimetic and synthetic sense the reader's guide through the allohistorical moment.[21] But his allohistorical child self, young Philip, lived through that deviation and only knows the world of the story. Rather than using these distinctions—of the present and the past, the contemporary "real" and the allohistorical—to divide the consciousness of the narrative voice and draw attention to the differences between child self and adult self, Roth engages what Marah Gubar has named a "kinship model" of child-adult relations. The kinship model requires "a delicate balancing act" that refrains from essentializing the child as other by "maintaining that children and adults are fundamentally akin to one another, even if certain differences or deficiencies routinely attend certain parts of the aging process" (299). The child is not seen as lacking, but rather as "first and foremost . . . alike" (300). When Roth's child figure wields a countersurveillant gaze, the adult narrator who tells of it wields it as well; because the child figure—and thus his countersurveillant gaze—is not estranged from the adult narrator, but rather integral to that adult's perspective, the gaze complicates the defamiliarizing effect of allohistorical storytelling because it is positioned as the link between the allohistorical United States of the novel and the contemporary United States of Roth's present. That is, if the fictional child cannot exist in Roth's contemporary US present, his gaze can—and, as the novel implies, should.

The text makes this implication via the narrative dynamics of its countersurveillant child gaze. Working through the profundity of his experiences, the narrator's impulse to tell and the shape of that telling rests upon child acts of countersurveillance, which become the filter through which he and Roth's implied reader must make sense of what they see. In doing so, the text's narration makes countersurveillance a necessary vantage point for considerations of US racial ideologies that target marginalized children and adults, and, as this novel makes clear, the country's integrity as a nation of ethnically diverse people that has an ethical obligation to all of its children. In this way, this novel aimed at adult readers also posits childhood as a valid entry point into the critique of US narratives of belonging.

Philip, a young Jewish American boy living in a predominantly Jewish neighborhood in Newark, New Jersey, engages modes of looking that are almost immediately thrown into conflict. The opening pages of the novel precede the vulnerability and shocked knowingness Philip soon experiences as a newly marginalized child. To cast that moment into high relief, the narrator early insists on the quintessential "Americanness" of Philip's early childhood—complete with stamp collecting, a view of the Statue of Liberty, a mom active in his school's Parent Teacher Organization, a corner candy store, the Pledge of Allegiance, Fourth of July fireworks, and Thanksgiving turkey (1–5). This version of childhood, which has steeped him in patriotic identification with hard-working Americans who speak in American English and think of America as their homeland (3–5), has cultivated a particular way of seeing for him—a way I will call "Bergerian," after John Berger's formulation that "the way we see things is affected by what we know or what we believe" (8).[22] Young Philip's swift dismissal of the "stranger" with a hat and beard who "appeared every few months after dark to ask in broken English for a contribution toward the establishment of a Jewish national homeland in Palestine" stems from the naive faith he has in America as a homeland, a place of safety for him, his family, and the people in his neighborhood. This way of seeing makes him complicit in the exclusion of this man from the purview of mainstream American concerns, and it is mirrored in Philip's distancing treatment of classmate Seldon Wishnow, whose subtle religious and gendered differences are dissonant with the triumphant narrative of American greatness he and his brother have imbibed since birth.

Myths of American greatness are central to this novel's project, as several critics have noted. Jennifer A. Slivka, for instance, reads *Plot* as a "counternarrative to the American (i.e., Christian) historiography that [Philip] reads in his schoolbooks" (135), and Jason Siegel argues that the novel "explore[s] and revis[es] the ways we represent and comprehend history" (131), specifically by exposing "the various possibilities inherent in any moment that reveal the divided consciousness of the body politic" (131). The image of one American great—Lindbergh—is quite literally the focal point upon which Philip's mode of seeing becomes complicated, enacting such a "divided consciousness." Precandidacy Lindbergh is hailed as so much of an American cultural hero—and Philip's family sees themselves as so American—that Philip's own parents intertwine their story of expecting their first child with Lindbergh's first transatlantic flight, a "mythology" (Roth 5) that Philip's brother Sandy captures in a sketch of his mother carrying him in utero while gazing up at Lindbergh's plane.

By thrusting this version of American heroism into the past via young Philip's shift into countersurveillant mode, the text affords the distance and perspective it needs to critique those who have formed it—just as the allohistorical genre affords the defamiliarization required to reconsider trajectories of US nationhood. That defamiliarization occurs overtly via several key scenes in the text that exhibit how once Lindbergh's anti-Semitism and fascist leanings have become visible on the public stage, the mode of Philip's looking fractures. Gazing at the portraits, which Sandy has deceitfully told his parents he has torn up, Philip notices that "now something external had transformed the meaning of these drawings, making them into what they were not" (26). The vague phrasing of "something external" underscores young Philip's confusion about how to name what he has experienced in becoming the target, rather than the agent, of American hegemonic practices. By focalizing this moment through the child's experience of seeing—and couching it in language left unencumbered by further clarifying commentary from the adult narrator—the text enacts the shocked confusion of the child, pulling the reader into a lived moment rather than a recounted memory, aligning them with the child against suspect narratives of American heroics.

The scene also calls attention to the significance of context—the external—in producing and destroying particular ways of looking. While Philip's earlier mode of looking was decidedly Bergerian, this moment is marked by dissonance: he simultaneously recalls what the paintings "were" and documents that they are "now . . . not." Philip has not changed, but his sociopolitical affordances have. That Philip feels heavily his status as a vulnerable child—it is in this scene that the narrating voice remarks "never before had being seven felt like such a serious deficiency" (26)—is also a source of dissonance, for his vulnerability is conflated within the world of the text, not with innocence but rather with knowingness, the knowingness of the marginalized child, the child who cannot enjoy the privilege of culturally ascribed innocence reserved, in this case, for European-appearing gentiles.[23] The recollecting filter of the narrative performs childhood's limitations and disempowerment even as it speaks to the child's savvy perception of the ethnic ideologies that other him. Philip may not be able to—or does not want to—name what has happened, but he does know that a shift has occurred, and his way of looking cannot any longer fully participate in that which glorifies American identity. As it is for Cassie and to a certain extent Charley, knowingness is now a condition of Philip's existence in the United States. Indeed, *The Plot against America* demonstrates overtly how a countersurveillant mode of seeing is itself Bergerian for the marginalized child.

The shift in Philip's way of looking is in direct contrast to official national messaging, even as it is born of its exclusionary tactics. One of Lindbergh's early radio speeches asserts the significance of engaging in a state-sanctioned gaze: "No person of honesty and vision . . . can look on their pro-war policy here today without seeing the dangers. . . . A few far-sighted Jewish people realize this. . . . But the majority still do not. . . . We cannot blame them for looking out for what they believe to be their own interests, but we must also look out for ours" (13). The shifts here, from "person" to "Jewish" to the "we" versus "them" bifurcation, suggest that modes of looking encode exclusive identities, and the "we" American viewpoint cannot accommodate the "they" prowar Jewish gaze. That Roth has taken these lines almost word-for-word from a speech the historical Lindbergh delivered in 1941 at the American First Committee rally in Ohio speaks to the seriousness with which Roth infuses young Philip's countersurveillant looking.[24] Combating Lindbergh's vision by staring back at its exclusionary tactics is important, necessary, and possible to be enacted by a child.

It is significant that the moment when Philip does first define for himself what has occurred in his country emerges via an act of looking resistant to national mandates—one that manifests in a dream that conflates child vision with insight. Philip's dream evokes and disrupts the quintessential American childhood now out of his reach. In it, he visualizes a transformation of his beloved Washington bicentennial stamps and his national parks stamps, two series that celebrate American myths of independence, leadership, and protected yet free land, respectively. The Washington portraits turn to images of Hitler, and across the image of each national park appears "printed a black swastika," covering "everything in America that was the bluest and the greenest and the whitest and to be preserved forever" (42). When Philip sees the portraits, he is "stunned"; when he sees the parks set, he "f[alls] out of the bed and w[akes] up on the floor, this time screaming" (43). The "truth" of Philip's dream is not the transcendent truth of the Romantic child of pure vision, but rather a horrible realization that carries over into his waking life, where he is trapped in and vulnerable to strengthening fascism in US politics.

Philip's gaze upon the stamps is so effective as a narrative strategy because it demonstrates that he recognizes the new aesthetic of post-Lindbergh America while at the same time rejecting it, casting the swastikas as unnatural intrusions into a heretofore pristine landscape. Here, and crucially, Roth does not position the child as othered by his country but the United States as othered by the child. Philip's dream rejects the state-sanctioned gaze promoted by Lindbergh, exposing the political crisis that draws the implied reader closer to him and further away from the America he refuses to condone.

Set in opposition to and in anticipation of forthcoming Lindberghian policies that enact surveillance, such as Homestead 24, the work of the Office of American Absorption, and the Good Neighbors program—which attempt to destroy Jewish communities and the possibility thereof by relocating individual Jewish children or whole families to non-Jewish regions—this scene emphasizes the impulse of the child to enact countersurveillant resistance. That impulse, though resulting in a terrifying vision, is the anchor of this scene. Child vision is the vehicle of the storytelling adult, and the child's and adult's continuity positions child perception not as immature or simplified but as crucial to countersurveillant resistance. And indeed, that the most clear countersurveillant moment for young Philip so far is conveyed in a dream emphasizes the narratorial dynamics at work in the novel, for the alterity of dream vision refracts the alterity of the allohistorical genre. Thus, Philip's dream—in its form as well as its content—offers metacommentary on the mode of looking readers must engage to see exclusion at work in the United States. Seeing with the child becomes a narrative imperative; the adult reader must inhabit the vulnerability as well as the power of the countersurveillant child living in a United States that breeds Nazi ideologies.

The brief synopsis and quotations I have used to describe this scene above do not do justice to the length with which Roth draws out the scenario; it spans several paragraphs, the text dilating with the child's eye, asking the reader to pause over the details that emerge when the child looks back at exclusionary visions of American identity. Indeed, the ekphrastic nature of the passage is clear down to the details on a "one-half-cent stamp" versus the "six" or "ten," the "two-cent red, the five-cent blue, the eight-cent olive green" background colors, the "white-faced roman" typography as well as the "cliffs, the woods, the rivers, the peaks, the geyser, the gorges, the granite coastline" (43). To a certain extent, the notional ekphrasis of this passage complicates the alterity of the dream, for it conjures an image of a series of stamps that actually exists in the real world, even as it defamiliarizes that series with the allohistorical nightmare of the swastika and the face of Hitler. Thus, the child's gaze is the vehicle of the scene's pathos: the reader is invited not just to view but to *recognize* an object from real US history and react with the shocked horror of finding it marred by a symbol that official US discourses deemed hatefully un-American. Note, too, that his dream constitutes a chapter end, its force doubled and underscored by the withholding of narrated analytical commentary. It is the careful looking—the act itself—in which young Philip engages that carries the weight and the momentum of the scene. The adult is actually not necessary to interpret the vision of the child, though he is, perhaps, necessary to put it into words. If grown Philip is our recollecting storyteller, then young Philip is our truth-seer.

It is not surprising, then, that when Philip's family takes what was supposed to have been a quintessential American family vacation to Washington, DC, countersurveillance takes over as the truth of Philip's new existence. The national monuments, key assemblages of national power, perform their work here, creating an American space that exalts American nationhood. Visual theorist W. J. T. Mitchell notes that public art, including monuments, contributes to the myth of a Habermasian public sphere, where "disinterested citizens may contemplate a transparent emblem of their own inclusiveness and solidarity and deliberate on the general good, free of coercion, violence, or private interests" (378–79). However, he wonders whether "violence [is] built into the monument in its very conception" (378). If the "fact" of the public sphere is not inclusivity but "the rigorous exclusion of certain groups" (379), then the spectacle of the monument raises the specter of exclusionary violence—a specter that becomes flesh in Roth's novel via Philip's countersurveillant gaze.

When young Philip sees the Lincoln Memorial, his initial reaction is that of the ideal citizen to an emblem of a united country: "The sculpted face look[ed] to [him] like the most hallowed possible amalgamation—the face of God and the face of America all in one" (63). But the protection or safety Philip had formerly associated with the United States does not sustain his gaze; instead, it is confronted by the blatant anti-Semitism of a fellow tourist, whose "long, gaping look" at his father precipitates his derogatory and dismissive comment "loudmouth Jew" (65) and his companion's "I'd give anything to slap his face" (65). In response, Philip's gaze again enacts a countersurveillant mode of looking that documents the effects of the new national leadership: "It was the most beautiful panoramic I'd ever seen, a patriotic paradise, the American Garden of Eden spread before us, and we stood huddled together there, the family expelled" (66). Again, Philip's gaze at the monument in juxtaposition to the treatment his family experiences enacts a countersurveillant condemnation of narratives of inclusivity that the nation's leadership and citizenship fail to uphold.[25] Seeing the American paradise at the same time that he sees his own family divided from it reverses, or counters, his pre-Lindberghian way of looking. The text makes clear that myths of American greatness serve not to protect and unite but to villainize and divide.[26]

The people who disdain the Roth family for their Jewish characteristics, it is clear, have not been newly taught how to recognize them; they elected Lindbergh on a ticket that capitalized on demeaning ethnic difference. Rather, Lindbergh's presidency has authorized the use of this recognition of difference to discriminate, hate, and threaten in public spaces supposedly tied to notions of national belonging. Indeed, anti-Semitism as part of US social fabric is earlier suggested in the text by the fact that the Roth family chose to stay in their Jewish neighborhood despite Mr. Roth's having been offered a lucrative job transfer to a gentile town. Furthermore, Philip's own pre-Lindberghian looking does not always amount to a pure hero worship of American sociopolitical practices, though it does downplay exceptions. What Roth accomplishes with his allohistory, then, is not a full turnaround of US visuality related to Judaism, but rather the emboldening of American anti-Semitism in real US history as well as the contemporary present to the extreme. Young Philip's countersurveillant looking in response to this more overt anti-Semitic visuality reflects the way in which real American children, past and present, who are subjected to cultural scripts that strip them of national belonging develop modes of social critique—including a countersurveillant gaze—that call for change to a national identity that is constantly being made and remade by the exclusion of their image.

It is important to note, however, that just as with Charley and Cassie, Philip's resistant countersurveillant gaze is ineffectual within the world of the text. None of Philip's looking actually protects his family or his neighborhood, and even his most blatant act of countersurveillance—that of following Christian men and observing their everyday lives—in the end proves dangerous to himself when a predatory man invites him and his friend in for treats. One may want to conclude that the child as an agent is, therefore, ineffectual. But young Philip's decision to try to "save" his own family by suggesting to his aunt that the Wishnow family be relocated rather than his *is* effectual, and in fact deadly. Seldon's mother is killed in anti-Jewish riots in their new town. Thus, the child is not without means to power, but that power can go horribly wrong. I wish to point out that in this case, it goes horribly wrong when it acts in complicity with, rather than in resistance to, the surveillance state that manages ethnic whitewashing programs like Homestead 24. As with Charley and Cassie, Philip's countersurveillant gaze performs on the level of narration what it cannot effect diegetically.

That performance is considerable. Roth published *Plot* during George W. Bush's presidency, and critics consistently interpreted it as a critique of Bush's exclusionary post-9/11 policies. Roth repeatedly denied the association, claiming instead to have written about an imagined trajectory for the United States that he was thankful did not occur when he was a boy. Still, critics drew (and continue to draw) the political connection to the contemporary moment,[27] and I suggest that has much to do with the narratorial dynamics accomplished by the child gaze couched in adult-as-kin narration. Roth's insistence that he was writing about a past that did not occur is belied by the narrative power of his fictional child self who gazes upon the material of US identity, especially since the child gaze substitutes quite powerfully, especially in the moments discussed above, for Roth's alter ego narrator's adult interiority. The weight lent to the mode of such gazing makes the text resonate as countersurveillant, and countersurveillance is portable in a way that an allohistorical early 1940s is not. Indeed, the potency of *Plot* continues after the 2016 US presidential election.[28] By way of the primacy of the child gaze in a novel that overlays the fictional past and real present of a nation and a self as well as engages the tensions therein, Roth suggests that hindsight is not the only method by which we can critique narratives of American nationhood. Watching and being the target of exclusionary practices in the moment may make us feel vulnerable and powerless, qualities we often culturally attribute to children, but bearing witness through countersurveillant vision cultivates a knowingness that can preserve and empower against discrimination and subjugation.

COUNTERSURVEILLING THE ADULT FOCALIZER IN LANGSTON HUGHES'S "RED-HEADED BABY"

Langston Hughes's "Red-Headed Baby" offers a case study wherein the countersurveillant child gaze matters much more on the level of narration than it does on the level of the child character, which places it on the opposite end of the spectrum of child interiority from texts like Roth's and Taylor's. Even Charley, though seemingly removed from narrative explorations of interiority during his acts of looking, is a character whose thoughts and feelings are given voice elsewhere in the novel. Hughes's child character, however, functions throughout his story more as symbol than character, acting as a cipher and fulcrum in a battle the text stages between focalizing character and narrative. As such, the story plays overtly with the subject/object relation that positions gazer and gazee in a power hierarchy that is ultimately destabilized by the countersurveillant child. Furthermore, the child gaze in this text, unlike in the texts discussed above, is effective both inside and outside the world of the story. It also carries heavy thematic and synthetic weight, calling attention to constructions of the child as well as the constructedness of the countersurveillant gaze as a tool for social critique.

Writing during the Jim Crow era about his contemporary moment, Hughes begins "Red-Headed Baby" with the hegemonic attitude and surveillant gaze of a red-haired white sailor on a brief leave on the Florida coast. Almost the entirety of the story is focalized through him as the principal subject who objectifies all that he sees, a narrative technique that makes it all the more powerful that Hughes sets up the titular child's intervening countersurveillant gaze as triumphant in the story. From the start, the sailor, Clarence, speaks and thinks—in a combination of monologue, dialogue, and free indirect discourse—in terms of the dismissive authority of his gaze: "Half-built skeleton houses. . . . Never finished. Mosquitoes, sand, n*****s. . . . What the hell is there to do except get drunk and go out and sleep with n*****s?" (121). Surveying the area, narrator Clarence asserts his dominance, even as the narrative calls attention to the unequal housing and public works distribution along racial lines: "No street lights out here. There never is where n*****s live" (122). On his way to visit a girl named Betsy, whose virginity, he boasts dubiously, he took three years ago, Clarence refers to her as a "mule" (123), derogatorily animalizing her mixed-race identity as well as her "working" status as a woman he can pay for. That denigration continues once he enters Betsy's home, where he surveys Betsy and the "old woman" and inventories their physical appearance (123–24). This portion of the story represents that his way of looking is the sole way of looking, whether the narrative is conveying his thoughts or speaking his words.

Clarence's command of the situation, however, is derailed by the entrance of a mixed-race child with hair and eyes the same shade as his. The manner of this entrance is pivotal, as it both emphasizes the primacy of the child's gaze and features the first and only clear moment of simple third-person narration in the story:

> . . . everybody drinking—when the door . . . slowly . . . opens.
> "Say, what the hell? Who's openin' that room door, peepin' in here? It can't be openin' itself?"
> The white man stares intently, looking across the table, past the lamp, the licker bottles, the glasses and the old woman, way past the girl. Standing in the door from the kitchen—Look! A damn red-headed baby. Standing not saying a damn word, a damn runt of a red-headed baby. (125–26)

The dash in the first line of this passage casts the opening door as interruption, precipitating Clarence's suggestion that someone's "peepin' in here" (125). Clarence is wary about being the object of the gaze rather than its subject. The lone third-person moment—"the white man stares intently" (125)—heralds a narrative shift and also calls attention to the craftedness of the story, which pointedly pits his white man's surveillant gaze against this potential countersurveillant one. The "Look!" that follows the next dash might be read in the voice of both the third-person narrator and the free indirect discursive perspective, for each here demands the reader train their attention—train their gaze—on the baby who "peep[s]," multiplying his significance. Furthermore, by introducing the child's gaze before the child himself, Hughes casts looking as his crucial action; and indeed, here and throughout the remainder of the story, that gaze has a disruptive influence on Clarence as well as the narrative itself.

As the gaze of the child shifts Clarence's attitude from enjoyment to extreme discomfort, the free indirect discourse that characterizes the narration changes its texture. The emphatic "Look!" (a verb repeated throughout the remainder of the story) and the repetition of "damn" convey his shock and distaste, while the use of "runt" (echoing the earlier "mule") suggests he will continue to try to assert his dominance and objectify the child. But the interjections, ellipses, and interruptions sprinkled throughout the text become more frequent and more intense as his will to power vies with the overpowering effect of the baby's appearance and countersurveillant gaze: "Betsy's red-headed child stands in the door looking like one of those goggly-eyed dolls you hit with a ball at the County Fair. The child's face got no change in it. Never changes. Looks like never will change. Just staring—blue eyed. Hell! God damn! A red-headed blue-eyed yellow-skinned baby!" (126). The narrative tension is stretched upon two poles here. One is Clarence's objectification of the child as a golliwog-style doll that was often used as a game target and prize in county fairs during the Jim Crow era, with its attendant concepts of white violence and racial caricature.[29] The denigration of this impulse is magnified by the fact that the boy is clearly his biological son, also named Clarence, who mirrors back to him some of his own features, made hideous to him through their unification with the child's "yellow" skin. The elder Clarence's free indirect discourse constructs the mixed-race child as monstrous and his entrance as threatening to the feeling of sovereignty he had been enjoying.

The other pole on which the tension is stretched is the gaze of the child himself, "staring" back at Clarence, unchanged, in the face of Clarence's attempt to objectify him. Yancy notes the feelings of exposure and anger that can occur when looks aimed back at an oppressor "communicate to them ... that they were not unseen, but seen ... specifically from an embodied Black subjectivity" (44). Clarence's sense of exposure is a key way the text constructs the child's gaze as countersurveillant; it is Clarence's reaction that imbues it with power both diegetically and extradiegetically. Throughout the rest of the story, Clarence returns relentlessly to the goggly-eyed doll image. Tellingly, the last time he does so, he suggests that he's never actually won this game—"you wham at three shots for a quarter in the County Fair half full of licker and can't hit nothing" (127)—thus foreshadowing his eventual loss to a child who looks countersurveillantly.

Jean Paul Sartre's thought experiment referenced in the introduction to this book is of use here as a comparison to the action of the story. A white man, feeling fully in charge of his surroundings and wielding the white gaze that manifests his power, encounters another figure whom he sees wielding a gaze unique to them, thereby asserting a perspective that "st[eals] the world from [him]" (Sartre 343). If Clarence has been in charge so far, it is the gaze of the baby that "corresponds . . . to a fixed sliding of the whole universe, to a decentralization of the world which undermines the centralization which [he is] simultaneously effecting" (343). And indeed, that the child is, as Clarence cries, "lookin' at me up at me. I said, *me*" (Hughes 344) causes Clarence to become, despite his being the subject through whom the narrative is focalized, an object to both the child and the reader—in Sartre's terms, "being-as-object for the Other" (344). That is, he is forced to feel himself placed in the object position, the one who is countersurveilled rather than the one who is doing the surveilling. The repetition and italicization of the object pronoun "me" emphasizes both his indignant rage and his loss of agency. This type of moment, argues Sartre, precipitates the experience of being "in a world which the Other has made alien to me" (350), and indeed, Clarence's next line attempts to take that space back: "Get him the hell out of here!" (Hughes 127).

Note that for Sartre, there is no need for conveyance of anything but the gaze on the part of the Other to create this situation; no words need be exchanged in order to shake the foundations of a person's principal authority in the world. Hughes's red-headed baby character is, according to his caretakers, deaf and potentially mute, and we have no access to his interiority. His key act in the text is that of looking, and it is the countersurveillance this act enables that allows the story to confront Clarence's power and control.

The baby is not otherwise oppositional outside of Clarence's perspective; indeed, the text gestures to his innocence by the fact that he simply stands in his own kitchen and toddles over to Clarence to hug his leg. He poses no literal threat to the white man, and therefore the narrative—despite being almost exclusively constructed through the perception of Clarence—opposes Clarence's construction of the child as monstrous. Indeed, that the child approaches Clarence, who repels him with shouts such as "Take your hands off my legs, you lousy little bastard!" (127), impugns Clarence for denying any fatherly obligations that should position him to protect the child, not "knock his block off" (127). Mobilizing readerly sympathies to the side of the child, Clarence's narration is his own indictment, for it exposes the innocence of the child as well as the knowingness Clarence chooses to read into the child's gaze in order to displace his own. That gaze carries the narrative weight of knowing opposition to Clarence—and prompts celebration of that opposition. Though he is the focalizing subject of the story, Clarence becomes the scrutinized object of the narrative, and the call for his objectification is made manifest through the entrance of a countersurveillant child gaze.

That the countersurveillant gaze of the child is only imagined within the world of the story, but is quite existent on the level of narrative, suggests that a child whom a text positions as looking countersurveillantly need not be a developed or even a knowing character on the mimetic level; the synthetic narrative can ascribe to the gaze a knowingness that resonates thematically. In this story, the undevelopedness of the child character allows him to function more overtly as a symbol of the mixed-race children resulting from white domination of Black women. The irony that Clarence contributed to the creation of this person and cannot admit it—though he knows and is repulsed by it, evidenced by the rambling "looking like me at me like me at myself like me red-headed as me" (127)—reads as a central indictment of white oppression that takes forms such as sexual objectification, negligence, abuse, and denial.

The child's countersurveillant gaze documents and disrupts this oppression while sending a clear message of Black survival and existence despite it. For the gaze of the baby, though not constructed to reveal his interiority, does suggest a resilient subjectivity. He is alive, and he "ain't blind" (126), as his mother emphasizes. Laura Dawkins argues that Harlem Renaissance writers embraced "the black baby [as] a beacon for the future, a sign of the strength and resilience of the African American—living proof that the race had survived both enslavement and the genocidal violence following Reconstruction" (175). By constructing this child not as, in Clarence's vision, a monstrous threat that needs to be objectified, but rather as a toddling baby with a countersurveillant gaze turned relentlessly on a white man, Hughes metonymizes "the endurance of people" (Dawkins 176) and makes a claim for the Black child as inheritor and future of American belonging. Sartre theorizes the look of the Other as a manifestation of the "Other's freedom" (351); in the end, it is not the child but Clarence who retreats, thus suggesting the space itself can be controlled by the child. The child's countersurveillant gaze—even though the child who wields it may not be aware he is doing so—is triumphant both within the world of the story and on the level of narrative, positing literary children as powerful conduits for social critique and social change.

CONCLUSION

The texts under discussion in this chapter exhibit the nuance with which the countersurveillant child gaze can be deployed as a narrative technique to signal resistance of exclusionary narratives of US national belonging. Jackson's *Call Me Charley*, through its subtle museum silent moments of Charley's countersurveillance, exposes institutionally approved anti-Black exclusion in the midcentury US North. Taylor's *Roll of Thunder, Hear My Cry* positions Cassie's emotional interiority and sometimes vocal protest as an overt narrative signal for approving and joining her countersurveillant gaze. Through the narrative dynamics of her looking, Taylor impugns the blatant anti-Black racism and violence plaguing Cassie's Depression era Mississippi community and schooling, as well as the anti-Blackness that persists into Taylor's historical moment. In *The Plot against America*, Roth employs a kinship model to bind adult interiority to the child's perception, creating a powerfully countersurveillant child figure whose gaze is transferable beyond the allohistory depicted in the novel. Representing the alterity of an overtly anti-Semitic US 1940s through the kin perspective of his child self allows the adult narrator to position childhood as a seat of social critique and the child as a serious lens through which to condemn shifting political rhetorics that favor ethnic exclusivity. And through the most opaque child character in this study, Hughes demonstrates the narrative power of a child's countersurveillant gaze by casting his titular red-headed baby as a disruptive force to the texture of the narrative itself. Limning the loss of racialized control in a white man when faced with the assertion of the existence of his own mixed-race child, Hughes wraps the potential for defeat of white oppression and spatializes demands for belonging in the body and gaze of a Black child.

One concept that energizes the documentation and critique of the various social orders represented in these texts is the Romantic notion of the child with purity of vision, the child who sees the "truth." But each text also works against the simplicity of this evocation. Charley's lack of commentary might connote confusion as much as it conveys ekphrastic clarity, and Cassie's rebellious nature counteracts an angelic read of her perceptions. Hughes's red-headed baby becomes a cipher for the fight between understanding the mixed-race child as monstrous or valued, a symbol that eschews purity as part of the story's stakes. And the first several pages of *The Plot against America* build up young Philip's heroic vision of America only so that the rest of the novel can indict it as dangerously exclusive. Purity is neither the object nor the objective of the child's vision in these novels.

Even if these texts do rely on culturally ascribed notions of purity to position the reader to heed the child's gaze—and I believe they all do, to a certain extent, capitalize on the readerly sympathies engineered by the figure of the child writ large—they also work against that construct by concerning their social critique with the fact that purity is irrelevant to the child marginalized by the national environment in which they live. As Althea Tait puts it, the real-life counterparts of these child characters are young people "whose daily political locations place them in overlapping cross fires of the inescapable imaginary and other fatal artillery" ("Empathy" 219). Their seeing is not marked as transcendent, in the ways we might associate with Romantic childhood vision; it rather imbricates the child in the real sociopolitical unrest perpetrated by the top-down surveillance of those oppressed by authority. That is, the countersurveillant child gaze is not a goal or ideal longed for with nostalgia or spiritual desire, but rather a means of intervening in real and often violently exclusive narratives of nationhood in the United States.

Note, too, that in three of the four texts under discussion here, the child who returns the gaze is figured as both innocent and experienced: innocent of the unworthiness with which surveillance charges them and experienced by way of noticing said surveillance. And in the fourth, the knowingness and power ascribed to the child's gaze (if not the child himself) via the narration makes innocence a nonfactor. That the countersurveillant child disrupts the innocent/experienced binary is particularly important for children of color and others who are subordinated in narratives that privilege white, male, Christian, middle-class citizens in the United States. Too much experience or knowingness can cast a child as "not child" and therefore unworthy of protection; authors of countersurveillant children thus tend to weave in markers of childhood that trade, by association, with innocence (such as play, benevolent adult intervention, naive or misguided efforts to intervene in larger affairs, a very young age) in order to recover such children into the innocence narrative. This combination of experience and innocence creates an urgency about the child's vision—a mattering that results from anxieties about the very binary the gaze threatens to dissolve. And the narrative energies spent couching these children in the paradigm of innocence also serve to emphasize their knowingness, not as a reason to cast them out of the category of child but as a nefarious product of their country's indefensible racial ideologies. The guilt belongs to the United States, not to the child who has seen what adults might wish they did not have to.

This notion of "having" to see speaks to the stakes here, as anxieties about child vulnerability and child power drive the construction of the countersurveillant child. As a figure that serves as a cultural touchstone, the child is so compelling as wielder of the countersurveillant gaze specifically because the gaze makes visible—and, by the logic of surveillance, vulnerable—the very agents who threaten them. This is not so much a transfer of vulnerability from child to nation as a radical sharing thereof. The children are in real physical danger, in every text under discussion here, because they live in a particular cultural moment in the United States, when hegemonic attitudes make their small bodies visible and therefore vulnerable. That they cannot rid themselves of this vulnerability is to the point. Their vulnerability is both historically accurate and narratively useful, for it engineers the readerly sympathies that make their pointed gazes so arresting. Their gazes may not be threatening within the worlds of their texts (with the remarkable exception of Hughes's story), but they do pose a risk to the mechanisms of exclusion in the world beyond the text, for they expose them and make them the target of the reader's gaze. Furthermore, given that children often signal notions of futurity, such exposure suggests the possibility of a future in which such children can survive and thrive.

Finally, the ekphrastic descriptions of the objects of the child gaze provide evidence for the circumstances that have necessitated countersurveillance, and the reader is called to look at these objects through the perspective of the child targeted by them—whether that perspective is rendered in first or third person. Dilating the text by way of the child's eye, these moments demand the notice the child has given to the object. The narrative weight of the gaze thus connotes a logos that balances out the child character's pathos by keeping it from conjuring the patronizing pity that might be reserved for a being entirely "innocent" or defenseless: for the gaze connotes a serious knowingness that allows the texts to call forth resistance as well as cast childhood as a viable position for spurring it.

Thus, when children look back—including Hughes's narratively opaque yet insistently gazing red-headed baby—at oppressive authority, they energize a narratively induced sense of righteousness and call for an ethical evaluation of the object of the gaze. Given that the surveilling gaze in such texts attempts to mark the child as monstrous, the achievement of the child's countersurveillant gaze is that it hurls the label of monstrous back on the surveillant. And although—or rather because—the child is threatened within the diegetic world of the text, the child's gaze is both protected and promoted at the level of narrative, obtaining its power by the fact that it is wielded by a child denied but deserving access to the protections of citizenship in a nation's social order.

Chapter Three

THE TRANSACTIONAL CHILD GAZE

Wrestling with Ideology in the Visual Surround

The previous chapters investigate modes of the child gaze that can coexist with various levels of awareness on the part of the looking child. That is, children who look appreciatively or countersurveillantly may be represented along a spectrum of "knowing" and "not-knowing" in relation to their gaze. Langston Hughes's titular red-headed baby, for instance, remains an opaque character, his looking implying (on the level of narrative) rather than intending (on the level of character) the countersurveillance that characters like Mildred Taylor's Cassie knowingly and insistently perform. Likewise, Sydney Taylor's all-of-a-kind girls engage in looking that is self-evidently celebratory but not often remarkable to them personally; the third-person narrative voice *describes* their appreciative looking, but it does not often convey the sisters' *awareness* of their gaze or its tonality. On the other hand, James Baldwin and Yoran Cazac's TJ does exhibit awareness of his ways of seeing, even specifically calling attention to the inconclusive curiosity of his own gaze—as, for example, when he ruminates over Blinky's glasses. In each of these texts, the level of child knowingness inflects the representation of their gazes, but it does not determine whether or not their gazes exist—nor does it correspond, inherently, to the level of efficacy their gazes achieve as narrative techniques.

This chapter turns to a type of child looking that requires not only the child's awareness but also the narrative's attention to the child's *consideration* of their acts of looking. I term this gaze the "transactional child gaze," which manifests when the child's awareness of and reflections on their acts of looking are key elements of their character arc. Characters who engage in transactional looking may do so countersurveillantly, appreciatively, both, or neither. Their looking is defined not by its effect but by its orientation: transactional, relational, concerned with the exchange between the child and the visual aspects of that child's ideological environment. The transactional gaze comprises a process-oriented looking by which the child negotiates the self in relation to their surroundings, surroundings often dominated by visual signs of cultural ideologies that, to use Louis Althusser's formulation, call forth the child's subjectivity and assert their power via interpellation.

Cassie Logan's gaze in *Roll of Thunder, Hear My Cry*, for instance, although discussed under the umbrella of the countersurveillant child gaze in chapter two, might also be considered transactional. As she countersurveils the white authority in her town, the text reveals the effect of such looking on her. The first-person narration makes it quite clear that what she sees causes her to deepen her understanding of how she is supposed to be positioned in relation to white power—and it makes clear that she knowingly resists such positioning and aligns herself with antiracist, activist thinking. Indeed, since the transactional child gaze is process oriented, it posits the child's subjectivity as dynamic. It therefore builds in the possibility of the child's resistance to the ideologies of their environment, even if its persistent result is conformity—as exhibited in Pecola Breedlove's character arc in Toni Morrison's *The Bluest Eye*, discussed below. That is, by engaging with the ideologies that work to formulate the child subject and by privileging the child's perspective thereon, the transactional child gaze exposes the unstable imbrication of the child and the child's hegemonic cultural surround. In US literature, a transactional child gaze posits the child as inextricably intertwined and yet always in conversation with the visual discourses of hegemonic ideologies, such as those concerning but not limited to race, ethnicity, class, gender, sexuality, and age. It works as both catalyst and vehicle for youth making sense of their values and choices in relation to such ideologies, and its repeated use over the course of a text continually opens up possibilities for a critique of dominant exclusionary discourses, especially as they affect the child's trajectory.

This opportunity for critique is a key facet of the transactional gaze's narrative power: it reveals the ways in which such ideologies work upon the child who is aware, at least to a certain extent and perhaps imperfectly, of this very working. It therefore allows scrutiny and interrogation of the interpellative process. While the child, via the heuristic of the transactional gaze, ongoingly *constructs* a negotiation of self in relation to and as part of the world, the text, via representation of that same gaze, *deconstructs* the process by which such negotiation occurs. Pivoting on the construct of the child figure as protean, vulnerable, malleable, and rife with possibilities, including the possibility of oppositional agency within hegemonic social structures, the transactional gaze invites a cultural critique focused not only on the specific scripts that are brought to bear upon the child but also on the ways ideologies are transferred through or interpreted by the child.

It is important to note that this gaze does not simply *locate* the child in the ideological environment. Moments of transactional gazing *enmesh* the child with the environment in the moment of seeing, binding them together in the ongoing alchemy of subjectivity and perspective. Instances of appreciative and countersurveillant child gazing can also perform along these lines, as noted earlier; however, those modes do not necessarily lay bare the deep alchemy that characterizes a transactional gaze. Consider the appreciative child gazing throughout *All-of-a-Kind Family*, mentioned above and discussed in chapter one, where the narration does not remark at any length (and often does not remark at all) upon the sisters' processes of subjectivity in relation to their seeing. A transactional gaze by necessity entails significant narrative devotion to child subjectivity as an ongoing process in relation to visual ideological markers in the environment.

The transactional child gaze, then, also belies the categories of "insider" and "outsider" that result from exclusionary fictions of the dominant cultural imagination and positions the child as always and ever *a part of* (rather than *apart from*) the very social contexts that may threaten to exclude them.[1] It also eschews the construction of the child as passive recipient of cultural mores, instead positing the young person as aware, at least to a certain extent, of social constructs and their implications—constructs their character makes visible through their acts of looking and implications their character makes manifest through their acts of transactional reflection. Whether the results of the transactional gaze are liberatory, oppressive, or a mix of the two for the child who engages it, this gaze imagines the child as extant and active within systems built to guide, control, or even destroy them. Thus, the relationship between child and environment is not necessarily deterministic; indeed, it is destabilizing, as the transactional gaze occurs in the progressive act of seeing, the ongoing dynamics of which always carry the possibility for both repetition and deviation. Given that this gaze is tied to character development, charting its instantiations over the course of a novel—which already contains built-in generic expectations for growth, especially when a young person is its main character—maps the environment as much as it maps the child's trajectory through it, and, indeed, as part of it. In highlighting this tension-laden dynamic between child and environment, it can also function as a narrative call for the renegotiation of the values and hierarchies that support exclusionary ideologies.

Since the child's critical stance within and toward visual signs of national and cultural ideologies—which may manifest dynamically along a spectrum of accepting, adapting to, resisting, or manipulating—is itself situationally inflected by the powers with which the child contends, the transactional gaze also invites an interrogation of that critical stance at any and all stages of the character arc. For even as the representation of this gaze allows the reader intimate access to the responses of the child and can encourage understanding or sympathy, it also provides an opportunity for the reader to observe the child's exposed point of view. Since transactions are unique, specific to the singular interplay between an individualized child self and the child's distinct environment, this gaze becomes a site for readerly critique of the subjectivity continually emerging from visual transactions with the ideologically infused environment. Thus, texts that employ the transactional gaze as a narrative technique do not just foreground a child's ongoing relationship with the visual markers of their environment's ideologies; they also foreground that relationship's implications for the child's subjectivity and call for scrutiny of the child's possibilities within the often-discriminatory systems that constitute that environment.

In theorizing and naming the transactional gaze, I draw on several fields of study containing ideas that map onto and mirror each other: education (specifically aesthetic transaction theory, otherwise known as the transactional theory of reading and writing), psychology (ecological perception theory), philosophy, and visual culture studies. I adopt the term "transactional" from the transactional theory of Louise Rosenblatt, herself informed by John Dewey's use thereof, in order to emphasize the ongoing, dynamic exchange between viewer and viewed; it does not, despite its use in business parlance and in scholarship on neoliberalism, refer to commercial exchange, but rather to the "ongoing process that characterizes the relationship between human and environment" (Rosenblatt, "Viewpoints" 40).[2] Though Rosenblatt's transactional theory was initially conceived in relation to reading and writing, she has argued for its significance to other realms, including the visual, in works such as "The Aesthetic Transaction." Her work and that of others concerned with perception, visual culture, and the social context of the human subject inform this theory of the transactional child gaze, especially regarding the relationship forged between viewer and viewed that is always situationally specific. In the section below, I review the connections among that body of work in relation to my formulation of the transactional child gaze before turning to three texts that allow a demonstration of its contours, specifically when it is wielded by a child in an environment suffused with exclusionary ideologies of national belonging in the United States.

While the transactional gaze can be a site of interrogation for any dominant system of power, here I exhibit its workings on texts that confront ideologies of race and ethnicity (and at times their intersections with gender) in order to create a stronger case for comparison as I tease out the ways this gaze works across a spectrum of diegetic and extradiegetic resonance. In the texts I discuss below, the process of choosing or learning to look is a key way the protagonist "grows" or "develops" within the context of an embattled relationship between the self and ideological environment. That is, the texts emphasize the transactional, hermeneutical nature of the child gaze, the way the child's acts of looking catalyze acts of interpretation of dominant US cultural practices even as the child (and the gaze) is interpellated by them. The differences among the texts, however, speak to the ways transactional gazing, depending on how it positions the trajectory of the child in relation to oppressive narratives, opens up a critical space to interrogate that trajectory and that relationship.

Sandra Cisneros's *The House on Mango Street* (1983) employs the transactional child gaze as a key characterization tool for its exceptional Chicana main character, thus emphasizing the resistant powers of the child in the face of the ethnically inflected gender expectations of her community. However, by foregrounding without irony or critique protagonist Esperanza's point of view, which focuses heavily on her need to leave her barrio, it also risks maintaining the primacy of white-dominated United States metastructures that influence the ideologies of her marginalized community. Cisneros's text demonstrates that while ostensibly liberatory for the child, the transactional gaze can reproduce as immovable the machinery of culture without critiquing it. Toni Morrison's *The Bluest Eye* (1970), on the other hand, actively critiques the superstructures at play in the world of its characters by highlighting the transactional gaze of a young Black girl sublimated by racist standards of beauty and value; it juxtaposes her gaze with the transactional gaze of her neighbor, who is able to resist but ultimately becomes aware of the ubiquity of the oppression she attempts to avoid. The children's subjectivities, victimized within the world of the text, become the novel's powerful exposure of the pernicious work of the very ideologies to which they fall prey. Finally, Jason Reynolds and Brendan Kiely's *All American Boys* (2015) employs the transactional child gaze to emphasize how one can reorient the self in relation to oppressive ideologies of race in order to combat from within the racist cultures built to enforce them. Containing alternating narration by two teen boy protagonists, one Black and one white, this text calls attention to the way transactional looking highlights the relationships among white privilege, racial victimization, and antiracist activism. Through the evolving transactions of its characters, however, it also emphasizes that despite the intensive and violent power of an anti-Black racist system, the transactional gaze offers a pathway toward empowerment—in the storyworld and on the level of narrative—against the exclusionary tactics that produce racial bifurcation.

THE TRANSACTIONAL CHILD GAZE IN THEORETICAL AND LITERARY CONTEXT

Humans see in context, and context must be understood to encompass the situations attendant upon viewer, object, and the act of seeing itself. Citing optical studies from the field of psychology, Rosenblatt builds her transactional theory on the finding that "perception depends much on the viewer's selection and organization of visual cues according to past experience, expectations, ends, and interests" ("The Transactional Theory of Reading and Writing" 9). Indeed, visual culture as a field attends to "subjectivities of identification or desire or abjection from which we view and by which we inform what we view" (Rogoff 18). This focus on the importance of the viewer's identity, experiences, and position to the act and effect of seeing is echoed across disciplines,[3] and literature as a stage for looking reproduces this phenomenon: its focus on characters in settings, for instance, disallows isolating visual perception as a mechanical act. Looking must carry the valences of an individual's situationally inflected identity and experience.

Looking also involves the object of the gaze, and that object has its own physical and social context. Together the object and its context produce "environmental information" that calls out to a viewer's attention (Arzamarski et al. 721). Thus, in addition to the viewer's context, "the nature of the perceived object itself" (Freeman 59) influences whether we see it at all and how we perform that seeing. For instance, a very tiny insect might go unperceived by the human eye altogether, unless it is positioned under a microscope the viewer is using; an insect that appears to be small and slow-moving might elicit a viewer to bend down close and peer, and a large insect with pointy appendages that move very quickly might elicit that same viewer to eye it suspiciously while backing away. Of course, in any of these cases, the viewer is also an influential component of the seeing act. The viewer must know to recognize the insect under the microscope; appreciate looking at small insects and feel physically able to bend down; and have some experience with large, pointy creatures as potentially dangerous. The enactment of seeing is inextricable from either viewer or object even as it is the key element linking the two. The dynamic interplay between viewer and object through the act of seeing—and their interrelated contexts—is the foundation of the transactional gaze.

Such a transaction is an alchemy. Rosenblatt describes the relationship between viewer and object in various complementary ways—as a "reciprocal, mutually defining relationship" ("Aesthetic" 122), as a "two-way, or, better, circular, stream of dynamically intermingled symbolizations which mutually reverberate and merge" (123), and as a "live circuit between perceiver and artifact" (127). Philosopher Eugene Freeman, who like Rosenblatt draws the term "transaction" from John Dewey, refers to a "triadic" perceptual process: "It brings together three inseparable ingredients which make up a perception: an 'organism' which cannot be separated from its environment, an 'environment' which cannot be separated from the organism, and a 'process' of mutual change and impact of one upon the other, involving the meanings of environmental stimuli as determined by the past experience, the present assumptions, and the future purposes of the percipient organism" (60). Art and visual studies scholar James Elkins focuses on this melding of viewer and object by claiming that the concept captured in the sentence "the observer looks at the object" is an impossible one, since the observer and object are immediately impacted—that is, changed—by each other in the moment of looking (18–19). Elkins locates that change in the transaction: "It's as if I have abandoned the place in the sentence that was occupied by the words 'the observer' and I've taken up residence in the verb 'looks,' literally between the words 'object' and 'observer'" (43). The transaction draws the viewer and object into each other's paradigms in the moment of looking, potentially creating a new paradigm in which both now must exist. Regardless of where on the spectrum of attraction to repulsion the transaction produces a reaction, in the instance of the gaze there is a binding that produces that reaction, a connection rather than a division that asserts the existence of both viewer and object in the interplay of the beholding. The viewer's link to the object is paramount; it is the catalyst.

The dynamism of character action and development in a literary text bolsters the power of transactional gazing on the page. Anthony Wall's extrapolation of character theory from Bakhtin holds that "the consciousness of that which we call a character is never a self-contained entity, but rather, like the living ideas that characters incarnate, it is in constant interaction with everything that surrounds it" (2). Characters are "unisolable" (45) from their worlds even as they are distinct actors within them. The transactional gaze is one way authors represent that unisolability, fusing the character and that which the character sees in the instant of the look. And no text can represent everything a character sees, which speaks to the significance of the visual details the text *does* represent. Because those details garner the attention of the character who looks, their importance is signaled to the reader—as is the importance of the character noticing them at all.

The introduction to this book as well as its earlier chapters spent some time discussing how a character's act of looking is a narrative event that directs the readerly gaze, so on one level, this signaling of importance is true of all character gazing. In terms of the transactional gaze, however, which occurs in those instances when the character does not just look but is aware of and reflects on their response to that looking, the study of perception events can also be what psychologists Shaw et al. refer to as "a study of mind" (281). Because a text employing the transactional gaze must attend overtly to the interiority of the character who looks, every instance of the transactional gaze, especially when it is extended as a network of gazes over the course of a text, exists as a flashpoint for examination of the looking character's stance, or perspective, as well as the visual artifact that has called forth that stance.

The fact that texts do not catalog all items its characters see, therefore placing special attention on those that they do see, also speaks to a concept that has gone by different names in different discourses: "attensity," "selective attention," or, in a more extreme version, the "punctum." In psychology's ecological perception theory, attensity is "the property of an environment-organism interaction that makes one particular part of the scene attention-grabbing for that organism" (Blau and Capetta 8). From all elements in the informational surround, the viewer focuses on those that are most important to them. That importance might be determined by a myriad of qualities related to the viewer, and in Blau and Capetta's estimation, representation of attensity in literary texts pertains to a fictive character's "World Line," which is made up of "the character's capabilities, intentions, and history" (6).[4] Following psychologist William James, Rosenblatt refers to this prioritizing of particular details as "selective attention," where selectivity determines "what is pushed into the background or suppressed and what is brought into awareness and organized into meaning" ("Transactional" 6). Roland Barthes's term "punctum," which he uses specifically regarding photographs, speaks to the emotionality at play in this "detail that attracts" (42). And while Barthes theorizes the punctum in terms of the idiosyncratic, psychological response of the viewer, such a response is not itself immune to the social and cultural ideologies that have a hand in shaping it. Indeed, Barthes's description of the punctum as that which one "stubbornly see[s]" (43), that which "rises from the scene, shoots out of it like an arrow, and pierces" (26), maps easily onto the ways poignant acts of looking are represented in literature, especially by characters whose fictionalized psychological interiorities are often constructed in relation to the cultural mores in which they are situated. The crucial point of contact between viewer and photograph, a punctum's relationship with the viewer recalls the transactional alchemy discussed above: "Whether or not it is triggered, it is an addition: it is what I add to the photograph and what is *nonetheless already there*" (Barthes 55). Elkins does not name the phenomenon so succinctly, but he does refer to the "irresistible effect" of some objects, "as if we were tied to them by little wires" (19). Both Barthes's and Elkins's formulations also emphasize the embodied nature of these wires. They are not simply imagined or strictly cognitive but lived and felt. They anchor the act of seeing in the "personal, social, [and] cultural matrix" (Rosenblatt, "Viewpoints" 46) of the transactional moment.

That moment then becomes a part of that character's life: an instance that matters to the subjectivity of the character and that will now matter as part of that subject's history in shaping subsequent transactions and even interpreting past ones. Given that transactions spur a "constantly self-revising impulse" (Rosenblatt, "Transactional Theory" 8), the effect of the transactional gaze changes over time in concert with the viewer's acquisition of new experiences. Indeed, the figure of the child is key to the power of this gaze as a narrative strategy, as it is a figure culturally and biologically steeped in the notions of change and growth.[5] The generic and cultural expectation that literary children will grow places them in a state of flux, doubling down on the orientation toward process that characterizes the transactional gaze.[6] Furthermore, as young people move out of early childhood toward adolescence, they enter a stage of life that in the United States is overtly linked to struggles with ideologies and institutions. Roberta Seelinger Trites argues that adolescent literature (by which she means literature written for youth or literature that features adolescent protagonists) posits negotiated relations with systems of power as "fundamental" to character growth, which reflects the way that Western ideologies position the adolescent in contention with institutional control and maturation out of adolescence as synonymous with "learn[ing] their place in the power structure" (x–xi).

The ideological concerns Trites places in the period of adolescence, however, often begin far earlier for young people and are especially pronounced for children who are marginalized. The main characters in several texts discussed in previous chapters evidence the reflection in literature of contentious child-ideology relations prior to adolescence: *Call Me Charley*'s titular Charley is twelve; *The Plot against America*'s fictional child version of Philip Roth is seven; *Roll of Thunder, Hear My Cry*'s Cassie Logan is nine, and *A Tree Grows in Brooklyn* follows Francie Nolan from age eleven. Likewise, the texts exhibiting the contours of the transactional child gaze discussed in this chapter emphasize ideologically aware looking in characters that range from age nine to age seventeen. Althusser claims that interpellation begins even before birth, by way of the child simply existing within power structures constantly at work to sustain themselves via the very subjects they interpellate (19). But the child is also often conceived as a figure who must be recruited into the understanding of cultural mores and behaviors; children are born into social communities with practices and belief systems the child does not immediately acquire wholesale, but rather learns over time. Indeed, as Karen Sánchez-Eppler argues, children are not only "objects of socialization" who are "taught to conform" but also "individuals inhabiting and negotiating . . . often conflicting roles" (xv). That negotiation is part of this time gap, so to speak, between birth and full interpellation, and it imbues the figure of the child with the elasticity to maneuver without full alignment with—though certainly still tethered to—hegemonic social narratives. Furthermore, this time gap need not be understood to enforce what Marah Gubar terms a "deficit model of childhood" (298)—a not-yet-ness that downplays the child's participation in the human scene. Rather, it invests the child with the possibility of personal power, with agency.

Child experience and child growth are bound up in ideological relations, and the transactional child gaze makes visible the profound implications of each for the other. In the perceptual psychology terms employed above, child characters enacting a transactional gaze exhibit an "education of attention," or a change, over time and because of experience, in "cognitive processes that raise the attensity level of a particular property of physical information over and above the average attensity level of the total available information" (Shaw and McIntyre 355). Thus, considering this "education of attention"—also called "attunement" or "informational reattunement" (Arzamarski et al. 721)—over the course of a text allows an interrogation of the child-environment relationship, which is itself dynamic and malleable. Indeed, the shifting visual perception of the child also calls into question the stability of the visual field itself, a concept established by visual culture theorists. As Rogoff notes:

> Much identity in the field of vision is formed through a process of negative differentiation: that whiteness needs blackness to constitute itself as whiteness; that masculinity needs femininity or feminized masculinity to constitute its masculinity in agreed upon normative modes; that civility and bourgeois respectability need the stereotypical unruly "others" . . . to define the nonexistent codes of what constitutes "acceptable" behavior. However, at the same time we have understood that all of these are socially constructed, "performative" rather than essentially attributed, and therefore highly unstable entities. (21–22)

Transacting with the visual markers that support ideologies guarding boundaries of exclusion, child characters expose for the reader's view the way hegemonic narratives of US belonging shape their responses and their patterns of growth, which can contend with and sometimes submit to the forces that shape them. In experiencing such alchemy through the transactional gaze, child characters reveal that contention or submission itself to be part of a dynamic process that dissolves the solidified boundaries to which normative social constructions pretend.

Whether the elements converging in the transactional gaze appear to hamper or hinder what is culturally considered to be positive growth for the child, they also expose the dynamic, self-revising, meaning-making activities in which the child subject engages—and in doing so, the transactional gaze illuminates, to some degree, the instability of the particular ideologies that come into its lens. Furthermore, not all ideologies are consistent over time and locale—though they often do *persist* in ever-changing shapes—and literary texts press against these ideologies in ways responsive to the cultural milieu in which they are produced. As Gabrielle Owen notes, the literature of social resistance "reflect[s] the forms of representation that emerge as possible in the present moment" ("Adolescence" 256). While the transactional gaze is not itself made possible or impossible by degrees of ideological instability, the texts that employ it do so with inflections related to the extent to which such ideologies are contested in the author's moment. Jason Reynolds and Brendan Kiely's *All American Boys*, for instance, employs the transactional gaze of a white boy and a Black boy concerning police brutality, transactions made possible on the literary page in the mainstream young adult market in 2015 precisely because of the rise of attention from dominant media outlets to the ongoing problem of racialized police brutality. Likewise, Toni Morrison's 1970 *The Bluest Eye* contests racist beauty standards in concert with the Black Is Beautiful movement coming out of the 1960s; it does so by representing characters victimized by normative realities infused by white standards of beauty, and it uses such victimization to expose the violence of such normativity and to call for change. Forty years later, accompanying a shift toward more inclusive notions of beauty in the West (a shift we might attribute in part to Morrison's text), a novel like Sharon Flake's 2010 *The Skin I'm In* takes up racist beauty standards by ultimately leaning on resistance instead of victimhood to orient the text against the standards it impugns, reflecting both the persistence of racist standards of beauty and the more widespread revision thereof.

Thus, the transactional child gaze carries the valences of the realities it represents and to which it responds. Sometimes that response has the potential to revise hegemonic social structures in the eyes of the child affected by them—and if not *in* their eyes in the world of the text, then *because* of their eyes in the world of the reader. Through the child character's transactional gaze, the texts discussed below interrogate the role of hegemonic national narratives in the growth of the US child, as well as the literary child's power—diegetically (Cisneros), extradiegetically (Morrison), or both (Reynolds and Kiely)—to disrupt them.

THE POSSIBILITIES AND LIMITS OF THE TRANSACTIONAL CHILD GAZE: SANDRA CISNEROS'S *THE HOUSE ON MANGO STREET*

The House on Mango Street's use of the transactional child gaze demonstrates how this mode of looking provides a platform for orienting the self in opposition to exclusionary ideologies but raises questions about exceptionalism as a viable way to trouble hegemonic structures. In Annie O. Eysturoy's words, Esperanza's character development involves "imagining herself beyond the confinements of the status quo" for a young Chicana girl embattled by the "socio-cultural context" of her barrio (Eysturoy 90). Eysturoy and others read the novel as a story of liberation, and certainly Esperanza's trajectory bears that out. I argue, however, that the way the narration represents her "imagining . . . beyond" focuses on the exceptional individual able to free herself from her neighborhood's limitations and that the text's use of the transactional child gaze also, and perhaps ironically, privileges the change in the child over a potential change in the ideologies of ethnic and gender discrimination that produce such neighborhoods. Consequently, the text runs the risk of naturalizing the systemic inequities that work to marginalize and degrade Chicana women in the United States. Still, that downplaying is mitigated by the exposure, through the representation of the transactional gaze, of Esperanza's critical stance, thus allowing an interrogation of that stance as influenced by the very oppression it rejects.

The House on Mango Street follows Esperanza's childhood experiences in poignant first-person vignettes about her Chicago neighborhood in what is likely the late 1960s or early 1970s. Throughout the text are allusions to the discriminatory ideologies that have created her barrio. The titular house, for instance, is "an emblem of the oppressive socio-economic situation that circumscribes her life and is the source of her feelings of alienation" (Eysturoy 92), and such circumscription affects Esperanza's trajectory as she comes of age and feels forced to choose between "cultural factions" (Roszak 61–62)—that is, between her ethnic enclave and the opportunities that exist outside of it for a Chicana girl.[7] Ultimately, Esperanza chooses to leave Mango Street so that she can thrive but revisit it via her storytelling, of which the text itself is a metaphorical embodiment. Critics have contested whether Esperanza's leaving is, on one hand, a rejection of her culture of origin or, on the other hand, a radical rescripting of Chicana identity as hybrid and binary dissolving, where the narrative's "full circle" ethos of returning to Mango Street enacts a commitment to the people who inhabit it.[8] This debate can be understood as one result of the text's use of the transactional child gaze, which affords a nuanced investigation of the trajectory of an exceptional child whose response to her environment sets her in opposition to the ideologies that seek to place her in a position of submission and spur her leaving—as well as her imagined return.

Few critics have paid specific attention to the role of looking in this text. Crawford-Garrett has argued for Esperanza's gradual move from a "participant stance" to a "spectator stance," by which Esperanza assumes an objective perspective through which she evaluates her surroundings (97). This reading, however, does not take into account that the text presents Esperanza's gaze as transactional, as inextricably linked to the relationship between herself and her surroundings, a relationship predicated upon and contributing to her subjecthood.[9] Yomna Saber's casting of Esperanza as a Chicana flâneuse moves a bit closer to the transactional paradigm, suggesting that the oscillating roles of "participant and observer produce the dialectics of [Esperanza's] flânerie" (76), the method by which she "forges her identity" (70). While I argue that the text collapses the roles of participant and observer specifically by way of a gaze that is itself a mark of the participatory subject, Saber's assessment speaks to the relationality at the foundation of Esperanza's gaze. Her identity formation and resultant actions—including what these critics call "observation"—are unisolable from the environment in which they are enacted.

Indeed, critics who have not focused on Esperanza's gaze have nevertheless expressed the nature of her relationship to Mango Street as "intersubjectiv[e]" (Hartley-Kroeger 277) and read "her identity as deeply imbricated in forms of relation" (Carden 151), "inextricably connected to [the sociocultural] context" (Eysturoy 89) that is Mango Street. The transactional gaze draws these components together, positioning Esperanza's looking as itself a type of dialogue. The gaze makes visible the ideological subject in context, eliciting sympathy for and celebration of Esperanza's trajectory even as it opens up to critique her perspective and her choices, themselves influenced by the ideologies she comes to oppose.

Esperanza is aware of how ideologies are tied to practices of looking in the United States, specifically in reference to race relations:

> Those who don't know any better come into our neighborhood scared. They think we're dangerous.
>   . . .
>   But . . . we know the guy with the crooked eye is Davey the Baby's brother, and the tall one next to him in the straw brim, that's Rosa's Eddie V. . . .
>   All brown all around, we are safe. But watch us drive into a neighborhood of another color and our knees go shakity-shake and our car

windows get rolled up tight and our eyes look straight. Yeah. That is how it goes and goes. (Cisneros 28)

Her sardonic comments "Yeah" and "That is how it goes and goes" asserts the presence, the repugnance, and the relentless perpetuity of ethnic and racial hierarchies that govern what and how one sees; even Esperanza's wry perspective does not sever her from the practices she describes, with the possessive "our" turning her "we" into someone else's "they." Observing and participating at once, rather than in turns, Esperanza and her visual transactions are a product of her subjective experience, steeped in the very relativism she sees at work in her world.

That relativism, however, also allows her trajectory as a unique subject within her shared context, a trajectory the text makes scrutable via Esperanza's transactional gaze. In particular, Esperanza's transactions with objects of attensity for her—namely, windows, apertures that both invite and limit vision through their frames—demonstrate that in Esperanza's assessment, the sexist ideologies that infuse Mango Street impede her from living the life she envisions for herself.[10] In an early vignette Esperanza lays out the "subtle beyond," to use Barthes's term (59), of the window as the punctum gripping her gaze. Thinking of her great-grandmother and namesake, a woman "so wild she wouldn't marry," Esperanza recounts the way her "great-grandfather threw a sack over her head and carried her off . . . as if she were a fancy chandelier." She adds, "And the story goes she never forgave him. She looked out the window her whole life, the way so many women sit their sadness on an elbow" (Cisneros 11). Objectified as a decoration and forcibly sexualized into a marriage of submission, Esperanza's great-grandmother enacts a window-gazing fate, the repeated story of which ("the story goes") has informed Esperanza's response to scenes involving women and windows. She claims, "I have inherited her name, but I don't want to inherit her place by the window" (11). The window thus becomes Esperanza's visual touchstone for her consideration of discriminatory expectations regarding gender, sexuality, and space in the barrio. With the window as punctum, she enacts what Chicana critic Gloria Anzaldúa calls "*La facultad* . . . [or] the capacity to see in surface phenomena the meaning of deeper realities . . . an acute awareness mediated by the part of the psyche that does not speak, that communicates in images and symbols" (Anzaldúa 60; italics in original). Since those who possess *la facultad* are "excruciatingly alive to the world" (60), Esperanza's consistent attention to windows over the course of the text speaks to the dynamic, reciprocal nature of her gaze.

The nuance of Esperanza's transactions with window scenes develops in tenor throughout the course of the novel, illustrating the relationship between her transactional gaze and her character arc. In the recounting of her great-grandmother's story, Esperanza wonders "if she made the best with what she got or was she sorry because she couldn't be all the things she wanted to be" (Cisneros 11). However, future vignettes suggest that Esperanza determines the window to be a sign of entrapment rather than small solace or reprieve. In the "all brown all around" section discussed above, for instance, the rolled-up car windows create a barrier between viewer and world, a sign of nonparticipation, of mutual exclusion between the person and the world outside. Such refusal to engage reflects the way her neighbor Mamacita, unwillingly brought to the United States by her husband, "sits all day by the window and plays the Spanish radio show and sings all the homesick songs about her country" (77).[11] Esperanza notices how another woman, Rafaela, "leans out the window and leans on her elbow" because she is "locked indoors" by a husband who believes her "too beautiful" to allow the chance to "run away" (79). Rafaela's window is particularly poignant for Esperanza, who remarks that she often "forget[s] [Rafaela] is up there watching" (79), a gesture to Rafaela's removal from the neighborhood. Indeed, that the only "transaction" possible for Rafaela at her window is merely a monetary one—she asks Esperanza and her playmates to take a dollar and bring her back some juice from the store, which they must hoist up to her on a clothesline—underscores her isolation as a woman under a man's control.

Anzaldúa has remarked that such abusive male behavior is tied to ethnic hierarchies perpetuated by white men that, in turn, position Chicana women as victims:

> [The] modern meaning for the word "machismo," as well as the concept, is actually an Anglo invention. . . . "Machismo" is an adaptation to oppression and poverty and low self-esteem. It is the result of hierarchical male dominance. . . . In the Gringo world, the Chicano suffers from excessive humility and self-effacement, shame of self and self-deprecation . . . [and] the loss of a sense of dignity and respect in the macho breeds a false machismo which leads him to put down women and even to brutalize them. (105)

Esperanza's transactional gaze, which makes visible the gender oppression she experiences in her marginalized US neighborhood, thus, at least arguably, invites critique of the legacies that support it. However, *The House on Mango Street* constructs Esperanza as unaware of such legacies; rather, Esperanza defines the origins of such ideologies on Mango Street as "Mexicans don't like their women strong" (10). Her subject position, informed by her limited understanding of gender dynamics in relation to ethnic exclusion, is made visible via her transactional gaze, the representation of which is limited to the material produced by her first-person narration, which, especially late in the text, is not represented as wanting. She is the unique artist who leaves Mango Street in order to write about it. Indeed, it is not until one of the final vignettes that the text quietly communicates Esperanza's burgeoning sense of the active neglect of her barrio by the powers that be, when she "laugh[s] out loud" at the idea that the mayor would improve Mango Street (107). Thus, the textual dynamics of Esperanza's gaze tend to complicate a critical stance concerning Esperanza's subjectivity. The overt attention to gender overrides the attention to ethnicity, leaving the critique of ethnic discrimination available only to readers aware of the broader intersection of ethnic and gender oppression in Chicana experiences in the United States.

Esperanza's assessment of Mango Street's ideologies are not necessarily incorrect, based on her experiences, nor is that the point of this analysis; indeed, they are the result of the alchemical transactions that have formed her subjectivity via the visual markers she deems indicative of the limits of women in her childhood neighborhood. And yet those assessments are nevertheless incomplete, and their incompleteness speaks to the critical possibilities set up by a transactional child gaze. Her transactions are a product of her lived experience in a nation where dominant powers work to make invisible the legacies by which they are upheld, and those transactions are limited to that which she can see. Chicana and Latina women at windows are a particularly attensive portion of her visual array; white men, especially interacting with Chicano men, do not even seem present in her purview. The segregated housing arrangements that punctuate the US landscape and her limited mobility within the borders of her "all-brown" neighborhood keep Esperanza from visually transacting with the forces underlying them, leaving her with, at best, a vague understanding of the nation's ethnically marginalizing social forces at work in relegating her female counterparts to their windows. Indeed, her few interactions with whiteness serve to solidify rather than destabilize the structures of dominance that contribute to her experience. "Ashamed" of "staring out the window" at the presumably white-owned "house[s] on the hill" where her father gardens, Esperanza determines to own a home herself. While there is a Chicana feminist sensibility in her claim that she will not "forget who I am or where I come from" (87), in the same breath she decides she will invite "bums" to stay in her attic as a way to stay honest to her roots. The sense of shame as well as the word "bum" for her invitee—whom she imagines separated from her in the house and mistaken by her imagined guests for "rats" (87)—maintain the hierarchy between where she comes from and where she intends to go, even as she sees herself as a bridge between the two.

Esperanza's enactment of the transactional child gaze allows *The House on Mango Street* to posit the child as aware of the immediate forces with which they contend and able to reject the very limits that, paradoxically, call forth that rejecting subjectivity. It may seem a tautology to say that Esperanza's leaving is made possible by her being there in the first place, but it is true beyond the logic of location and direction. Her subjective experience on Mango Street, and in particular the transactional gazing she performs in that environment, precipitates her decision to leave. In Anzaldúa's vision, "Nothing happens in the 'real' world unless it first happens in the images in our heads" (Anzaldúa 109). In striving to be "free of the tainted biases of male dominance" and "seek new images of identity" (109), Esperanza's transactional gaze asserts the importance of Esperanza's subjectivity, selfhood, and agency as a Chicana girl, especially in a nation where, in Manzanas Calvo's words, "those who are not Anglos are immediately reduced to the category of non-being" (21). Indeed, Manzanas Calvo's reading of Esperanza's attention to Mango Street aligns with the ethos of the appreciative gaze discussed in chapter one: "Cisneros explores and presents whatever is negated by the dominant culture to demonstrate that even when Mango Street isn't, it *is*. *The House on Mango Street* reveals in this way the lives of those who—as seen by the Anglo world—are invisible" (21).[12] However, the transactional dimension of Esperanza's gaze troubles such appreciation, for it villainizes the ideologies of Chicago's Mango Street for thwarting Esperanza's developmental trajectory without emphasizing the larger national and colonial ideologies that underpin them. Absent from her transactional gaze—which controls the text—is a larger critique of ethnic marginality in the United States.

Certainly, Esperanza's triumph can be understood as set against such ideologies, which maintain their grip over "the ones who cannot out" (Cisneros 110). But the representation of her gaze as transactional rather ironically casts that triumph as worth interrogating—especially in relation to the metastructure of forces that perpetuate Mango Street's oppression, particularly of its women. Thus, while the use of a transactional child gaze to chart character development in texts like *The House on Mango Street* serves to celebrate the agential child, it does so with the troubling implication that "not making it out" may be due to personal failure rather than to oppressive ideologies. Such an implication can serve to maintain structural inequities that promulgate the practice of praising those who, because of their rejection of their milieu, "deserve" to be able to exercise agency in liberating ways. Difficult questions, then, arise from Esperanza's trajectory, questions that are enabled by the very gaze that underpins it. Does the liberatory bent of Esperanza's transactional gaze place her worth above those of her neighbors? If Esperanza is a figure of hope, is there no hope for those "who cannot out"? And finally, is such agency a prerequisite for liberation, thus seeming to excuse the oppression of those who seem to accept it? If the transactional gaze is, as the above theory and analysis have shown, intensely individual, then its relation to exceptionality needs to be a part of the context in which we read and interpret it.

INTERPELLATED VISION AND NARRATIVE RESISTANCE IN TONI MORRISON'S *THE BLUEST EYE*

Toni Morrison's *The Bluest Eye* exhibits how the transactional gaze can prove less liberatory for child characters in the storyworld even as it functions on the level of narrative to critique the ideologies to which its child wielders fall prey. While Cisneros writes a child whose gaze carries the logos of the text, Morrison uses two child characters whose gazes, at least at face value, do not. Their visual transactions in the mimetic world of the story result in their succumbing to rather than escaping from anti-Black standards of beauty and value.[13] However, the troubling interpellation brought about by their gazes—as well as the narrative levels on which each is represented—energizes the text's clear indictment of those standards.

In *The Bluest Eye*, Toni Morrison foregrounds two child characters whose transactional gazes work on different registers as well as in tandem to denounce the dangerous implications of racist paradigms for the young Black child, especially those pertaining to female beauty. One of those girls is Pecola Breedlove, a supposedly "ugly" eleven-year-old Black girl abused at home, at school, and in her social circles. Pecola is confronted repeatedly with visual regimes rooted in American ideologies that deny not only her beauty but also her worth. These ideologies—made visible in Morrison's text via their images as well as the ways of seeing they maintain—meet with Pecola's eyes in an alchemical transaction that leaves her victimized and eventually broken. The tragedy of Pecola's transactional gaze, however, also performs as a tool of resistance; while her gaze fails Pecola's interests in the diegetic world of the text, extradiegetically, its depiction works to perform the novel's indictment of anti-Blackness in the United States.

In addition, the novel achieves a distance between its point of view and Pecola's due to the narrative levels it employs to negotiate them. Pecola does not narrate her own story but is, rather, narrated in turns by a third-person omniscient narrator and the first-person voice of her neighbor Claudia MacTeer, nine years old at the time of the diegetic events but somewhat older in her remembering and retelling of them. Because the visual regimes of Claudia's environment overlap with those of Pecola's but Claudia does not bear the same abuse as Pecola does, Claudia functions as a bit of a foil for Pecola: she manages to resist some of the "truths" that Pecola accepts and therefore performs as a model for the reader regarding such resistance. Claudia, however, does not perform the role of the exceptional child against which Pecola should be measured; rather, her looking-in-progress over the course of her narration culminates in an acknowledgment of the influence on her own subjectivity of the same ideological regimes that victimize Pecola. Key to Claudia's transactional gaze in the novel is that Claudia does not find refuge in alliance with such regimes; she, rather, indicts such an alliance even as she admits her at least partial enforcing of it, thus performing, through her transactions with what she sees, a method of rejection that deconstructs the very ideologies that prove indestructible. Thus, Morrison's novel exhibits the ways the transactional child gaze, in carrying out both resistance and submission within the diegetic world of the text, functions narratively to confront exclusionary narratives that work persistently to oppress young Black girls.

Morrison foregrounds the visual regimes that interpellate Pecola's and Claudia's subjectivities via a thrice repeated Dick and Jane primer section that provides a sort of prologue to the text. Numerous critics have pointed out the ways in which these passages orient the text in dialogue with the "national masterplot that defines Americanness within the parameters of innocent white middle-class childhood" (Vásquez 56) and demonstrate that the novel "challenges America's complacent belief in its benevolent self-image" (53).[14] I wish to call attention not only to the exclusionary representations of American childhood manifest here but also to the imperatives to see, written directly into the primer, that champion its features even in the eyes of those who may not gaze upon its real counterparts in their own lived experiences. The commands to look—"See Jane. . . . See the cat. . . . See Mother. . . . See Father. . . . See the dog. . . . Look, look" (Morrison 3)—that structure the primer relentlessly direct the reader to imprint the "ideal" American childhood at the expense of any other. Its repetition over three passages maintains its attensity for the primer's imagined child audience as well as Morrison's implied reader. Indeed, in representing the transactional gazes of both Pecola and Claudia within the context of exclusionary American childhood, *The Bluest Eye* delves into the implied "you" subject of these commands, considering what happens to such subjects when their gazes transact with a world that denies their belonging in the childhood experiences supported by the Dick and Jane ideal.

The textual representation of the primer's words gives some insight into the perspective wrought in the transaction between the Dick and Jane images and the "you" subject's gaze. The passage is repeated three times in succession: the first with conventional spacing, capitalization, and punctuation; the second without punctuation or capitalization so that all of the sentences run together; and the third without spacing so that all of the words run together in a block text that both repels and forces the reader through its paces. With each repetition, the imperatives become more concentrated, until the final version both unmasks the nonsense of this "unreality"—according to Ortega, it might be read as an enactment of Claudia's deconstructive response (131)—and enforces the mantra-like, unstoppable script that is the hegemonic power of Dick and Jane's imagined life. In this second sense, the final repetition might be understood as representing Pecola's consciousness in a sort of free indirect discursive moment, revealing her transaction with the text. Indeed, the only character to reference such a primer in the text proper is Pecola, when she first considers how she might exchange her eyes (Morrison 46) and when she finally asks her split self whether her new blue eyes (a devastating figure of her imagination) are "prettier than Alice-and-Jerry Storybook eyes" (201).[15] If Claudia deconstructs the narrative, Pecola internalizes its storybook imagery. The absence of its packaging in a punctuated, syntactical arrangement of individual words reflects the invisibility, to her, of the cultural packaging Claudia perceives and can therefore reject. The stream of images and the commands to see them interpellate Pecola's subjectivity completely.

That Pecola's gaze is transactional is a key element of the novel's force. She is not a *passive* receiver of the visual cues around her but an *active* assessor of their meaning. It is this *activity*, not *passivity*, that emphasizes the tragedy of her character arc. Pecola engages in the dynamism of the transactional gaze, and the result of that dynamism is the subjugation of her agency to the ideological structures that shape it. Early on, she admires a Shirley Temple cup, and at first her "fond" gaze might be read to reflect a cognitively empty "admiration" of Temple's "cu-ute[ness]" (19). However, the obsession that leads her to drink gallons of milk just to get it served in the cup emblazoned with her Shirley punctum indicates a deep manifestation of the imbrication of her subjectivity with the visual ideologies of her world, which she has actively surveyed and contemplated. The "blue-and-white" (19) Shirley cup functions like her Alice and Jerry storybook, her gaze upon each prompting her devastating transaction with her own physicality:

> Long hours she sat looking in the mirror, trying to discover the secret of the ugliness, the ugliness that made her ignored or despised at

school, by teachers and classmates alike.... [Her teachers] tried never to glance at her. ...

. . .

It had occurred to Pecola some time ago that if her eyes, those eyes that held the pictures, and knew the sights—if those eyes of hers were ... beautiful, she herself would be different. (45–46)

The ongoing nature of Pecola's transaction—"long hours" begun "some time ago" and characterized by a recurring "praye[r] for blue eyes" (46)—speaks to her subjectivity as, paradoxically, always in process but also always fixated by images of exclusion. Her "conviction that only a miracle could relieve her" is "binding" (46) in that it is inextricable from her response to images away from which she cannot turn.

The text's representation of Pecola's ability to formulate resistance within some of her visual transactions makes her outcome all the more tragic. Her recognition that a particular sidewalk is well disposed to roller skating while another is not implies discernment as a feature of her very active transactions with her visual world, a world she "saw and experienced" with its "codes and touchstones . . . , capable of translation and possession" (47). Such "owning . . . made her part of the world, and the world a part of her" (48). Further, her rumination about dandelions—"why, she wonders, do people call them weeds? She thought they were pretty" (47)—illustrates a way of looking that responds via confrontation rather than acquiescence. Pecola's transactional gaze marks her as active and manifests her existence; her rejection of her own eyes is really her attempt to reject her transactions, which have continually placed her at the bottom of a social hierarchy. With her gaze as heuristic, she has assessed her position in the world as a problem, and the poignant tragedy of her character arc is enforced when Soaphead Church deems Pecola's request for blue eyes "the most fantastic and the most logical" (174) bid he has ever heard.

The cruel power of Pecola's transactional gaze is that rather than liberating her from the ideologies that provoke it, it indentures her to their hierarchies. That is, she rejects her subjective experience, not the forces that have elicited it. While Pecola rightly ties her experience to the eyes of white people, she cannot tie it to the *ideologies* of whiteness that promulgate it and faults instead her own blackness for the relation she perceives. Consider her musings about the local storeowner's reaction to her:

> She looks up at him and sees the vacuum where curiosity ought to lodge. And something more. The total absence of human recognition—the glazed separateness. She does not know what keeps his

glance suspended. Perhaps because he is grown, or a man, and she a little girl. But she has seen interest, disgust, even anger in grown male eyes. Yet this vacuum is not new to her. It has an edge; somewhere in the bottom lid is the distaste. She has seen it lurking in the eyes of all white people. So. The distaste must be for her, her blackness. All things in her are flux and anticipation. But her blackness is static and dread. And it is the blackness that accounts for, that creates, the vacuum edged with distaste in white eyes. (49)

The reasoning in this passage enacts Pecola's transaction. From "and" to the em dash to "perhaps" to "but" to "yet" to the sentence-of-its-own "So"—each shift traces her thought process in response to the visual information of her environment, exposing her trajectory toward awareness of the discrimination that surrounds her, an awareness limited to naming blackness rather than whiteness as its cause. But though Pecola finds the fault within herself, the text does not, which exhibits the ways a transactional child gaze can create room for critique that diverges from the gazing child's assessments. Dilating over Pecola's moment of looking, the text both explains and laments her transaction, shielding Pecola from the reader's degradation by pointing to the visual cues of exclusionary ideologies—the "lower lid[s]" of the "eyes of all white people"—that have shaped her ways of thinking.

Certainly there is an element of dramatic irony attendant upon transactional gazes that do not depict the type of thinking the text purports to elicit, and such irony aids in the critical assessment of the transaction by distancing the reader from the subjectivity of the child *even as* the reader is invited into its most intimate recesses. It is a move that can provoke sympathy rather than pity, measured consideration rather than abrupt dismissal. In representing Pecola this way, Morrison is able to draw Pecola's complex responses close to the reader even while keeping her conclusions distant from the character.

To a certain extent, the third-person point of view allows this distance, as Pecola's perspective, though often focalizing the narration, is not ultimately the privileged point of view.

Claudia's first-person account achieves a different kind of distancing, as she tends to provide a meta-awareness of her visual transactions. She not only transacts with the visual markers of exclusionary ideologies in her and Pecola's world but also actively investigates the roots and implications of them. Claudia is first set apart as Pecola's foil by her "hatred" for Shirley Temple (19). Claudia's much safer and nurturing homelife, led by a mother who is tough on her but nevertheless loving, a woman who sings the blues and "provide[s] Claudia with examples of strong Black women who were capable of directly confronting emotional pain . . . but never becom[ing] a prisoner to it" (Yancy 212), is one way to attribute the possibilities for her resistance. But the text also provides another reason, which finds power in the developmental stage of the child. The narrating Claudia asserts her youth as the reason for her ability to reject Shirley: "Younger than both [her sister] Frieda and Pecola, I had not yet arrived at the turning point in the development of my psyche which would allow me to love her" (Morrison 19). Not yet fully interpellated by the visual cues that privilege blue-eyed, blond-haired, white beauty, Claudia's hatred is "unsullied" (19). Her gaze upon Shirley Temple prompts a transaction that rejects the white imaginary and in fact privileges Black kinship: "She danced with Bojangles, who was *my* friend, *my* uncle, *my* daddy, and who ought to have been soft-shoeing it and chuckling with me" (19). Positioning Bojangles as Claudia's punctum, her transactional gaze casts Shirley as stealing rather than eliciting attention from the Black child. In contrast to Pecola's perspective, Shirley's eyes, to Claudia's, are not coveted but "squint[y]" (19).

And yet Claudia's transactional gaze reveals that she is also impacted by the same forces that interpellate Pecola, and often in the same ways. She, too, wonders about "what made people look at [little white girls] and say, 'Awwwww,' but not for me?" (22). She is "bemused, irritated, and fascinated" by the "high-yellow dream child with long brown hair" who "enchanted the entire school," so that "black girls stepped aside . . . , their eyes genuflect[ing] under sliding lids" (62). However, while Pecola's gaze settles upon blue eyes as the ultimate answer, Claudia's transaction persists in questions: "What was the secret? What did we lack? Why was it important? And so what?" (74). Her tearing apart of a white doll in order to "*see* of what it was made, to discover the dearness, to find the beauty, the desirability that had escaped me, but apparently only me" (20; italics added) exhibits how she is willing to manipulate her visual landscape in order to transact with new information.[16] To use the language of ecological perception theory, Claudia "manipulate[s] an object in a certain manner . . . [to] unveil inertial properties of that object . . . that are lawfully related to to-be-perceived properties" (Arzamarski et al. 732). In her quest for answers, she investigates the doll for the mysterious property it seems to contain. However, Claudia cannot find anything but sawdust and a sound disk, for the relationship between the doll's adoration and its materiality is not "lawful"—that is, not reflective of a natural, innate correspondence. The whiteness she seeks is ideological, deployed and sustained through the image of the doll, but not inherent or embedded in it.

Thus, while Claudia's "remov[ing] the cold and stupid eyeball" of the white doll in her quest for deconstruction orients her transaction toward examining the source of white worship in the outside world, Pecola's wish for blue eyes orients her gaze toward transplanting its source into herself, deeming herself as the problem. By casting Claudia as narrator without the same level of dramatic irony accorded to Pecola, Morrison foregrounds her way of seeing for the reader's agreement. She also constructs a child as capable of critical analysis of the visual text the world presents, allowing her to find fault in *it* rather than in the child's own status. Claudia's tearing into the doll involves a gaze that transacts against the grain. She knows "adults, older girls, shops, magazines, newspapers, window signs—all the world had agreed that a blue-eyed, yellow-haired, pink-skinned doll was what every girl child treasured" (20), and she demonstrates the need to reject that agreement in, to use bell hooks's terms, a "political struggle to push against the boundaries of the image . . . when [she is] seeing what most folks don't want" (hooks 4). Her rejection is thus aligned with the political project of the text, which pushes against the mandate of Dick and Jane by saying, "See *Claudia*! See *Pecola*!" Her gaze also cements the tragedy of Pecola's wish for blue eyes, which is also formulated via transactions in accordance with the messages on "every billboard, every movie, every glance" (39). The girls even consider their own viewing power in opposite ways. Pecola thinks her own attempts to disappear are thwarted by her brown eyes, which held "all of those pictures, all of those faces" (45) that have worked upon her. Claudia, on the other hand, wonders "where the world went when [she] closed [her] eyes" (97), in a Cartesian assertion of the self controlling the sensory world—rather than the other way around.

And yet Claudia's self-asserting resistance is not thorough, and thus Morrison's depiction of her transactional gaze keeps the text from upholding Claudia as a pure alternative to Pecola's submission. It also keeps the text from aligning with Cisneros's depiction of the exceptional child. Since Claudia's story is not one of triumph, the text emphasizes indictment of racist ideologies rather than praise for a child who escapes them. That becomes clear through the character arc that leads Claudia from hating the image of Shirley Temple as a young girl to eventually "learning to worship her . . . , knowing, even as I learned, that the change was adjustment without improvement" (23). The repeated reference to "learning" emphasizes her interpellation. Claudia's "growth" is one of "adjustment" to the world's messaging rather than "improvement" of herself. The significance of Morrison's withholding of triumph from Claudia is also exhibited in her ongoing transaction, even as an older person, with the image of Pecola's ugliness: "All of our beauty . . . she gave to us. . . . We were so beautiful when we stood astride her ugliness" (205). Claudia's difference from Pecola is not a difference of exception; it is a difference of degree. Diegetically, Claudia's gaze is still caught on Pecola; narratively, her transaction exposes herself as prey to and participant in the ideological network that the text condemns for its interpellation of both of them. Through Pecola and Claudia's different levels of awareness as well as their different transactions, which exist along a spectrum of rejection and acceptance of their visual array, *The Bluest Eye* exposes the nuance with which anti-Black US narratives of raced and gendered beauty victimize Black girls and women. The power of the transactional child gaze—not liberatory, but rather limiting for the child within the diegetic world of the text—is thus the platform for the novel's critique of the very powers that relentlessly interpellate the subjects performing the gaze.

JASON REYNOLDS AND BRENDAN KIELY'S *ALL AMERICAN BOYS* AND THE ACTIVIST ENERGIES OF A TRANSACTIONAL CHILD GAZE

Jason Reynolds and Brendan Kiely's *All American Boys* also employs the transactional child gaze to impugn anti-Black racism, but this novel's iteration empowers the child to work against them both diegetically and potentially extratextually. It also emphasizes the process-oriented nature of the transactional gaze precisely because the two main characters follow a significant developmental arc over the course of the text in relation to their transactions with their visual environments. Esperanza's and Pecola's transactions are ongoing but repetitious even as they deepen, which works to confirm their findings over a span of time; Claudia's persistent queries about the power of whiteness characterize all of her transactions. Rashad and Quinn of *All American Boys*, however, engage in questions about the relation of the self to the racial inequities in their world with answers that shift significantly in tenor over the course of the novel—in Rashad's case from withdrawal to activism and in Quinn's case from ignorant privilege to aware intervention. Thus, the transactional gaze in this novel zooms in on that which is worth noticing as well as that which such noticing can prompt in terms of antiracist thought and action. *All American Boys* exhibits the agential power of the transactional gaze for the child who wields it, not as a way to evade interpellation by the ideologies most threatening to their current experience but as a method to formulate a powerful stance against them. In representing the transactional child gaze this way, the text makes its call for change in the world of the reader, who can take either or both boys' gazes as models for coming to power against anti-Black ideologies in their local and national communities.

The text's dominating narrative feature is its alternating narration. Black teen protagonist Rashad and white teen protagonist Quinn recount their experiences during and after Quinn's ersatz older brother, police officer Paul Galluzzo, beats Rashad for a crime he did not commit, which results in Rashad's hospitalization for a significant period of time. Within those narratives, Reynolds and Kiely employ the transactional child gaze to track the ways each character works through the moment of police brutality. Focusing on the visual elements of their environments that contribute to and reflect the discriminatory ideologies in the United States that contextualize the use of excessive force on the nation's Black populace, the text demonstrates how the transactional gaze leads each boy to an assertion of subjectivity positioned in resistance to such ideologies: a resistance that manifests not only in theory but also in activism.

Perry Nodelman writes that the use of alternating narration in young people's fiction "moves attention away from what the characters experience onto *how* they experience it. . . . A second focalizer seems to demand an awareness of how the two different characters represented are in fact different—how they perceive and think about their experience in different ways" (7; italics in original). I argue that while *All American Boys* certainly draws on alternating narration's ability to emphasize how two characters "perceive and think about their experiences" differently, the novel does not displace attention to the "what" of their experience because it is an event with great attensity for their evolving "how."[17] So many of the visual transactions for both boys recirculate the images of Galluzzo's attack or Rashad's injuries, which means they are continually foregrounded for the reader—and offered as catalyst for their transactions. Such recirculation is itself achieved through acts of looking, such as Rashad's engagement with his own injured body in mirrors, in the media, and in his drawings as well as in Quinn's slowly changing witnessing stance via in-person, remembered, and video-captured occurrences of Galuzzo's brutality. Following and then later attending to the comparative implications of each character's visual transactions with this moment reveal the manner in which the transactional child gaze can be a tool for positioning the child as activist disruptor of exclusionary ideologies.

Rashad's transactions with the image of his body in mirrors, the media, and his own drawings punctuate his character arc toward activism in the novel. Even before he is attacked by Paul, Rashad calls attention to what he terms "Mirror-Looking 101" as endemic to the adolescent experience: "Springfield Central High bathrooms were never empty. There was always somebody in there at the mirror studying" (Reynolds and Kiely 10). The humor here serves to emphasize that the adolescents are in a state of becoming, as folks are studying for "whatever facial hair was finally coming in" (10). They watch their physical bodies as spectacles of change, the gaze transacting with the image of the body and highlighting how both are in process. After his attack, however, Rashad's hospital mirror becomes a site where he finds it difficult to renegotiate his vision of himself, which is articulated through his inability to gaze steadily:

> I had just flushed and washed my hands while performing the strange task of looking at my bruised and broken face, but only in glimpses. That's all I could take. A few seconds at a time. Three seconds, then back to the sink. Then back to the mirror for three more seconds before darting my eyes over to the paper towels. Anything longer than that made me . . . uncomfortable. (88)

Rashad's discomfort with his beaten face in the mirror is echoed by his discomfort with seeing himself on television. He repeatedly grapples with the fragmentation of his sense of self because the coverage of the attack confronts him with the image of himself as victim: "I couldn't believe what I was seeing. I mean, it was me, but it wasn't. But . . . it *was*. I didn't know how or what to feel. Like how could I be that boy—a victim" (94). The newscaster's remarks that "it was *a developing story*" (95; italics in original) conveys information about the status of the news report as much as it reflects Rashad's process of coming to terms with his experience as victim in a racist society. The use of ellipses in these two passages above—a feature of many passages in the text—also speak to a "figuring out" state of mind as he attempts to articulate his experience.

Indeed, Rashad's visual transactions trace the emotional difficulty of fitting this new image of himself into the ideological schema that produced it: "I had seen this happen so many times . . . on TV. People getting beaten, and sometimes killed, by the cops, and then there's all this fuss about it, only to build up to a big heartbreak when nothing happens. The cops get off. And everybody cries and waits for the next dead kid, to do it all over again" (59). Rashad's cynicism about the cycle he has witnessed in media attention to police brutality informs his distancing of his own image as victim, which is now wrapped up in his indictment of the ineffective political symbolism of the dead Black child.[18] Furthermore, the media images discount the complexity of his selfhood. On the news he sees alternating photos of himself in his ROTC uniform and images of the moment of attack, which are only partial representations. As Elkins points out, such partial representations have implications for sense of self:

> Photographs clip out instants in time, and since we see in overlapping moments and usually base our sense of a person on a fluid sequence of moments and motions, a single photograph can often seem wrong.... But there's something else at stake as well: a photograph pushes a small part of the person forward and presents it as the whole and adequate person, and that will tend to hurt the subject's sense of herself. (28)

Thus, Rashad's response to what he sees on the news, that he "didn't want all that" (Reynolds and Kiely 59), is the result of his earlier transactions with images of Black child victims in the media, his confrontation of his injured body in the mirror, and his denial of the distillation of his existence into the "peculiar caricature" (Elkins 28) effect of news media coverage. His wish to remove himself from the cycle of police brutality targeting the Black body and its attendant media coverage is the early resistance he enacts with his transactional gaze.

Such removal is made impossible, however, by the ideological schema that already contextualizes his attack, and Rashad's character arc throughout the novel is largely achieved by way of his changing transactions with visual elements that attend upon it—elements that will not change without intervention. One way the text traces this arc is through his drawing, a visual manifestation of his transactional gaze. By combining his childhood obsession with the circular, lenslike frame of Family Circus comics (Reynolds and Kiely 142) and the style and figures of Harlem Renaissance painter Aaron Douglas (143–44), Rashad has developed an artistic technique that he tweaks further throughout his stay in the hospital and in conversation with the mirror and media scenes in the text. His creation and revision of a self-portrait sketch reveals the way his visual transaction moves from distancing his attack and its context to acknowledging and directly responding to it. In doing so, he moves from understanding himself as a victim to asserting himself as a survivor:

> I wasn't sure what I was drawing.
>   That's not true.
>   I knew exactly what I was drawing. The only thing I could. (144)

The simple, one-sentence paragraphs reflect his halting recognition that the drawing manifests his response. "Re-creat[ing] the scene" (144) from the vantage point of his survivor's gaze, Rashad slowly visualizes and revisualizes his response, exploring the alchemy of his gaze: "First the outline. A teenage boy. Hands up. No. Erase. Hands down. No. Hands behind his back" (144), and so on. The constant revision that marks his artistic process also marks his coming to terms with how to understand this moment as part of his subjectivity, as a moment in which he existed and with which he will have to continue to exist. It also demonstrates how the transactional child gaze is capable of reshaping meaning and engendering action.

The drawing evolves over several days, and a key transformation occurs for Rashad as artist and as subject when he has a nightmare in which he reconfigures—that is, transacts with—visual elements of the scene of the attack: "I adjusted my eyes to see my own reflection, my own face. But I couldn't. I mean, my face was there, but . . . it wasn't. There were no eyes. No nose or mouth. Just blank brown skin" (229). This gazeless, voiceless face is a representation of both the depersonalizing white gaze on the Black body that the police officer made manifest in violence and Rashad's own struggles to come to terms with his existence after the attack. The next time Rashad picks up his sketchpad, it is just after he has forced himself to watch the video of his attack, and he "start[s] drawing like crazy," crying onto the page as he renders the scene of a man pulling out the heart of another, where "for the first time [he] broke away from Aaron Douglas's signature [faceless] style" and "began to draw features on the face of the man having his chest punched through" (246). The facial features of the man in the drawing—a version of himself who is now, because of his individuality, "impossible to ignore" (273)—make Rashad's drawing an existential act articulated through the transactional gaze. It recasts his orientation to the ideological environment by visualizing resistance against the forces that would erase him.

Rashad's corresponding decision to join the protest and die-in that his brother has organized exists in opposition to his earlier comment that he "didn't want all that" (59); furthermore, in a move that draws his artist gaze into one of his final visual transactions in the novel, he once again stands at a mirror, this time to remove his bandages. Despite his "hate" for the new contours of his bruised face, he asserts, "I wanted people to see me. See what happened. I wanted people to know that no matter the outcome . . . I would never be the same person. I looked different and I would be different, forever" (303). Positioning his face once again as a visual text for himself and, now, for others, Rashad confirms the significance of transacting with the visual markers of racist ideologies in ways that impugn their violence. Embodying the ethos, logos, and pathos of his drawing, Rashad enters the protest as someone "people started to recognize" (304) and as someone who now sees in ways informed by the gazing he enacts over the course of the text: "I looked out at the crowd. People, young, old, Black, white, Asian, Latino, more people than I could count. It was straight out of an Aaron Douglas painting, except there were faces. Faces everywhere" (305). Rashad's affirmation of his own importance also affirms the individual power in each person coming together to stand against ideologies of erasure.

Rashad's face becomes a visual anchor of resistance for Quinn in this final scene as well, who remarks, "All I wanted to do was see the guy I hadn't seen one week earlier. The guy beneath all the bullshit too many of us see first—especially white guys like me who just haven't worked hard enough to look behind it all" (309). This is the arrival of Quinn's character arc, a white boy who saw Rashad's beating and who spends the entirety of the novel transacting with his moment of witness in order to arrive at the statement above. In recognizing the "bullshit" screen of racist ideologies that often prevent "white guys" from truly seeing people of color—and in referring to the "work" it takes to look beyond them—Quinn here encapsulates the possibilities of the transactional child gaze of a white character when it comes to social justice work surrounding race and ethnicity.

Quinn's initial moment of witness is infused with his visceral responses, detailed as they unfold to emphasize the process-oriented nature of the transactional child gaze. As different aspects of the scene come into his consciousness (that is, gain attensity for him), his cognitive and emotional reactions adjust. At first, he sees "a cop" pushing a "younger guy" out of a store and "press[ing] him face-first into the concrete" (37–38); then he notes the "guy on the ground was black" and "around [his] age" (38), which prompts him to move from a distanced stance of description to a personal wondering: "Did he go to our school?" (38). But drawing Quinn most firmly into the witnessing moment is his recognition of the cop, who at first is only "white" and then, upon raising his head, is "Guzzo's older brother, Paul" (38). Here, the text creates a paragraph break and uses italics to emphasize the emotional attensity of this recognition: "*Holy shit!*" (38). Now noticing how "the blood kept coming" as Paul "pummel[s] the guy," Quinn's focus remains on Paul, whom his "gut" wants him to "help," though his logic tells him to "stay out of police business" (38). Quinn's siding with Paul here is born of the significant relationship he has with him. Paul is the guy who took him under his wing when Quinn's father was killed during military service overseas. Quinn's subjectivity—informed by both his emotionally important affiliation with Paul and his experience as a white boy who leaves "police business" alone—drives this initial transaction.

And yet the denouement of this first scene also evidences elements of Quinn's transaction that begin to work upon his subjective orientation to the world. He "stood there, sorta frozen, just watching, transfixed.... [He] couldn't look away; [he] didn't even want to" (38). But the text, through Quinn's gaze, disallows the reading that Quinn is simply admiring Paul. He "didn't know what the hell was going on" (38) and decides "it's fucking ugly and [he] need[s] to get the hell out" (39). He tells Guzzo and another friend what he has seen when he almost literally runs into them as he flees, but Quinn inwardly rejoices that "no one saw [him]" there so he can "pretend . . . like it didn't happen" (39). These opposing instincts—to side with or against Paul, to speak or erase his gaze—spur his character development over the course of the text.

Quinn's wish to erase his gaze and all evidence of it so he is *not even seen to have seen* is a manifestation of the white privilege of "looking away" at an inconvenient truth. It also implies a suppressed struggle to come to terms with the fact that he knows what he saw "was bad" (40) and nods to his potential turmoil about "that look of rage [he]'d seen on the face of a man [he] knew and thought of as family" (40). That Quinn goes on to spend several chapters avoiding rewitnessing the beating, refusing to watch the cell phone videos circulated by the news and social media, reflects his confusion about how to make sense of—that is, how to transact with—Paul's attack on Rashad. His avoidance of his moment of witness is an avoidance of confronting the flaws in the ways of looking and transacting with which he has become comfortable.

When Quinn finally commits to watching the videos of the attack, he arrives at the choice through a slow process of social critique emanating from questions at the intersection of gaze and privilege that recur throughout the text. The drawn-out progression documents the brutality of an oppressive system of power that excludes people of color from paradigms of value and operates through emotional conduits such as fear. The narrative's recounting of Quinn's transactional gaze emphasizes the signs of divisive ideologies that acquire attensity for him over the course of his ruminations. First, he begins to feel distant from Paul, as if rather than being present with him, he's "watching [a] whole damn party [at Paul's house] unfold[ing] on TV" (62). Then, Quinn begins to use race as a lens through which to view the power dynamics of his town, as evident when he sees a fight break out at a pizza joint: "The crowd outside Mother's was white, black, Latino, Asian, just like Springfield. The four guys being cuffed were white. The cops, almost all of them were white, but two of them were black. It was impossible not to think about this as Paul slamming that black kid into the sidewalk the night before replayed in my mind" (81). Quinn is undergoing what Shaw and McIntyre refer to as "the education of attention" (355). Different aspects of his visual array begin to hold more attensity for him as he begins to realize their significance to his concerns. Thus, his noticing a shift in his own impulses to notice race leads to a fuller examination of the racialized nature of his transactions and the forces attendant upon them, specifically regarding the ways ideologies have informed his ways of looking as a white boy.

Contemplating Paul's use of fear tactics, for instance, causes a visual memory to surface for him, with which he proceeds to transact:

> I was a freshman and I saw a [Black] senior walking down the hall ... wearing an old-school Public Enemy T-shirt: *Fear of a Black Planet*—the bull's-eye logo poised to eclipse the Earth. Fear. The T-shirt was right. Like the way Mrs. Cambi talked about our neighborhood now. Fear. Like the way Ma told me to cross the street to the other side of the sidewalk if I was walking home alone and I saw a group of guys walking toward me. Guys. That wasn't the word she used. Thugs. Fear of thugs. Just like what some people were saying on the news. Rashad looked like a thug. (132)

The progression of his transaction traces Quinn's dawning realization of how white control of national ideologies and institutions is maintained via the instillation of fear of the Black body and Black Power. He connects the image of the T-shirt to the incipient white flight in his neighborhood and the language used to condemn its Black residents. When he finally arrives at the image of Rashad as promulgated by the media, he has come to apply a more precise lens to the police brutality he witnessed and the reactions of his white neighbors.

That Quinn continues to hone this lens through subsequent transactions over the course of the text speaks to the "work" it takes to "look behind" the "bullshit" (Reynolds and Kiely 309) exclusionary ideologies attempt to smear over that lens. After being schooled by a Black basketball teammate who is friends with Rashad about how such attitudes manifest in Quinn's everyday life and actions (176), Quinn reaches a key insight that spurs his move from private confusion to public condemnation of the anti-Black systems at work in United States: "I could just walk away from it all like a ghost" because "my shield was that I was white" (180). He also comes to this metacognitive corollary: "I realized something worse: It wasn't only that I could walk away—I already had walked away ... not watching the video was walking away too, and I needed to watch it" (180). In undertaking this work, Quinn changes his intentions from granting himself the white privilege of denying his moment of witness to undertaking his ethical responsibility to own it.

As Arzamarski et al. point out, "a change in intention expresses itself as informational reattunement" (721), and Quinn's moments of rewitnessing—which do not involve the text redescribing the brutal scene but rather Quinn's reactions to it—center instead of denying the cycle of racialized trauma and his role in it. Through the arc of Quinn's transactional gaze—emphasized in the incremental steps by which he adjusts his ideas in reaction to what he sees, compounded by noticing visual features of his environment new to him because of such adjusting—Quinn's narrative portion of the text makes a call to action, for white readers in particular, to confront and dismantle the ideologies that prejudice their perceptions. Indeed, it is this moment that spurs Quinn's choice to be part of the demonstration and die-in organized by Rashad's supporters. At the end of the story, when Quinn and Rashad share a mutual gaze that is rendered on the page like poetry, it is clear that the transactional gaze that has characterized his arc leading up to and at the protest has manifested his ability to see Rashad as subject, the guy "who, even with a tear-streaked face, seemed to have two tiny smiles framing his eyes like parenthesis" (310). The individual facial characteristics noted here—rather than a depiction of Rashad's battered face—seem a response to Rashad's call for a gaze that recognizes his existence as he asserts it via his eyes.

Both Rashad's and Quinn's types of looking are invoked in the text to interrogate the belonging implied by its title: *All American Boys*. Quinn's claim to American identity comes not just through his father's military service and sacrifice but also through his white identity, the privilege it bestows upon him, and the racism in which it trades. His continual transaction with his moment of witness allows him to question the dynamics of racial privilege and discrimination and start committing to working to dismantle it. Rashad's transactional way of looking ultimately asserts his claim to existence as an American boy, the individual faces he sees opposing a monolithic notion of American racial belonging. Thus, this text exhibits how extended visual transactions with instantiations of violent ideologies—and the ultimate choice to look, and to look steadily, in the face of fear and in the face of trauma—can direct the reader to understand the transactional gaze as a powerful catalyst for youth negotiating their vision, values, and voices regarding the politics of race in twenty-first-century America.

Nodelman has pointed out that "novels for young people with alternating narratives tend to characterize cultural registers of difference, and especially class and race, as barriers to be ignored or transcended" (188) and that "the racial barrier that divides [the narrating characters] . . . prevent[s] them from perceiving what they share" until they "end up like-minded friends" (188). *All American Boys* engages neither of these paradigms, avoiding the amity solution by allowing only the eye contact (rather than a burgeoning friendship) at the end of the story and emphasizing the significance of racial barriers too dangerous to ignore and too systemic to transcend. Commitment to changing the ideologies and practices that maintain those barriers is the ultimate resolution each boy achieves via their transactional gazes.

That such gazes are themselves raced raises important questions about the different registers by which Quinn's and Rashad's gazes spur activism, however. In the case of Quinn, the assertion of the choice to look in antiracist ways does not at first present itself as "common sense" to him, as his subjectivity has been formed by his interactions as a white boy unused to thinking critically or even pointedly about race. Rather, it represents a dedicated, process-oriented shift in his personal value system in relation to state violence against Black bodies, a shift that promulgates his own foray into activism at the die-in but is nevertheless a shift that does not put his life in jeopardy. More troubling, Quinn's personal triumph of values seems to require the in-person witnessing of an attack on a peer of color, which he notes is different from a mediated experience in a "video game or a movie" (81). Furthermore, in Rashad's case, that the text begins with his body appropriated as a visual touchstone for police brutality means he has no choice, other than the erasure of the self with which he is viscerally confronted, but to engage with the violence perpetrated against him. His early trepidation about attending the protest is less about his personal value system than about the fear of further erasure; at no point can he even consider simply walking away (quite literally) from facing anti-Black ideologies. Such differences in privilege are limned by the fact that almost the entirety of Rashad's story happens in his hospital room, while Quinn is free to roam the halls of his school and the streets of his city.

Taken together, Rashad's and Quinn's racialized subjectivities, gazes, and character arcs invite a comparison that postures the text to prompt the interrogations invited by the transactional gaze, confronting and providing pathways to dismantling the deeply violent ideologies at work—albeit with different results—on all people in the United States. As a text aimed at young readers, themselves often involved in "Mirror Gazing 101" and thus positioned for the examination of the self the text highlights, *All American Boys* reflects the contemporary American scene as part of that examination of the self, for its dual narration emphasizes how selves are always situated in cultural context. If, as Trites argues, twentieth-century texts for adolescents tended to privilege character trajectories implying how "adolescents can learn to exist within institutional structures" (7) without "deal[ing] directly with the role of the state" (22), then works like Reynolds and Kiely's *All American Boys* participate in a different trend wherein young people's "learn[ing]" actually confronts the "institutional accommodation" Trites theorizes (15) as a mode of being.[19] The transactional gazing of both boys reflects the power of young people to confront those ideologies by actively intervening in their perpetuation, including the ways of looking they support.

CONCLUSION

The transactional child gaze allows an interrogation of the ideological scripts that are brought to bear upon the child as well as the visual methods by which they interpellate the subject. It is a technique that, like the appreciative gaze, can uphold or reject exclusionary narratives or do a bit of both. Binding the seer and the seen in the idiosyncratic relationship forged by the act of seeing, which is always contextualized by the ideologically infused situation of the transaction, the transactional child gaze emphasizes both a continual process of becoming and the relationality that underpins such becoming for both child and environment.[20]

The readings in this chapter demonstrate how the transactional gaze responds to particularly robust US ideologies of racial and ethnic discrimination with various outcomes for the child and thus varying implications for the implied reader. Cisneros's text, in highlighting the exceptional visual transactions of her Chicana protagonist, runs the risk of reinforcing the ethnic hierarchies that contribute to her experiences even as the transactional gaze liberates the child from gendered oppression. Morrison's text sacrifices its Black girls to relentless anti-Black racism, and their transactional gazes bear witness to the tragedy of interpellated subjectivities. It is the failed liberation of the diegetic transactional gaze that resonates extratextually as the text's foundation for its call for change. *All American Boys* exhibits different trajectories for white and Black boys, inviting a comparison between the types of learning and coping forced upon each by the racist ideologies that structure US neighborhoods. Each boy, via a transactional gaze, navigates the visual discourse of systemic racism and arrives at empowerment within the social structure, inviting the reader to join them in action against exclusionary forces that inflict violence on the bodies and minds of US citizens.

I mention in the introduction to this chapter that the transactional child gaze functions on a different register from other ways of looking examined in this project because of its dependence on a child character who is aware of and *reflects on* their acts of looking. But I also state that the transactional child gaze is not necessarily mutually exclusive of the appreciative or countersurveillant child gazes. The analysis above, though focused on the language I use to describe the transactional gaze, implies that Claudia, Quinn, and Rashad all engage in countersurveillant looking as well; indeed, some of Pecola's looking might be understood in this category too, especially in terms of the extradiegetic force of her gaze. Likewise, Rashad engages in moments of appreciative looking, as when he surveys the crowd at the protest or when he sketches facial features into the survivor drawing, making visible a person too often blurred out by a hegemonic lens. And though I focused on Esperanza's transactions with her windows, there are moments when she views the women inside of them—and other features of her neighborhood—with the nuanced sympathy and respect that marks appreciation. Indeed, it is the very mixing of the two that propel Esperanza's choice to remove herself from the situation of those women, even as Cisneros dedicates her text "A las mujeres / To the Women."

Also noted at the start of this chapter is that some texts examined earlier in this book contain gazing that could be labeled transactional, but others do not. A few quick notes on those not already discussed above will suffice to emphasize the rather emphatic nature of the transactional child gaze. For instance, Philip Roth's *The Plot against America* often details young Philip's transactions with what he sees both during the act of looking and after, via memory, fusing the transactional gaze with countersurveillance. Betty Smith's *A Tree Grows in Brooklyn* is dominated by Francie's transactions with the sights of her Brooklyn neighborhood, fusing the transactional gaze with appreciation. Neither would have been out of place in this chapter, but texts like Jesse Jackson's *Call Me Charley* would not fit, since Charley's transactions are only subtly implied—contributing to the subversive technique of "museum silence." The transactional gaze tends to be an overt technique, less flexibly subversive than the other two, and in fact its boldness is its modus operandi: it leaves little room to "read past" the child's acts of looking, as the transactional gaze automatically both attributes and *explains* the attensity of the object in view, transferring its attensity to the reader as well. The transactional child gaze fuses acts of looking with character arc; no child who wields this gaze can seem ideologically neutral or fully unaware, for their reflections speak to consequences. And finally, in foregrounding the ideological formation of the subject, whether in concert or contention with the forces that act upon them, the transactional gaze also foregrounds the active cognitive and emotional life of the agentive child subject. As a narrative technique, it demands the reader consider the role that the child plays in cultural transmission and critique.

Chapter Four

COMICS FORM AND MATERIALIZATION OF THE CHILD GAZE

In the image below, young Bass Reeves participates in a shooting match at the command of an enslaver. Having trained Bass to be a top marksman, the enslaver exploits the odds of folks betting on an enslaved person and plans to reap the financial reward for Bass's skill. The speech bubble in the right-hand frame contains a minstrel face rebus—one of Joel Christian Gill's signature moves as a comics artist—to signal the derogatory language the enslaver uses to label Bass and to encode the visual history of racism that provides the historical and contemporary context against which Gill writes his comics series *Tales of the Talented Tenth*.[1] The child gaze in these panels, however, also works as part of the verbal-visual grammar of the two-panel sequence, and it signals Bass's reaction to the enslaver's words as well as the text's attitude toward them. This gaze-directed interplay is a key way that Gill joins a tradition of African American biographers whose work extends to a child audience and who place, according to Rudine Sims Bishop, a "strong emphasis on African American history [that] functions as a corrective to the historical neglect, distortion, or omission of that history in school curricula and a manifestation of the belief that knowledge of their history will function as anchor, compass, and sail for African American children" (249). Anchor, compass, and sail accurately describe the weight, directionality, and energy of Bass's countersurveillant gaze.

A more detailed examination of the textual dynamics at work here reveals that weight, directionality, and energy. The moment-to-moment transition between the panels and the change in zoom level emphasize Bass's eyes as a key visual cue on which the reader can base their closure—that is, their sense of coherence—of the narrative segment. In the first panel, Bass's eyes

Figure 4.1. Bass gives some side-eye (Gill 11). Fair use.

focus on his target through his gun's sight, indicating his marksman's aim; in the second panel, his eyes shift in the opposite direction, back to the area from which the speech bubble emanates (as made clear by its tail). In the gutter between the panels—that space of "encounter" that energizes the active readership comics requires (Chute, *Why* 23)—an implied action takes place: Bass's eye slide movement, the dynamic enactment of his counter-surveillant gaze. Implicating the speaker of the derogatory language, Bass's countersurveillant eye slide is the "action" of these panels. Indeed, given the nonlinearity of comics reading and the fact that the second panel is more visually arresting than the first (because of the close-up of Bass's face as well as the minstrel face above a colorful bowtie), many readers are likely to find their eyes drawn to the right panel first and then move to the left, then again to the right, and so on, repeatedly engaging the panels and the relationships between them as their own eyes move back and forth to mirror Bass's sliding gaze. Bass's dynamic side-eye is also anchored by the centering of his eyeline in the second panel, indicating its significance to the progression of the story.

This chapter examines the ways in which graphic narrative—a form often associated with the child (Chaney 57ff)—materializes such gazes with and without the ekphrastic verbal intermediary of prose narrative. Derek Parker Royal points out that while comics uses "images that serve as referential icons [and can] fall prey to the same kind of semantic slippage found in linguistic codes . . . , there is something relatively 'direct' about an image's ability to affect reader response. The figures that make up the comics rub up against reality in ways that words cannot" (7). Indeed, the immediacy of the child gaze in graphic narrative conveys significant visual illocutionary intent. Eyes draw other eyes to them, and in the child-affiliated comics form, the child's eye is a particularly evocative visual cue—difficult to pass over and viscerally arresting.

The aim of this chapter is not to argue that comics is a better or more profound form than prose regarding the way the child gaze operates as a narrative technique; rather, it argues that because comics involves a heightened level of attention to the visceral qualities and physical positioning of the child gaze, which is literally depicted on the page, it deserves special attention. In materializing the embodied child as one who looks in the spatialized layout of the comics medium, graphic narrative asserts the child as physically enmeshed in the space of a visibly ideological world and as participating and reacting to that world in an embodied state made visible to the reader. The gaze of young Bass above, for instance, is a physical marker of his agency within the slave society into which he was born, the ideology of which might be said, metaphorically, to permeate the air around him, filled on the space of the page by his owner's oppressive speech. The stakes for graphic narrative's representation of the child gaze, then, have to do with the role of the child as a physical agent within an ideological discursive surround—one visualized and verbalized on the comics page and one that, in US graphic narratives, often metonymizes the American reader's own.

By representing the child gaze in a visual narrative medium, comics provides a platform for a negotiation between reader and depicted child. Comics' ability to guide the reader's gaze physically casts the child gaze as doubly visual: first as a visual representation of looking within the diegetic world and second as a visually oriented interlocutory pathway between the comic and the reader. When the depicted child's gaze is juxtaposed with an ideologically saturated verbal-visual surround, that visual interlocutory pathway has great potential to disrupt hegemonic narratives of US national belonging. Hence, not only does young Bass's eye slide depict him directing his eyes at a speaker; it depicts him *looking back* at a speaker employing *anti-Black discourse* meant to dismiss him from *the personhood his eyes overtly assert*. Children on the comics page can look in various evocative ways, including countersurveillantly (like Bass), appreciatively (like the children in *March*, discussed below), transactionally (like Jin in *American Born Chinese*, also discussed below), or a combination thereof.[2] In each case, the key to the power of their gazes in relation to US hegemonic practices is that the visual discursive surrounds at which and in which they look are ideologically marked, thus demanding that the reader consider such ideological markers in their acts of closure as they view the comics pages.

The depicted child and the reader can even, as in the case of comics' employment of a direct gaze, approximate eye contact with each other, an effect that is not reproducible in prose narration. In comics, this moment of eye contact can colocate the reader with the supposed object of a character's gaze, reach out directly to the implied reader, and, in some cases, produce both effects simultaneously. Drawing the reader and the comics child—as well as the reader's world and the comics' world—closer together, these moments enable a type of second-person graphic narration that breaks the fourth wall to work diegetically, extradiegetically, and extratextually, eliciting the reader's reaction even as they register the character's own.

The graphic narratives I discuss below represent the gazing child in visually ideological spaces created on the comics page to simulate a cultural surround of hegemonic verbal-visual discourse—discourse tied, to continue a common thread from earlier chapters, to exclusionary narratives about race and racial representation in the United States. In that racialized discursive surround, the child's ways of looking allow for indictment—directly or indirectly—of racism in the United States, and in each text the child gaze does so in a way of looking theorized earlier in this book. John Lewis, Andrew Aydin, and Nate Powell's *March* engages an appreciative gaze to perform its antiracist and commemorative cultural work, while Joel Christian Gill's *Bass Reeves: Tales of the Talented Tenth* employs the child's countersurveillant gaze in the anti-Black US Civil War era. Gene Luen Yang's *American Born Chinese* traces the tension in main character Jin's life through his transactional gaze—in concert with a direct gaze that invites the reader into a critical transaction with anti-Asian attitudes and Jin's experience therewith.[3] Each text's antiracist project is carried out through the way the child gaze directs the gaze of the reader, who is invited to provide the closure that makes sense of the relationship among child, discursive surround, and sometimes, in the case of the visual technique of the direct gaze that breaks the fourth wall, the reader.

The first volume of Lewis, Aydin, and Powell's *March* materializes a model for the reader through the physical posturing of a child's act of looking: in this case, a child who gazes appreciatively. Employing a partial frame story for John Lewis's autobiographical account of his role in the US civil rights movement, Lewis, Aydin, and Powell guide the reader into the role of the educable, interested child. The frame provides crucial direction to infuse the text with the curiosity and appreciation of the child ready to learn about and eager to see themselves as part of the legacy of movements for social justice.

Joel Christian Gill's *Bass Reeves: Tales of the Talented Tenth* employs the child gaze as the vehicle for the text's countersurveillant mode and anchors antiracist agency in the child who looks back at the visual and aural vocabulary of oppression. By creating his main character's discursive surround on the comics page via the verbal-visual minstrel face rebus mentioned above, as well as the depiction of particularly racist white people as crows, Gill positions the child gaze as a strong base from which to reject stereotypes associated with blackness and transform them into markers of racist white oppression.

Gene Luen Yang's *American Born Chinese* exhibits the use of a transactional child gaze to direct the reader to consider the impact on Chinese and Chinese American children of acculturating forces of whiteness and the circulation of Chinese stereotypes in US schools. Its depiction of the acts of looking of Chinese American protagonist Jin engages the tension of gazing at and with white and Asian peers—a tension made plain in Jin's gazing within the comics world and one that confronts and is even transferred to the reader in moments of a direct gaze. In such moments, this ambiguous second-person narrative technique ramps up reader participation beyond the act of closure and places it in the realm of viewer-character intimacy. That is, *American Born Chinese* demonstrates how the direct gaze as a recurring trope elicits reader participation in the child's transactional gaze.

This chapter's examination of comics' powerful materialization of the child gaze employs concepts laid out in the previous chapters and also builds on three key characterizations of the comics form: its cultural relation to the child, its visual pedagogy, and its history, especially in the United States, of engaging and transforming racial stereotypes. I now move to a discussion of the scholarship that situates comics as a key site for antiracist "teaching" interventions through the figure of the child before a close reading of the texts that demonstrate the theory in action.

COMICS, THE CHILD, VISUAL PEDAGOGY, AND (ANTI)RACIST WORK

Children matter in comics of the United States. Even in comics aimed at adults that do not depict children, the idea of the child is culturally bound to graphic narrative. Michael Chaney argues that the child is "the default face of American comics" (*Reading* 16) and the "archetype of its mediation" (57). Citing their tie to the history of the form through their depiction in early comic strips as well as their controversy-raising reading practices of the mid-twentieth century, Chaney also argues that children—and, more specifically, the figure of the child—"incarnates" the notion of "synapses or the space between" (62) in a nod to the meaning-making formal elements of graphic narrative. If the child, as he posits, "rises to the level of an imperative in the comics" (62), then that cruciality energizes the child gaze as an organizing, meaning-making directive. When depicted, it carries out the imperative of the child's role in the text and for the reader.

The connection between comics child and reader, then, is also crucial to this imperative. Indeed, if an "association with all things juvenile" connotes the "form's ethos as teacher" (Chaney, *Reading* 3), then we can consider how the comics page continually positions the reader in the role of the educable child, taught to see, read, and make sense of the text by its very own features. Hillary Chute refers to the "narrative scaffolding" comics deploys ("Comics" 452) that allows the reader to engage in a "participatory, even slowed-down practice of consumption" (*Why* 28); each gutter on the comics page "gestures conspicuously to the reader's active and involved reading" (23). Jared Gardner calls comics a "profoundly collaborative form," one that "must always show and tell only a fraction of the information required to make narrative sense of the information being presented" (138). The "formalistic tutorials in seeing" enacted on their mises-en-page allow comics to prompt readers' acts of closure, for there is an "inherent necessity for any comics text to teach its viewers how to process its under-language" (Chaney, *Reading* 10, 145). Gwen Athene Tarbox and Michelle Ann Abate emphasize how contemporary comics written for children and young adults exhibit a "heightened appreciation for generic and artistic experimentation" that includes "a furtherance of the expectation that readers need to be challenged to fill in interpretive gaps on their own" (5). The reader's role in the visually pedagogic form of comics art persists across age of intended readership, and the child gaze is one way graphic narrative scaffolds the reader to be able to perform the act of gap filling required by the form.

While making sense of comics means making sense of the combination of visual and verbal elements on the page, the combination itself is decidedly not kin to the conventional trajectory of verbal communication and prose.

It is nonlinear, spatial, and taken in via the viewer's wandering eye. Theirry Groensteen notes that the figures and panels in comics are laid out in a network of "*situated* coordinates" (168); it is the situatedness of the relations on the comics page that leads, pushes, pulls, and focuses the viewer's eye and that does not just contain but encodes the lessons graphic narrative conveys to its reader-viewer. Given this "ocularcentric" form (Chaney, *Reading* 5), I argue that the appearance of a child gaze within the network of the mise-en-page provides a metavisual cue for the viewer's "learning" processes. It takes on a leading role in the governing optics at work on the page, optics that catch the reader-viewer's eye and direct—and sometimes hold—its gaze.

One area in which the visual pedagogy of comics has intersected with ideologies of exclusion in the United States is in the depiction of race. Comics as a medium often relies on stereotype to convey character and is thus a particularly fraught space for the dissemination of racist caricature (Eisner 11). Of interest to this chapter are those caricatures of African, African American, Asian, and Asian American peoples prominent in the historical archive of American comics. Frances Gateward and John Jennings point out in their introduction to *The Blacker the Ink: Constructions of Black Identity in Comics and Sequential Art* that "The first images of black people in comics were loosely based on the stereotypes generated in blackface minstrelsy, stereotypes mired in the notion of fixity" (5), and Jeet Heer notes that these early caricatures "took the existing racism of society and gave it vicious and virulent visual life" (par. 8). When African American audiences resisted the "minstrel-style" drawings and the American response to Adolf Hitler during and after World War II somewhat tempered the circulation of blatant anti-Black racist visuals, many comics writers and publishers did not respond by correcting such caricatures. Rather, they often took them out, leaving 1950s comics more "lily white" than before (Heer). Tim Caron and Qiana Whitted both note the dearth of complexly represented Black bodies and experiences in comics (Caron 142; Whitted, "And" 92).

Asian American representation in comics through and beyond the nineteenth and twentieth centuries follows a similar pattern of racist caricature. Min Hyoung Song points out that "slant-eyes, short stature, sallow skin . . . , claw-like fingertips, and long menacing queue" (80) were reproduced in popular media, political signs, and comics, creating a "powerful visual vocabulary for imagining the Chinese as from elsewhere and as therefore not belonging in the United States" (80). Gardner notes the shift from earlier stereotypes of the "bestial, violent . . . savage" to "postwar fantasies of the quiet, studious and robotlike Asian Americans," which contended ambiguously with the white ethnocentric notion of an "Asian Invasion" (134). Indeed, the notion of foreign threat remains prevalent through the turn of the twenty-first century with regard to "Asian American youths as stellar students" (Song 80).[4]

In these and other racially damaging images, comics' persistent use of "reductive iconography—the big noses, the bug eyes, the buck teeth, and the generally deformed features that have historically composed our visual discourse on the Other" (Royal 8)—exploits "ideas about race everyone is supposed to 'know'" (Caron 142). The "everyone" here is a white ethnocentric hegemonic construction. Drawing on the visual vocabulary of racism in the hegemonic cultural imaginary, comics have been complicit in an "abiding endurance of racist iconography" (Caron 142) that manifests overtly as well as subtly.

Yet the comics page can also confront the resonance of such iconography and, in such confrontation, can invite the reader into its stance and "teach particular ways of looking at things" (Rifas 27). In Nathalie op de Beeck's words, some graphic narrative "may be understood as instilling critical and political literacy" in a "countercultural function" (476); that is, its visual pedagogy can steer viewers away from what everyone is supposed to "know." Whitted argues that comics can make a "cultural intervention" because the form has a built-in opportunity to "repurpose hegemonic racial discourse and re-envision the spectacle of difference" ("And" 97); Gardner asserts that the sequential aspect of graphic narrative—requiring that readers fill gaps between panels as they perform the act of closure—manifests an "ability to *destabilize* racial stereotypes" (135; italics in original), and Royal points out that "the spaces of graphic storytelling ... foreground relational perspectives between and among individual objects. Such visual strategies are an essential component of multiethnic graphic narrative, writing that by its very nature relies upon themes of cultural context and contingency to generate meaning" (10). Rebecca Wanzo continues this line of thinking, positing, "The building blocks of caricature and sequentiality are in conversation with each other, destabilizing conventional readings of bodies, space, and things in relationship to time" (85). Understood next to these statements, Hillary Chute and Patrick Jagoda's claim that comics calls upon a "fullness of ... concentration ... to absorb its narrative or discursive procedures" (4) is perhaps doubly true in comics depicting racialized characters, where such "aesthetics of attention" (4) has the capacity to compound or disrupt the hegemonic gaze.

Lara Saguisag's research on comics of the Progressive Era emphasizes how US comics have long employed childhood not only as a standard connotation of the form but also as a depicted stage of life that can interrogate or uphold notions of citizenship, especially in relation to class, race, ethnicity, and gender—and often in concert with stereotypes (1–5). While

Saguisag finds that comics of that era eventually tended toward assimilation and the privileging of white, middle-class masculinity (6), the early twenty-first-century texts examined in this chapter demonstrate that, roughly a century later, comics use the figure of the child for stronger resistance of narrow parameters of national belonging and that one method of that resistance is the child gaze. Each of the following texts engages most specifically with the legacy of race in the United States by way of visual pedagogies that harness the power of the looking child. The appreciative child gaze that frames *March* eschews anti-Black stereotypes, turning the depicted children's and the reader's eyes upon the civil rights work of John Lewis and modeling, through its rendering within the spatialized ideologies on the comics page, appreciation for his inspirational work. *Bass Reeves* and *American Born Chinese*, however, engage stereotypes directly, representing in order to wrestle—in Reeves's case, countersurveillantly, and in Jin's case, transactionally—with an oppressive ideological surround permeated by the visual vocabulary of racism. *Bass Reeves*'s spatially embedded ocular signals in relation to that surround engineer the text's indictment of anti-Black stereotypes, while *American Born Chinese*'s direct gaze signals the need for intimate witnessing and empathic transfer of Jin's struggle with the anti-Asian, acculturating forces of white American youth culture.

FRAMING CIVIL RIGHTS ACTIVISM WITH APPRECIATIVE CHILD LOOKING: JOHN LEWIS, ANDREW AYDIN, AND NATE POWELL'S *MARCH*

March, John Lewis's three-volume graphic memoir cocreated with Andrew Aydin and Nate Powell, employs the appreciative child gaze as a crucial narrative frame for the story of the civil rights activist. Indeed, the text is dedicated "to the past and future children of the movement," signaling the centrality of the child to the work of the movement as well as to the activist energy the memoir attempts to capture and transfer to its audience. To investigate the way comics materializes the appreciative child gaze as part of this effect, I focus specifically on the frame technique Lewis, Aydin, and Powell use to introduce Lewis's first-person narrative: the visit to Lewis's office by two children and their mother on the morning of President Barack Obama's inauguration. Throughout the scenes depicting the young boys in Lewis's office, the physical posturing of the children's acts of looking as well as their location within the spatialized ideologies depicted on the page conjure an aura of interest, awe, and curiosity. Even the text's use of both visual and verbal humor in some of these panels contributes to the construction of the

Figure 4.2. The entrance of the visiting boys and their mother (Lewis, Aydin, and Powell 17). Fair use.

child gaze as a conduit for guiding the reader into an appreciative stance regarding civil rights work and its ongoing legacy in the United States.

Several critics have mentioned the general attitude the text requests its reader take, but none have yet investigated the way the child gaze overtly performs and transfers that attitude to the reader through the dynamics of comics panels. Johannes C. P. Schmid, for instance, argues that the text is "inspirational and even instructional to activists of the present" (para. 8), acting as a sort of "initiation ritual" as Lewis "pass[es] down his memories to teach the next generation" (para. 10), and Joanna C. Davis-McElligatt notes that the text "urge[s] young readers to identify themselves with" the visiting boys (309). Such initiation and identification, I argue, is modeled through the visiting children's acts of appreciative looking. The children's entrance both initiates the story proper, by providing John Lewis with two interlocutors with whom he talks, and organizes the story's direction and effect, by activating the text's eliciting of interested consideration and inspirational celebration. It achieves the latter specifically through their gazes, which demonstrates how child looking can dynamically intervene in an image's significance and become a tool for teaching in the pedagogy of the comics page.

The way the entrance of the children is drawn first establishes the significance of this gaze and then highlights the ideological surround of Lewis's office, which has elicited that gaze (17; figure 4.2). The midleft close-up of the office door slightly ajar conjures the notion of a peering subject—a child-height sight line into Lewis's office that corresponds with the height of the children in relation to the doorknob in the panel to its right. Indeed, note how that panel engages a viewing perspective no higher than the boys' own faces, the angle prioritizing them and their gazes. Their eyes are turned slightly upward, emphasizing their child stature in relation to the adults surrounding them and signaling their curiosity about the space they are entering, both of which prefigure their "looking up" to John Lewis as role model. Thus, when the bottom panel dramatically shifts to an aerial perspective, the boys' initial reaction has already been registered (and centered, quite literally, on the page). The bottom panel's display of Lewis's space marks the interior as a site of antiracist activist ideologies through the large, framed image of Rev. Dr. Martin Luther King Jr. partially obscured but nevertheless prominent on the wall behind the desk.[5] From this moment, Lewis turns his attention to the children as his diegetic audience for over half of the volume, signaling the significance of their role in the narrative's texture both physically and metaphorically.

That attention creates a feedback loop of appreciation between Lewis and the boys. The interplay of their looking and talking establishes Lewis as a storyteller just as it establishes the children as dynamic recipients, and even co-organizers, of a story meant to be thoughtfully considered and admired. While the mother makes clear their purpose, "we stopped by because I wanted my boys to see their history—I wanted them to know . . . how far we've come" (18–19), the text has even before this declaration prioritized the children, whom Lewis bends down to greet and invite into his personal office. The humor employed there via Lewis's description of his office as "a little junky," one boy's agreement "yeah . . ." and his brother's chiding "shh!" (19; figure 4.3) establishes the three of them as a triad of conversants, with one child a bit more forward than the other. That junkiness—assumedly piles of paperwork and such—is not shown in the image, which allows the humor to function as an assertion of the child's ability to interact with an important congressperson rather than a slight to Lewis's organizational skills or a nod to the demands of his job. Rather, the depiction of Lewis's personal office is dominated by the wall of framed photographs he begins pointing out to the children, which instantly

Figure 4.3. Lewis's personal office wall (Lewis, Aydin, and Powell 19). Fair use.

positions the children as witness not only to Lewis but to the networks and legacies of which he has been a part and into which he is welcoming them.

Though Lewis begins with references to well-known civil rights era leaders such as President Kennedy and Dr. King (19), the photograph tour he embarks upon foreshadows the way the text goes on to tell Lewis's story while widening the civil rights archive to include underrepresented figures, such as Diane Nash and Bayard Rustin. Given the narrow version of the civil rights movement and its key players often communicated to children and to the general public via school curriculum and popular media, this tour makes overt the pedagogical corrective performed by this graphic narrative, positioning the gazing children and the reader as its students. However, exactly who or what each photograph depicts does not matter at this point in the story, which is limned by the lack of clarity in their rendering. While several of them contain vague human forms, they are all drawn in blurred, sketched lines overlaid by diagonal cross hatching meant to indicate the sheen of their glass frames. What seems to matter most is simply that they *are* framed photographs—which itself matters immensely to the antiracist and appreciative work the text is doing, especially by positioning the Black child as inheritor of the legacies depicted in the text.

bell hooks's work on the role of photographs in African American families and communities emphasizes the significance of this positioning, and two dimensions of her analysis are key here: that photographs of Black subjects in Black spaces are part of a long practice of reclaiming visual representation from the hegemonic white gaze and that such photographs are a source of empowerment to the young people who view them. In an overt reference to comics-style art, hooks claims that in photographs, "we saw ourselves represented in these images not as caricatures, cartoonlike figures; we were there in full diversity of body, being, and expression" (*Art* 61). Against the insistence of derogatory visuals of blackness like those disseminated in comics, photography was a way to "document a reality" (60), "a political instrument, a way to resist misrepresentation as well as a means by which alternative images could be reproduced" (60). Photographs on the walls of private homes—or in this case, Lewis's personal office—are about asserting and celebrating the ability to intervene in the visual narrative of blackness in the United States as well as sharing such images for the strength and inspiration of the community. In a metatextual narrative way, as Chaney points out, Lewis's walls "resemble a comics page, gridded with rectangular image-frames, each one bordered by gutters" (171). Thus, in this scene, *March* emphasizes the "curatorial process" (hooks 61) that Lewis engages, both on his wall and in this graphic memoir. And it reclaims comics as a space for positive, nonstereotypical representation.

Positioning the child in front of such a wall is crucial to the project of *March*: to tell the story of civil rights through the lens of the lived experience of a Black activist in ways that inspire appreciation and continuance of the movement. As hooks notes, such walls of photographs are "empower[ing]" (61) to the child, even if the child is unaware (as hooks's herself was) of the link between Black "self-representation" and the history of racial oppression in the United States (*Art* 60). Indeed, in detailing part of that oppression through the story Lewis narrates to his reader-viewer, *March* metonymizes that link and also forges another between the child and the reader-viewer. Note how on the page above, the reader-viewer is brought closer to the photographs as the panels progress along a trajectory aligned with the sight lines of the children. The first two panels keep the viewer behind the children in what film critics refer to as over-the-shoulder shots, but the last three position the viewer overlaid with the children (or even closer than the children themselves are) in point-of-view shots, as if we have stepped forward to follow Lewis's tour with our own gazes. The perspectival positioning the page accomplishes in relation to the ideological space created with this wall of photographs conflates the reader with the child as we join in gazing at Lewis's wall of images, each of us marking the accomplishments of civil rights activists.

The text does not completely remove the children and transition to Lewis's direct narration to the reader-viewer at this point, however, reasserting the primacy of the child's spirit of appreciative, active curiosity achieved via the text's dependency on the child gaze. While one of the children directs his eyes at the photographs as Lewis speaks, his brother's rogue gazing—depicted at length, across several panels in gaze shot/point-of-view shot combination—results in a question prompting a new direction in Lewis's interaction with them: "Why do you have so many CHICKENS?" (20; figure 4.4). The question is not coded as rude; rather, the page space devoted to visually exhibiting the boy's curious interest before he verbalizes it legitimates the boy's wandering gaze.

Furthermore, the humorous valences of the curious child stepping outside the bounds of assumed social mores in important government spaces are here cast as productive. The child notices a strange pattern in Lewis's collection and wishes to consider its relevance to the office space he has been invited to explore. Such relevance is even signaled by the way Lewis's speech bubbles float through the panels featuring the boy's searching eyes and the chickens they land on, and it is confirmed when the question is appreciated by Lewis himself: "Ha! Well, that's a good question" (20). Chaney points out that the question "unveils the memoir's proper chronological structure" (171) as it launches the narrative back into Lewis's childhood past. I add that it not only unveils the future direction of the piece but also touches back to a

Figure 4.4. Chickens (Lewis, Aydin, and Powell 20). Fair use.

segment that occurs just prior to the children's entrance. At the top of the first page on which they appear, Lewis's sister Rosa has been telling a story to someone in Lewis's office—perhaps his aid, Andrew Aydin. The protagonist of the story is unnamed, but later in the narrative, when Lewis recounts his childhood experiences, it is revealed that Rosa was talking about Lewis, as a young boy, hiding under his porch to get out of farm work and catch the bus to school (16–17; 50–52). In the diegetic world of the text, this story would not have come up were it not for the boy's question about chickens, so the order of these details in the text position the child's appreciative gaze as a crucial meaning-making activity that aids the reader's ability to find coherence in a narrative knitting together past, present, and future.[6]

That the children still do not fully disappear from the narrative—despite having launched its "proper" direction—limns the ways an appreciative child gaze self-reflexively posits the worth of the children. Their curiosity matters, as does their place in the legacy of civil rights, which the text urges them and their real-life counterparts to take up. Their frame resurfaces thrice more—once when they ask about school (35), once when they ask about Lewis meeting King (63–64), and finally when prompted by their mother to say goodbye and thank you (74). And though their mother scolds one boy for an impertinent question about failing tests in the first of these resurfacing frame moments, in the next she raises her hand, mimicking her son's earlier motion (20; figure 4.4), making her own curious inquiry and thereby emphasizing her son as a model of appreciation. Each time, all gaze interestedly at Lewis, their scenes extending, interspersed with the story proper, over more than half of volume one.

Chaney argues that when the family leaves, the "temporarily framed narrative . . . is abandoned . . . in exchange for a disembodied voice of reminiscence" (173). However, given the boys' integral role on which the comic has visually, verbally, and spatially insisted, it is perhaps more fitting to interpret their leaving before the story ends as a sign of transference rather than abandonment. That is, it makes room for the reader-viewer to take on their stance wholly, which has been modeled by the boys throughout. That the children do not return to continue or "close" the frame in this volume or any of the others is metonymic for the text's eliciting of appreciative *readerly* closure. The comic itself becomes the reader's version of the boys' experience of the photographic wall, its narrative synonymous with Lewis's tour through the images that claim appreciative visual representations of blackness and the ongoing struggle for civil rights in the United States. Thus, *March*'s materializing an appreciative child gaze in the ideological space of Lewis's congressional office becomes a portal through which it guides a reader into an ideology of appreciation for its content.

COUNTERSURVEILLING THE VISUAL VOCABULARY OF RACISM IN JOEL CHRISTIAN GILL'S *TALES OF THE TALENTED TENTH: BASS REEVES*

Joel Christian Gill's *Tales of the Talented Tenth: Bass Reeves* grounds its countersurveillant mode in the agency of the child's gaze, which interacts with the verbal-visual discursive surround on the comics page to transform the visual vocabulary of racism in the United States into an indictment of white oppression. The comic tells the life story of its titular character, Bass Reeves (1838–1910), who escaped slavery to become the first African American deputy US marshal. Gill's depictions of the child gaze interact with recurring tropes to implement a pedagogy of looking that materializes racist practices

Figure 4.5. Young and grown Bass are accosted (Gill 6). Fair use.

in order to resist them. The following close reading of Gill's comic traces *Bass Reeves*'s use of minstrel faces and crows in relation to both young and grown Bass's eyes, exploring how their spatialization on the page troubles, resists, and subverts anti-Black visuals in the United States.

The image with which I introduced this chapter exhibits the mechanics of one instance of Bass's countersurveillant gaze, performed in relation to a racist discursive surround depicted by the visual slur in the speech bubble. Earlier instances of this visual slur in the text allow an examination of the pedagogies of looking enacted by the comics page that lead up to and scaffold the reader's reaction to the moment in figure 4.1. The mise-en-page corresponding to the minstrel face's initial appearance reveals several potent ways in which Gill orients the reader to receive the child's countersurveillant gaze as a powerful signal to dismantle the visual slur's historical power. Here, a young Bass of the past and a grown Bass of the narrative present are both accosted by white men who use the minstrel face slur several times (Gill, *Bass* 6; figure 4.5). As Gill himself has pointed out, the minstrel faces, which resonate in a particular *cultural* context, do not look like the characters to whom the speakers intend them to refer within the *local* context of the page (NPR Staff). Immutable even as it traverses time, the minstrel face is depicted the same way in each evocation: an overexaggerated caricature with bug eyes, large lips, a wide nose, and a red and white polka-dotted bow tie. Even to the most inexperienced reader, it is clear that the minstrel face bears no resemblance to the young or grown Bass, especially contrasting the top right depiction of young Bass, whose surprise and fear are conveyed in quite differently drawn wide eyes—eyes positioned in a direct gaze exchange with the reader, invited to share Bass's fear.[7]

Moreover, while the top and bottom frames rhyme, especially insofar as the bodily postures and placements of each character, the facial differences between young Bass and grown Bass emphasize the absurdity of the minstrel face's capacity to refer to either or both of them—and, by extension, to anyone. Manthia Diawara notes that "stereotypes always rob people of their history and shun their realism" (9), and Gill rejects the stereotype on this very ground and teaches his reader to do the same. By way of the interpretive gap created by the comparison of the various Black faces on the page, the reader is asked to conclude that the minstrel face is, despite its fear- and anger-inducing cultural context, an inaccurate signifier, disempowered in its ability to refer to either version of this historical person.

The visual discrepancy that keeps the racist marker from mapping onto its intended object also undermines the authority of its speaker, and the text destabilizes the intended signifier/signified relationship further via a formal convention of the comics medium: speech bubbles. In comics, a speech bubble's tail functions as an arrow pointing not to the receiver of the speech but to its originator, directing the reader to understand to whom the words belong. In Groensteen's terms, "One of the fecund schemes that organizes the reading of comics" is the "relationship between the speaker and the enunciation that is uttered" (75). In Gill's comic, because the minstrel slur does not attach clearly to the receiver and because the speech bubble sutures its utterance to its speaker, that tail activates the anti-Black depiction in reverse, contrapuntally implicating its speaker rather than the person to whom the speaker intends it to refer.

Figure 4.6. White men capture young and grown Bass (Gill 7). Fair use.

While the speakers are not fully visible on the above page (figure 4.5), the speech bubble tails are, and the breakdown of the opposite page tightens the connection between the two by drawing the speakers into the frame (Gill 7; figure 4.6). Here, the white men (one of whom is depicted as a crow—more on that below) are the only ones who speak. Young and grown Bass's faces are turned away from the viewer, further disassociating them from the minstrel face, which is still in full view in three of the four speech bubbles that point directly to white men. Indeed, that the visual slurs first appear disembodied from their speakers and yet unattachable to their intended referents before becoming visually sutured to their speakers on the next page guides the reader through a two-step process: first, an acknowledgment that the minstrel face is no marker for Black identity and second that it is a racist construct insidiously propagated by users who participate in its derogatory discourse. In this way, the minstrel figures are both diegetic (part of the character's words and therefore part of the action) and extradiegetic (part of the comics' reader-facing narrative texture), and pedagogically so. They depict the characters' own speech as a vehicle for metacommentary upon them.

In this scene, Gill also foreshadows Bass's countersurveillant gaze with subtle precursors to its later overt signals. Note the subversive depiction of the seven minstrel faces present on this spread. On the left page (figure 4.5), the four minstrels are identical to each other, down to the detail of their irises, which look to the middle left. On the right page (figure 4.6), they are also identical to each other, but this set casts their eyes *downward* and left. This shift is not accidental; on the left page, the middle-left gaze follows the direction of the speech bubbles' tails, suggesting the minstrel face is looking at the speaker. On the right page, the downward left irises function similarly, gazing at the speaker in two instances and at an interlocutor who later uses the same visual slur in a third. Via subtle representation of the minstrels' countersurveillant gaze, which points to the racism of their speakers, Gill also directs the reader's gaze to the white men by way of the very vehicle that propagates their racism. When young Bass performs his first eye slide above (figure 4.1), he eyes the speaker in tandem with the minstrel figure on that page as well, signaling that he has joined a tradition of countersurveillance established in the visual discourse of the early pages of the text. Indeed, Bass actually takes on the lead role for the remainder of the text, for this frame is the last in which the minstrel figure's eyes gesture to any character. As if having transferred the gaze to young Reeves, Gill relieves the minstrel figure of some of its performative duties, signaled by the absence of his showman-style bowtie in subsequent pages. Instead, the minstrel face gazes directly at the viewer, his wide stare seeming to ask us to share his exasperation. From this point on, it is Bass Reeves's eyes that become the markers of countersurveillant agency, orchestrating a visual pedagogy that indicts anti-Black rhetoric by guiding readerly attention to the perpetrators of oppression and reversing the signifier/signified relationship inscribed in the racist image.

Just after this moment, the page layouts emphasize Bass's countersurveillant child gaze as the core of his strengthening resistance. In a sequence that traces the growth of young Bass into young adult Bass, Gill's repeatedly closer shots of Bass's face focus less and less on the gun he holds and more and more on the lines of his eyes, thus positing the gaze as crucial to developing

Figure 4.7. Bass's growth sequence (Gill 19). Fair use.

antiracist agency (Gill 19; figure 4.7). The text on the page also highlights the dissonance of double consciousness that will spur Bass's escape from the enslaver: "Bass also got bigger and more aware of his place. All the while his master continued to think of him as his little [minstrel face]" (19). On this page, though the minstrel face is placed directly next to the final close-up version of young adult Bass that depicts his face only from his eyes up, Bass's eyes instead glare ahead toward the page turn, indicating thoughts of a future that depart from his characterization as [minstrel face].

Figure 4.8. Bass's direct gaze (Gill 22). Fair use.

Bass's movement to freedom—he escapes from the enslaver's Confederate war camp in 1863—is directly tied to Bass's countersurveillant looking. Just before the encampment scenes, the text includes several reaction panels of Bass's response to the enslaver's calling him a "family pet" (Gill 22; figure 4.8), and those panels indicate, again, a progressive power in Bass's acts of looking. In the middle panels (depicted at the top of the partial image of the page in figure 4.8), the shifts in zoom level, discursive surround, and eye expression energize a new stage in Bass's countersurveillance. Here his gaze actually reaches across the gutter—and cues the reader's eyes to follow—to implicate the enslaver's racism; no speech bubble tail in the panel depicting his eyes assists. The lack of the speech bubble tail converts the speech act into a metaphoric image of the attack on Bass's mental state, the speech bubble's hovering around his head signaling the pervasiveness of Bass's oppressive verbal-visual discursive surround. However, that hovering also centers his human eyes and face in opposition to the "pet" comparison. The final panel's close-up—spanning the entire bottom of the page—delivers a different eye movement than the characteristic slide that has organized the text's earlier visual pedagogy. Here, his eyes shift back to center in a direct, insistent gaze, one that seems to reach through the text's fourth wall and lock eyes with the reader-viewer, who is invited to nod in agreement. The decisive quality of his direct gaze both elicits the reader's closure and provides closure to this segment of the text; the following page shifts in time and space to the 1863 Confederate war camp and three pages later, a double page splash depicts Bass with a similar viewer-facing gaze as he punches the enslaver in the face (28–29)—thus cementing Bass's opposition in eyes and in body. The superhero colors (bright red, orange, and yellow) and composition of this splash (Bass with upraised fist, the enslaver flying back and down to the bottom left of the page) infuse the image with righteous triumph, connecting the countersurveillant gaze to immanent victory.

The pattern of visual pedagogy enacted by Bass's eyes in the text also signals that the countersurveillant gaze Bass cultivates throughout childhood and young adulthood continues to be his seat of antiracist power when he is grown. The earlier images that juxtapose young Bass with a grown Bass wherein both are giving side-eye to the speaker of the minstrel face rebus suggest this link, but it is more forcefully carried out in grown Bass's interaction with a particularly villainous character depicted as a black crow, Gill's visual marker for exceptionally racist white men. The crow itself is a literalized allusion to Jim Crow oppression and a metaphor for the power and monstrosity it encodes in the individual racist figure. The crow often appears anthropomorphized, wearing pants and a vest, and sometimes it holds a gun in its wing-hand. In one of Bass's final encounters with his nemesis crow, however, the image

Figure 4.9. Bass against the furious crow (Gill 54). Fair use.

transforms into an animalistic depiction of evil, and the comic employs Bass's countersurveillant gaze—now accompanied by fists—to defeat him.

In the figure below, the crow has captured US Marshal Bass and snapped his silver star badge, but Bass's indomitable reaction sends him into a fury (Gill 54; figure 4.9). Several visual cues convey the monstrosity of the crow in this scene. No longer anthropomorphized, the crow has lost its human vestments and is instead depicted as a purple-gray wraith figure. Surging toward Bass, the crow moves with a rapidity and aggression indicated by the feathers that shoot forward from its sides, and its red eye indicates its rage, which is mirrored in the red background. This emotive use of color erases the actual background depicted in previous frames, lifting not just the crow but also this entire moment out of the realm of the actual and into the realm of the symbolic—and limning the emotional intensity of the moment. Furthermore, the right to left motion of the crow pushes against the glance curve, passing some of the force of impact promised by the attack onto the viewer. hooks argues that "whiteness makes its presence felt in black life ... most often as a terrorizing imposition, a power that wounds, hurts, tortures" ("Representing" 169). Depicted here, then, is not just Bass's own long-standing feud with an individual racist man but the terrorizing force of an anti-Black racist system.

Bass's stance, however, works against this force, representing resistance through his raised fists and his powerful glare—one drawn with the strength of a gaze cultivated in childhood. Note how in the first two frames of Bass's reply, his hat brim is pulled low over his eyes. His eyes, however—were they exposed—would be the center point of the image, and thus the reader is prompted to focus on their existence and anticipate their unveiling, as the progressive close-ups recall the panel progression in figure 4.8. The moment of their opening in the elongated bottom frame provides visceral and visual punctuation to his verbal reply that resounds with the countersurveillant groundwork Gill has laid to this point. After taking a beating (the action of which is obscured by a classic comics-style dust cloud, shifting the scene away from the metaphor back to the concrete), Bass finds that he can use the ragged edge of the broken star to cut his bonds, subdue the crow and his sidekick, and escape. In essence, he exploits the crow's oppressive actions as weakness.

Furthermore, it is Bass's opposition to the crow's use of the visual slur that evokes the crow's outburst in the first place. The crow's "Ain't no [minstrel face] got the right to wear a star that should be reserved for a white man" (53) is spat with the illocutionary (that is, intended) force of subjugation; Bass's reply, however, prevents the crow's utterance from becoming perlocutionary (that is, successful in its intent) by both refusing to repeat the visual slur and launching a verbal attack that exposes the crow's weakness: "I didn't think you broke it 'cuz I'm black. . . . I figured that you broke it on account of the fact that you're a dirty, nasty, yella coward and you're a chicken when it comes to the U.S. Marshals" (54). The separation of the two sentences via the gutter—at the point of the suspense-laden ellipsis—emphasizes the pivot. Indeed, the crow's fury and use of the visual slur eventually do contribute to his own defeat in this volume and, tellingly, in concert with the articulation of a Black child's documenting gaze. A young Black girl who witnesses the accidental death for which Bass has been charged with murder testifies to what she saw—that is, articulates her gaze—and the crow's fiery outburst of "[Minstrel face]s!!" (113) prompts the white judge to throw him out of court and issue an apology and thanks to Bass. The white judge, in turning his countersurveillant gaze on the crow, follows the Black child's lead and thereby emphasizes the power of the child, who owns the right to look back, with impugnment, at anti-Black ideologies in the United States.

THE DIRECT GAZE AND THE TRANSFERENCE OF TRANSACTIONAL CHILD LOOKING IN GENE LUEN YANG'S *AMERICAN BORN CHINESE*

In *American Born Chinese*, Gene Luen Yang employs a direct child gaze as a recurring trope over the course of the text, a gaze emphasizing the transactional nature of Jin's response to the ideological surround of his diegetic world and one that invites a complex transaction with the reader-viewer. While such moments are used sparingly in texts like Gill's, which largely keeps the reader-viewer outside the fourth wall save for a few poignant moments of eye contact to elicit acknowledgment and agreement with depicted characters' implied feelings, Yang's text's ongoing use of the direct gaze deploys several layers of engagement with the viewer. These layers extend the significance of both Jin's and the implied reader's elicited transactions in contentious relation with US ideologies of racial belonging.

American Born Chinese is a text that mines the depths of transformation and synthesis, as Tomo Hattori, Elisabeth El Refaie, Ning Ma, and Song have pointed out; it is also concerned with visibility and invisibility (Davis; Song). Such matters are reflected in the novel's storytelling, for three narrative strands both hesitate to acknowledge each other and eventually synthesize: one about the legendary Chinese Monkey King, one about Chinese American youth Jin who transfers to a predominantly white California suburban school, and one about a seemingly white American's cousin, Chin-Kee, a character composite of Asian stereotypes in the United States.[8] By the end of the novel it is clear how they relate, but for some time the reader follows each character distinctly, emphasizing a tension between reader and text as the text simultaneously hints at and withholds information crucial to closing the gap between the stories.

Such intertwining has garnered significant critical attention, but here I focus on the ways the narrative tension occurs even within one strand, particularly that of Jin, the character most analogous to a presumed child reader.[9] Specifically, I attend to the ways Yang exploits the visual possibilities of comics—including zoom level, verbal-visual tension, perspectival positioning, and visual rhyme—in order to harness the protean valences of the direct gaze as a visual second-person address. In *American Born Chinese*, such direct address elicits the reader's understanding, and sometimes evaluation or condemnation, of the complicated phenomenon of internalized racism for Asian American young people as a result of the anti-Asian ideologies coloring everyday life in the contemporary United States.

The direct gaze in comics has received surprisingly little critical attention, but Kai Mikkonen's formulation provides a helpful entry point to Yang's use of the trope in his text. Before I delve into Yang's work, however, I use examples from *Bass Reeves*, familiar from the discussion above, to provide some preliminary explanations. Mikkonen argues that the direct gaze "realis[es] a hypothetical 'you' . . . , increas[ing] narrativity by suggesting a heightened level of involvement for the reader" (76). Taking the meeting of gazes through the fourth wall as a second-person "you" moment opens up a range of interpretive possibilities, especially since second-person narration in prose has been theorized as having particularly dynamic valences—what Monika Fludernik refers to as the "involving, dialogic function of you" (469). Magdalena Rembowska-Płuciennik views second-person moments through the lens of social cognition theory to arrive at a concept of "narrative cooperation" (166), predicated upon "the ability of the 'you' form to offer imaginative access to joint actions and shared experiences" (161). Such narration moves the reading experience from one of "immersion" to one of "participation" (163), requesting the reader behave with reference to the "social context of cognition and to our everyday social interactions" (160). Consider the earlier mention of the direct gaze technique in figure 4.8 from *Bass Reeves*, which depicts a close-up shot of Bass's direct gaze in the lower panel. Bass's eyes energize an interpersonal moment between Bass and the reader, a meeting of the gaze that occurs across the boundary of the fourth wall. This second-person experience is quite differently inflected from a third-person stance that positions the viewer to watch Bass perform as a figure within his storyworld. When the viewer's eyes meet Bass's, as the text requires them to do, the text slips out of—or at least overlays—its otherwise third-person narration with a second-person command: to interact with Bass as a figure able to communicate directly to the reader and to understand the reader as a person called to interact with Bass. Thus, second-person address implicates the reader in a complex interplay with the text.

This interplay rests on ambiguous ground, partially due to what Helmut Bonheim calls "referential slither" (71). Is the "you" (literal or implied) the narratee or the reader? In the image of Bass referenced above (figure 4.8), it is clear that Bass cannot actually look at the reader in his storyworld; he is, rather, glaring into the distance as he overhears the way the enslaver talks about him. Indeed, we can easily substitute in our imagination the enslaver as the object of Bass's gaze in order to anchor his emotional reaction. In second-person prose narration, the narratee is often a character in the story—in the strict sense of the definition, its protagonist, though there is debate about whether the narrator or narratee is the protagonist or even whether second-person narration is just a subdivision of first-person narration. In all cases, however, the "you" designation keeps implicating the reader in the narrator-narratee relationship. In comics, the direct gaze facilitates a meeting of eyes that is difficult to avoid. It involves the viewer no matter whether the viewer aligns themself with the object of the gaze or not. In the case of Bass, the text seems to position us as sharing Bass's anger rather than being targeted by it. On the other hand, being positioned as the object of Bass's gaze emphasizes the power of his anger as it is directed at the enslaver, or at least at the enslaver's assessment of Bass. The reader-viewer must negotiate the overlapping roles in which the comic places them.

In comics art, the range of "slither" is quite wide. Any direct gaze moment on a comics page might position the reader-viewer in the place of an object or person upon which the character gazes; might place the reader in the position of a different character's vantage point, making the directly gazing character the other character's object (as in the point-of-view shot in film); or might leave quite unclear (which is rare in prose narrative) whether the character is, indeed, looking at anything aside from the viewer-reader. Any direct gaze moment might be undertaken by a minor or a major character, regardless of whether they are also narrators, and neither need ever speak or be positioned as a "you." Indeed, the dynamic visual narrative of a comics page might include any of the combinations above, even synthesizing several at once or in sequence (as in a shot/reverse shot dynamic that carries out an intense encounter between two characters).

Furthermore, the rapidly shifting visual perspectives of which a comics page is capable—as well as its difference from film in the "all-at-onceness" (Chute, *Why* 25) of a multipanel comics page's visual effect—compounds what David Herman calls "the ontological hesitation" resulting from second-person prose narration's "constant repositioning [of] readers" (379). Such readers are often "suspended between a fictive world and [their] own real world" or, more precisely, "stand simultaneously inside and outside the fiction" (385). Indeed, the fourth wall the direct gaze breaks can be understood as a permeable gutter between the reader and the character, each gesturing beyond their own frames (which are also situated in relation to other frames on the page) in a dance of textual and readerly dynamics. Jarmila Mildorf discerns between textually playful second-person prose narration, like that of postmodern metatextuality, which invites an intellectual "aesthetic-reflexive involvement," and more emotive instances of second-person narration that elicit an "affective-emotional involvement," which she aligns with notions of empathy (148). The comics page is able to combine Mildorf's dichotomy of aesthetic-reflexive and affective-emotional involvement, for the closure the reader performs in a direct gaze moment is an intellectual as well as an interpersonal act, often carried out on several levels of interpretive and emotional possibility at once.

Yang's text is not a second-person text per se; its narration is constituted by a combination of first and third person, with Jin's section in the first person, past tense. Thus, the direct gaze moments are a rhetorical trope that does not permeate, but rather punctuates, key moments in Jin's and the implied reader-viewer's transaction with his ideological environment. Aiming his transactional gaze at the reader, Jin's direct eye contact develops in a pattern that demands nuanced reactions to his fraught experience as a Chinese American boy in a predominantly white public school in the United States, a reaction that blurs the reader's ontological position as part of and yet apart from Jin's world and the ideologies that permeate it.[10] Thus, through the direct gaze, the text implicates the viewer in the same ideologies with which Jin wrestles, and it implicates them as partner in his struggle. Energizing the reader's transactional gaze, Jin's second-person visual addresses thwart voyeuristic or objectifying readerly experiences even as they also signal the need to both understand and critique Jin's behavior, and all the while they indict the ideologies that conspire to influence them.

Consider, for instance, Jin's first introduction to his classroom (30–31; figures 4.10 and 4.11), which over its two-page spread positions the reader, in various turns, as (1) one of many students in the class, (2) a confidante sharing a "knowing glance" with the quietly frustrated Jin, (3) Jin himself being spoken to by a classmate, and (4) an undetermined person (could be Jin or a classmate) locking eyes with his classmate Suzy. On the right-hand page, direct eye contact with the reader occurs in every panel but the last. In the first and third panel on that page, the reader is positioned as part of the class of students staring at Jin. The attitudes of his new class and his teacher align with anti-Asian sentiment in the United States; one student asks an ethnocentric question about Jin's cuisine, and the teacher, even before her ignorant remarks on this page, has already mispronounced Jin's straightforward name and claimed he moved from China rather than San Francisco (30; figure 4.10). The reader, then, must handle the cognitive and emotional dissonance of these second-person moments, which physically position them as sharing the ocular vantage point of racist white Americans but also expose—as communicated via Jin's eyes—their effect on Jin. Jin's direct gaze might be read as concerned, his eyebrows slightly arched as he looks out at his classmates. As an address to the viewer, however, his gaze might also be interpreted as a plea for solidarity as he endures the anxiety-producing experience of being the new kid in a racially hostile environment.

Furthermore, the reader-viewer's identification with the class is also destabilized by the middle top panel, which positions them as Jin facing the uninviting gaze of his aggressive classmate. The oscillation between Jin and not-Jin carried out in the top panels imbues the perspective-taking the text elicits with the same tension about "Asian" and "American" that drives Jin's later transformation into Danny—the resulting image of his ethnic rejection. Thus, while the transformation into Danny does not happen for some time, the conditions that create it are made manifest and visceral from this moment in the text. In addition, given Ma's assessment of Jin as a "semi-autobiographical image crystallizing Yang's own experience of growing up in a racial climate wherein he has been too often treated as the object of race" (67), Jin's direct gaze can be read as a poignant confirmation of Jin as subject, and his subjectivity—and the visual transactions influencing it—as a key concern of the text. Indeed, using complex eye expression and gaze implications to depict that subjectivity is itself an antiracist stance in a story about a boy whose nation often uses derogatory eye references to denigrate its Asian population. Given that the storyline involving Chin-Kee rarely depicts Chin-Kee's eyes as anything more than slits, *American Born Chinese*'s depiction of—and positioning the reader as partaking in—Jin's direct gaze denies the one-dimensionality Jin's peers and social surround might force upon him and instead affirms the complexity of his experience.

The hierarchy of American over Asian as produced in Jin's school is further limned by the third panel, in which the reader is visually addressed by both Jin's teacher and Jin. Here, the reader must negotiate between the teacher's confident eye contact as she delivers her uninformed insight into Jin's family's habits and past and Jin's concerned gaze, positioned physically beneath hers, as if he is peeking trepidatiously over the gutter

Figure 4.10. Jin introduced to his new class (Yang 30). Fair use.

at the reader. That the frames cut off his mouth twice signals his voicelessness in a discursive space visually filled by the teacher's and classmates' dialogue. And finally, in the bottom panels, we might be Jin or Jin's white classmates, both away from whom Suzy Nakamura might turn her eyes in avoidance of participating in the class's assumptions about arranged marriages and Asian people. Thus, Suzy also turns her initial gaze—which might be interpreted as trepidatious, interested, or hopeful—away from us, not just conveying but eliciting the feeling of a lost connection due to the exclusionary ideologies at work in the school. The sudden lack of eye contact with the reader-viewer in this final panel closes the page on a note of isolation, setting the reader adrift even as it instills a sort of distant intimacy with both Jin's and Suzy's experiences.

Figure 4.11. Jin introduced to his new class, cont'd (Yang 31). Fair use.

If Jin's direct gaze in this panel exhibits only a possible plea to the reader due to the reader's often shared vantage point with his classmates, Yang strengthens the viewer-Jin transaction in a subsequent scene, where Jin has been forced to be friends with an unhygienic bully a grade above him. The verbal narration in this sequence is tonally neutral if taken by itself; only in conjunction with the images exhibiting "Peter the Eater" consuming boogers—and Peter's speech bubble text threatening he'd make Jin join him—does the narration achieve its deadpan delivery (34). On one page, that delivery is further augmented by Jin's direct gaze, which collapses older, past-tense narrator and younger, present action Jin into one narrative force with no one other than the reader implicated as narratee (35; figure 4.12). As Peter engages Jin in games that harm or offend him, Jin's insistent eye contact with the viewer in the top three panels

Figure 4.12. Peter the Eater with Jin (Yang 35). Fair use.

is the method by which the text exhibits Jin's exasperation. In essence, these moments of direct gazing function as theatrical asides, drawing the reader close to Jin without the other character's knowledge.

These second-person moments in this scene perform closest to the way Mikkonen theorizes a particular aspect of the direct gaze: it engages the reader-viewer "in a make-believe exchange of looks and create[s] an effect of shared subjective perspective" (86). Peter, as Jin conveys and the reader is positioned to understand, is neither a desirable nor a good friend. To phrase the effect via Goffman's work on linguistic interaction, the reader here becomes a fully "ratified participant" (10) in the reader-character relationship, one acknowledged by the (visual) interlocutor, Jin. Thus, no longer inhabiting the ambiguous, potentially "unratified" position resulting from the "superimpos[ition]"

Figure 4.13. Wei-Chen introduced to Jin's class (Yang 36). Fair use.

(Herman 381) of their role over that of someone else within the diegetic world of the text, the reader is positioned to emerge from this scene as a legitimate second-person recipient of Jin's direct gaze, an experience that orients their subsequent responses to Jin for the duration of the text, whether they are subsequently superimposed or not. The knowingness with which the reader-viewer is prompted to come away from this moment speaks, too, to the tensions embedded in Jin's ability to form relationships. Peter and Jin's "friendship" (Yang 34) is a result of Jin's ethnic estrangement even as it is the method by which Jin and the reader cement their transactional bond. The lower panel (figure 4.12) exhibits the loneliness Jin feels when Peter has moved away at the same time that the page breaks eye contact with the viewer, removing the intimate connection with Jin and emphasizing that feeling.

The bond between Jin and the reader is troubled by the acculturating forces of Jin's environment at work upon his relationship with his racial identity, involving an ongoing transactional gaze with the comic's visual markers of anti-Asian ideologies. Those markers begin to include Jin's own figure, as such ideologies manifest in his attitudes toward people at school and are often implied or emphasized by his gaze. Yang's portrayal of new classmate Wei-Chen's arrival in Jin's class—in a scene that visually and verbally rhymes with Jin's first day at school—employs several layers of second-person superimposition (36; figure 4.13). Melissa Schieble points out that in Wei-Chen's introductory moment, "Yang positions Jin as aligned with his classmates (both in stature and expression)," signaling, along with the verbal text about Jin's desire "to beat him up," Jin's "internalized oppression of the characteristics he sees in Wie Chen [sic] that remind him of his own shame about his Chinese identity" (51). Certainly Jin's internalized oppression is at play here, but Jin's face requires further investigation, especially as his gaze compares to its appearance in the earlier panel (figure 4.10). Here, Jin's eyebrows lower into a straight line rather than maintain an arch of concern, and they do not mimic his seat partner's wide-eyed look of surprise; his mouth is also not cut off but set in a slight frown—as is the mouth of the rude question asker in the previous scene. These signals suggest that the reader is positioned not to respond empathetically to Jin's concerned plea for understanding, as in the first scene, but rather to respond to Jin's hard look in our direction, which, read this way, seems to refuse the connection the text has heretofore elicited.

The visual layers here run deep. The panels may rhyme, but it is imperfect rhyme. Jin has visually taken the place of the initial question asker, who shared his frown, and our vantage point aligns us with Wei-Chen, fending off the unwelcoming gaze of his new and more powerful classmate. Further, when we are aligned with current-Jin's ocular perspective in the bottom left panel, Wei-Chen proxies as past-Jin, for whom the earlier scene elicited our empathy. Wei-Chen, however, does not make the direct eye contact with us that Jin does during his class introduction, so Jin remains our narrator and our main visual interlocutor. The visual pedagogy of this page, leaving our understanding of Wei-Chen's feelings as a foregone conclusion, seems instead to prompt a certain level of exchange with current-Jin, whose direct gaze, in its hardness, might also be taken as an expression requesting a shared nod of understanding and perhaps a head tilt of evaluation. Indeed, such understanding is not the same as the agreement elicited regarding the Peter the Eater situation; this understanding leaves room for the critique of interpellated subjectivity that the transactional gaze makes possible. Jin's face here matches Tomo Hattori's description of the "mask of attempted white normalcy that conceals [Asian American youths'] quiet racial desperation as their souls are crushed by the systemic racial discrimination of classmates, teachers, and society" (29). Jin is attempting to claim his belonging in a white American space by rejecting a version of himself, and his direct glare forces us to register the logic of his actions, even as it signals the cruelty of the stance. The fourth wall gutter between the reader-viewer and the character is the space in which the text employs the transactional gaze to offer Jin's subjectivity for examination. That gaze, in pushing us away as Wei-Chen, also brings us closer as confidante of Jin.

This push and pull persists throughout the text, punctuated and reoriented over and over by direct gaze moments. To name a few, Jin looks to the reader-viewer when he achieves the courage to ask the girl he likes on a date (105), when his white friend implies his unworthiness (180–81), when he emerges transformed as white-presenting Danny (194), and when he returns to his depiction as Jin (214).[11] Throughout the text, direct gazes align the reader with various and contrasting subject positions through physical vantage points, transferring ontological instability onto the reader-viewer. Transacting on many levels across the fourth wall gutter with the text's evolving characters, the reader-viewer is continually implicated in and confronted by the diegetic world's representation of ideologies of race in the United States. As Jin works through his thwarted sense of identity within exclusionary structures of hegemonic belonging, his moments of second-person visual address check in with a reader asked to understand and yet critique his choices as products of those very structures. Indeed, his gaze is itself a visual marker of ideologies that threaten to cut off his connection to his community; its demand to be met is part of the text's resistance to the isolation and division wrought by social hierarchies of race. The transaction is the goal. Turning away is not possible or productive.

CONCLUSION

Various elements endemic to the comics' form make it a site for potent materialization of the child gaze. Comics create a dynamic representation of eyes, sight lines, and objects of the gaze that the reader-viewer must follow and interpret as active participants who make meaning of the complex relation among visual cues. Furthermore, comics' relation to the figure of the child in American culture and its history of racial representation provide contexts that energize the visually coded interventions each of the above texts make in narratives of national belonging in the United States. Particularly important to this study is the way the visual, panel-to-panel narration of the medium creates conditions for the pedagogical directing and visceral eliciting of the reader-viewer's gaze, which is tethered to the child as locus.

This potency liaises in potentially promising ways with the trajectory of readers' encounters with the antiracist work accomplished by the child gaze in contemporary comics. Currently, there is an upswing in comics production from mainstream publishing houses, especially for those aimed at young readers, a phenomenon beginning in the later decades of the twentieth and continuing into the early decades of the twenty-first centuries (Tarbox and Abate 3). Graphic novels often appear on lists of exemplary texts for young people and, indeed, populate their own form-specific lists. Subgenres within the form abound—superhero, history, biography, fantasy, historical fiction, memoir, and so on—and librarians and educators, once positioned against the frivolous, immature, or even depraved reading thought to be inherently tied to comics,[12] now promote graphic narrative as a form tied to enjoyment as well as twenty-first-century critical thinking skills. Indeed, there is considerable research on the ways graphic narrative is particularly useful for working with reluctant readers, as well as much that positions comics not as a remedial means for reading intervention but as eliciting a type of literacy particularly important to contemporary readers living in worlds steeped in visual and multimodal rhetorics.[13] Comics' promotion of critical literacy, with specific attention to visual storytelling, recommends the form to classroom spaces as well as leisure reading.

Such a stance, especially for educators, is not without contest, however,[14] and comics scholars often criticize the way the term "graphic novel" came into parlance in order to raise comics to the elite or normalized status they were for so long denied (Hatfield 100ff). But we might look at the comics form as energizing from its very marginalization—like the child—the critique it manifests in the child gaze. Current calls for and celebrations of diversity in graphic narrative also suggest that the trends at work in the texts discussed above will continue to perform their important—and necessary—interventions (NCTE, with Laura M. Jiménez). Redirecting viewer attention from hegemonic narratives at the center of a more conservative American canon, the pedagogy of the materialized child gaze in the comics form offers a corrective to narrow understandings of race, racial conflict, and the ways the marginalized child can be tied to the ideals of rebellion and value in the United States.

Epilogue

ENVISIONING AVENUES FOR FURTHER STUDY

The child gaze is a powerful narrative tool at work in twentieth- and twenty-first-century US literature, specifically in its capacity to interrogate exclusionary notions of national belonging. By turning away from, targeting, or transacting with visual markers of discrimination, the children in texts like those studied here provoke a critique of US structures that gatekeep power in a country that continues to privilege white, Christian, middle-class lives over others. The child enters this conversation, however, through its own subversive relation to the country, tied to the ideals of rebellion and youthfulness on which the nation is also supposed to be built. Across several different genres and forms aimed at adult and child audiences, child figures wield the subversive, nonvocal discourse of the gaze appreciatively, countersurveillantly, and transactionally, manifesting a narrative technique intervening in narrow paradigms that need to be widened and dangerous hierarchies that need to be flattened.

The primary texts studied in *The Child Gaze: Narrating Resistance in American Literature* were chosen for their representativeness of literature evoking the ways of looking I theorize and examine. At first, when confronted with the task of selecting such texts, I was overwhelmed by the potential choices. I expected that child characters would perform acts of looking in just about every text I picked up. Eye and gaze imagery are quick, efficient ways to make clear how characters orient not just spatially but attitudinally in their worlds, and they are also quick, efficient ways to convey the visual qualities of that world for the reader. My task was to find those moments of looking that seemed electric, charged with those ideological repercussions discussed throughout the preceding chapters of this study. As it turns out, not all books with child characters engage the child gaze in casual ways. Thus, texts that I assumed might "fit" here, it turns out, do not:

Jacqueline Woodson's *Brown Girl Dreaming*, for instance, largely because of the relative lack of literal attention to child looking. And some texts that do offer pointed attention to child looking do so in ways that fall outside of the scope of this project, either in terms of the categories of gazing I articulate here or in regards to the specific sociopolitical interventions—race, ethnicity, and class with overlapping considerations of gender and creed—that knit together the representative texts I discuss. It is to those other types of texts that this conclusion now turns in order to envision possibilities for further investigation into the child gaze as a narrative technique. They pose a valuable question: what other modes of the child gaze are at play in literature that complement or depart from those theorized here?

The theoretical work on the rise of the valued/valuing child laid out in chapter one's examination suggests that even outside of the appreciative gaze's scope, the child as a cultural figure possesses considerable capabilities for directing attention. I focus on texts that perform disruption of hegemonic narratives of national belonging, but some texts employ the child gaze to uphold them. My discussion of Betty Smith's *A Tree Grows in Brooklyn* reveals some of that power, and works like Laura Ingalls Wilder's *Little House on the Prairie* and Carol Ryrie Brink's *Caddie Woodlawn* are also complicit, through the children's acts of looking, in upholding some of the hegemonic values against which the gazes detailed in this project contend. In another mode that is perhaps less engaged with the "priceless" child construction, George from *Call Me Charley* also exemplifies this stance, performing a surveillant child gaze that reflects the dangerous cultural transmission of discrimination within family and neighborhood. As Jennifer Ho points out, we need work on "the way whiteness operates, narratologically" (216), and the child gaze is a possible avenue for exploring how texts sanction white supremacist ideologies.

Considering literature that troubles the notions of childhood brought to bear upon this project also widens the possibilities for study. My work relies on fairly widespread understandings of childhood in the United States, but other conceptions of childhood demand attention. For instance, how does literature by Indigenous writers employ Indigenous-centered constructions of the child and Indigenous-centered practices of looking—as well as draw on Indigenous narrative techniques—to enact a child gaze with valences of social critique? Recent works such as Tim Tingle's *How I Became a Ghost* and Angeline Boulley's *The Firekeeper's Daughter* contain child looking that matters intensely to the progression of their stories; how have Indigenous authors put forth ideas about child and gaze that enact narrative cues?

In addition, this book refrains from a discussion of sex and sexuality in relation to the child, but the May 2021 Let's Talk about Sex in YA conference at the University of Cambridge as well as developments in queer theory concerned with the child suggest that acts of looking in relation to sexuality liaise with complex considerations of youth, desire, embodiment, and identity. Melinda Lo's recent *Last Night at the Telegraph Club* is saturated with curious and desirous gazing, both blatant and covert, and while touchstone texts like Judy Blume's *Forever* and James Baldwin's *Go Tell It on the Mountain* are heavily analyzed for their representations of teen sexuality and queer perspectives, respectively, specific attention to literal acts of looking can help us map new narratologies of burgeoning desire. For instance, transactional gazing is often in play in such texts, sometimes with attensities outside of the scope of ideological visual markers. But there are also silences that remove the gaze from the transactional mode, refraining from exploration of subjectivity—either in mimicry of the child's inability to articulate what they are feeling or to quiet but still signal taboo thought in eras and locales rife with dangerous discrimination. It is intriguing to consider what type of child gaze theorization such texts make possible.

Disability studies has also focused on the gaze—often a stare—trained upon those with disabilities. Scholarly work on such looking, ranging from Michel Foucault's concept of the clinical gaze to Rosemary Garland-Thomson's theories on staring as site of both power struggle and potentially generative interpersonal engagement, readies scholars for explorations of child looking from a disability studies perspective.[1] What does literature offer in terms of these formulations of staring on the part of the child, especially as a point of deflection, reflection, and transformation of the gaze? Further, what connections among disability, race, and sexuality arise in the literary archive of the child gaze?

Keener attention to the work of the gaze within particular genres is worth consideration as well. For instance, *March* and *Bass Reeves* provide inroads to thinking about nonfiction texts, but allohistory and some of the narrative threads in *American Born Chinese* not discussed at length here are as close as this book's archive gets to speculative or fantasy fiction. The latter is a genre where hegemonic structures are often reproduced with defamiliarization and thus worth considering in relation to how speculative fiction employs a child gaze as a subversive element of social critique—or as a narrative cue to maintain the status quo. In Madeleine L'Engle's *A Wrinkle in Time*, for instance, the children look with horror upon the extreme conformity enforced on the planet where their father is being held prisoner, and in Lois Lowry's *The Giver*, acts of looking resonate narratively and thematically in a society where the ability to see in color begins an ethical and political revolution for the young protagonist. Akwaeke Emezi's *Pet* and Nisi Shawl's *Speculation* literalize and thematize intergenerational ways of seeing that reveal untold stories and facilitate magical revelations that resonate politically.

Furthermore, what does memoir provide in terms of raw material for the study of the child gaze? Many memoirs begin in childhood, and they contain early scenes that create poignant moments of insight or discovery, some of which matter significantly to the subject's later life. bell hooks roots her theories of the gaze in her experiences as a Black girl, for instance (*Black*). What modes of looking occur in these works of literature and with what effect?

Chapter four discusses how comics' use of the child gaze draws from the power of verbal-visual narration to energize its implications, and other forms contain unique elements that can lend weight to children's acts of looking. I only discuss one picture book in this study, and picture books—with robust scholarship thereon—provide an exciting archive to connect to and build on this work. Forms like drama and film are also intriguing, for their spatial, audio, and visual dimensions create rich opportunities for studying the directorial effects of the child gaze for an audience. I think about how Lorraine Hansberry's *A Raisin in the Sun*'s curtain rises to reveal a stage where the lone young child character, Travis, is positioned at its literal center. What does his way of looking contribute to the story—both in Hansberry's unabridged script and in its many stage adaptations—of this intergenerational household dreaming beyond the bounds of racist housing segregation?

Finally, it's worth considering at further length the vantage point of the child in relation to that upon which they look. In all of the texts in this study, the child on which I focus is a part of the community or identity category that their gaze, implicitly or explicitly, promotes or defends. However, texts such as Matt de la Peña's *Last Stop on Market Street*, which I earlier reference as a text that inherits the orientation of the appreciative gaze, merit further attention since protagonists can gaze in appreciation upon a community that is actually not theirs. In *Market Street*'s case, this is so by way of class and geographical position in the neighborhood. And of course, if we step outside the boundary of US literature from the 1930s to the present, other literary landscapes provide opportunities to examine the child as a potent wielder of the gaze. Some nations contain similar or analogous hierarchies to those of the United States, combined with their own constructions of the child and their own mores of looking. How does a child gaze signal, narratively, in other sociopolitical contexts both like and unlike the one under study here?

The above discussion, often interspersed with questions, suggests that elements of this study may be portable to other types of literature, but it also emphasizes that this work is only the beginning of the breadth and depth with which literary and cultural studies might consider the child gaze as a site of analysis for narrative and its relation to cultural critique and hegemonic dominance. As general categories, appreciation, countersurveillance, and transaction may cross through borders of time and space, but they manifest differently in the storyworlds and narrative affordances of their texts. It is the nuances with which they do so—and the ways they may liaise with other modes of looking that bolster or complicate them—that open up avenues of study for ongoing inquiry into the child gaze.

NOTES

INTRODUCTION: THE POWER AND POSSIBILITIES OF CENTERING CHILD SIGHT LINES

1. See Anna Mae Duane's *Suffering Childhood in Early America: Violence, Race, and the Making of the Child Victim*; Caroline F. Levander's *Cradle of Liberty: Race, the Child, and National Belonging from Thomas Jefferson to W. E. B. Du Bois*; and Karen Sánchez-Eppler's *Dependent States: The Child's Part in Nineteenth-century American Culture*.

2. See Julia Mickenberg's *Learning from the Left: Children's Literature, the Cold War, and Radical Politics in the United States*; Katharine Capshaw's *Civil Rights Childhood: Picturing Liberation in African American Photobooks*; Nazera Sadiq Wright's *Black Girlhood in the Nineteenth Century*; Lara Saguisag's *Incorrigibles and Innocents: Constructing Childhood and Citizenship in Progressive Era Comics*; and Emily A. Murphy's *Growing Up with America: Youth, Myth, and National Identity, 1945 to Present*.

3. This is not to say that there is no difference, of course; it is rather to say that differences within the categories "child" and "adult," as Marah Gubar points out, are extraordinarily diverse and that the texts included in this study suggest the spectrum of nuance along which even fictional representations of children view and participate differently in the world.

4. See, for instance, Alban; Berger; Butler; Browne; Du Bois; Elkins; Fanon; Foucault, *Discipline*; Mitchell; Mirzoeff; Mulvey; hooks, *Black*; Rony; Said; Yancy.

5. For a discussion of focalization, see Genette; Rimmon-Kenan.

6. While "diegetic" and "extradiegetic" are terms often associated with the position of a narrator—e.g., whether they are a participating character in the story or part of the storyworld or an entity that does not participate in the story or exist within the storyworld—they are terms useful in relation to other elements of a narrative as well. When I use them to refer to the context and effect of the literary representation of a child gaze, I use "diegetic" to refer to its occurrence within the storyworld and "extradiegetic" to refer to its use as a narrative tool. "Extratextual" refers to actual or potential impact outside of the text altogether; in the case of the child gaze theorized here, "extradiegetic" and "extratextual" are closely related in terms of cuing the implied reader's response. See Rimmon-Kenan 92 for another use detached from narrator positionality.

7. See Herman et al. 111 and the works of Rabinowitz and Phelan for further information about the mimetic, thematic, and synthetic dimensions of character.

8. For related discussions, see Frederick Luis Aldama's edited collection *Analyzing World Fiction: New Horizons in Narrative Theory* and Hyesu Park's monograph *Alterity and Empathy in Post-1945 Asian American Narratives: Narrating Other Minds*.

9. I discuss this moment and others in Jackson's novel at further length in chapter two, suggesting that the withholding of Charley's comment works to create a sort of "museum silence" that fosters acute readerly attention.

10. See Day's *Reading Like Girl: Narrative Intimacy in Contemporary American Young Adult Literature* and Cadden's *At Arm's Length: A Rhetoric of Character in Children's and Young Adult Literature* and *Telling Children's Stories: Narrative Theory and Children's Literature*.

CHAPTER ONE: THE APPRECIATIVE CHILD GAZE: VALUING VISIONS OF MARGINALIZED CHILDHOODS

1. See Gary D. Schmidt's *Making Americans: Children's Literature from 1930 to 1960* and Leonard C. Marcus's *Minders of Make-Believe: Idealists, Entrepreneurs, and the Shaping of American Children's Literature* for a broader discussion of the library and publishing worlds' uneven engagement with progressive values leading up to and during this time.

2. Public school curricula continue to be battlegrounds for hashing out which viewpoints best befit "an American," not the least because what is at stake is whether such viewpoints should be infused into the child as a student and US citizen.

3. Mickenberg notes several exceptions, which she emphasizes as such, in her fourth chapter.

4. See Kenton Clymer, "The Ground Observer Corps: Public Relations and the Cold War in the 1950s."

5. Reflections of cultural gifts attitudes abound in this text, and as Cummins has demonstrated, Taylor practiced progressive politics ("Leaning Left"). That orientation is not surprising for a Jewish woman who came of age during the cultural gifts movement, in which Jewish activists played a crucial role (Selig 11). As Mickenberg has pointed out, children, and therefore children's publishing, remained a "repository for the social vision of the 1930s" (131) and well into the Cold War era, when *All-of-a-Kind Family* (and later books in the same series) was published. The Association of Jewish Libraries claims in a 2004 "companion" booklet for the novel that the text "gave non-Jewish readers a glimpse of Jewish life," and "it helped Jews feel accepted in American culture" (5). Their inclusion of "discussion questions," "extension activities," and recommendations for similar novels suggests the text's continued relevance over fifty years after its initial publication.

6. Boggs argues that the text, "talk[s] b(l)ack to the hegemonic discourse of standard English through the violation of standard rules of grammar, syntax, and vocabulary" ("Of Mimicry" 130). Certainly Baldwin's use of Black English confronts conventionally approved standards of writing, but not through mimicry or violation. As linguists have demonstrated and as Baldwin himself has argued, Black English has its own grammar and vocabulary that cannot be reduced to mimicry or violation and that rather constitutes a powerful language of resilience and artistic expression (Green; Baldwin, "If"). *Little Man, Little Man*'s Black English narration underscores the text's honoring of the Black child's voice and perspective.

7. Boggs puts forth a different reading of focalization in the text, mentioning that it employs a "roving narrative voice [that] approximates" various child characters through free indirect discourse couched in the voice of an unnamed Black child ("Baldwin" 132; "Of Mimicry" 130). While the picture book's avoidance of an intradiegetic first-person narrator may make this reading possible metaphorically, my analysis is grounded in the way the narratorial dynamics of the text continually and consistently foreground TJ's perspective without modulation among characters.

8. For an examination of the way music also contributes to *Little Man, Little Man*'s construction of Black childhood, see DeCoste.

9. All use of bold text throughout the remainder of the document reflects the original typography of *Little Man, Little Man: A Story of Childhood*.

10. Boggs has focused on Blinky rather than TJ as a model for looking in the text due to the attention given to her glasses. Boggs's convincing reading of Blinky posits her gaze as "queer-sighted," disrupting narratives of Black masculinity and allowing the text to "speak to the unrepresented lives of those queer children in Harlem who have been silence and marginalized by historical and institutional forces because of their 'deviant' sexualities" ("Of Mimicry" 124).

11. As scholar Amy Fish points out in her Public Books essay following the republication of the picture book in 2018, the children in the text "receive the care, however imperfect, of neighborhood adults."

12. The text abounds with many more complex situations that receive the care of both narrative voice and illustrator, consistently gesturing to the weighty consideration TJ invites. In particular, see the scenes with Mrs. Beanpole (Baldwin and Cazac 49ff) and the final scene with Mr. Man and his wife (83ff).

CHAPTER TWO: THE COUNTERSURVEILLANT CHILD GAZE: LOOKING BACK AT AUTHORITY

1. See, for instance, Epstein et al.; Goff et al.

2. Surveillance studies is an interdisciplinary field characterized by contributions from scholars of political science, criminology, economics, philosophy, sociology, and other areas of study. See, for instance, the work of Browne; Marx; Lyon; and Monahan.

3. For further discussion of Till in relation to dangerous looking, see hooks, *Black* 118.

4. For instance, at least one of the students who filmed the school resource officer's assault that I describe at the start of this chapter was arrested for her act and taken to a detention center. Her name is Niya Kenny, and she is now part of Represent Justice, an organization devoted to using media to raise awareness about the need for change in the justice system ("Niya Kenny").

5. See Melamed 51–70 for an examination of racial liberalism in relation to the race novel; see Capshaw 4–7 for a discussion of interracial friendship as a preferred race liberal narrative (especially for children) during the Cold War; see Schmidt and Marcus for the whiteness of the twentieth-century children's publishing industry, a whiteness that persists today.

6. The text spells out the racial slur in its entirety, as do other texts under discussion here. As a white researcher and writer who has no business reproducing verbal violence

in my own writing, I have chosen to use stars to indicate that the slur exists in the text. There is, however, one image in this chapter (figure 2.1) that contains a variant of this slur. Because it is a crucial part of an image reproduced as it appears in the text under discussion, it has not been altered.

7. There is even a full-page illustration of George performing such surveillance; see Jackson 31.

8. Note that the text equivocates about Charley's confrontation with George by casting his response in the language of boyhood rivalry. The same is also true of scenes where George's confrontations are openly racist, as when he hurls derogatory language at Charley in the first chapter, and Charley's responses are in line with general name-calling retorts: "My name is Charles. . . . Nobody calls me [slur] and gets away with it" (8). When George persists, "Charley's lips moved as if he were going to say something and had changed his mind" (8), in the text's gesture toward that which is unspoken.

9. Ecological theories of perception are discussed further in chapter three's theorizing of the transactional child gaze.

10. See Greenwell for a reading of the way this scene and others in *Call Me Charley* make a subtle protest against segregated recreation.

11. As James Phelan notes in *Experiencing Fiction: Judgments, Progressions, and the Rhetorical Theory of Narrative*, a reader's experience of inferring the judgments a narrative implies is one of the great pleasures of reading textual subtleties (14).

12. See Michelle H. Martin's "Let Freedom Ring: Land, Liberty, Literacy and Lore in Mildred Taylor's Logan Family Novels" for remarks on how Taylor's series "emphasizes to readers that despite their age, young people just as often fall prey to crimes of injustice as do adults and ought therefore to fight prejudice wherever they find it—even if they happen to be, like protagonist Cassi Logan in *Roll of Thunder*, only nine years old" (374).

13. This novel and others in the Logan family series are well known; *Roll of Thunder* continues to be a key text taught in public schools or housed on classroom and school library shelves today (Martin; Schwebel). For a discussion of the important role of Taylor's Logan novels in the history of African American writing for young people, see Rudine Sims Bishop's *Free within Ourselves: The Development of African American Children's Literature*. Most recently, Erin Wyble Newcomb has emphasized the "transformative agency" working as a call to action in the pursuit of justice in several of these novels. Though Newcomb's work does not discuss the gaze, it remarks on how the text "mak[es] transparent the sociocultural apparatuses that skew justice and reinforce systems of oppression" (382).

14. For an analysis of the busing initiative and controversy, see Delmont.

15. See Rickford; Capshaw 159–61.

16. The American Legion wrote a flag code in 1923 that stipulated that the American flag be flown above all others. This code was widely distributed, and a standardized practice of ordering flags became law in 1942. Taylor's use of the word "transposed" suggests that Cassie is aware of the code (and perhaps suggests her reader is as well) and equally aware of the Jefferson Davis County School's choice to disregard it. It is also worth noting that the Mississippi flag remained unchanged into the era in which

the novel was written and well beyond; just recently, in 2021, the state adopted a redesigned flag that dropped the Confederate symbol.

17. See figure 2.1. I have included this image specifically because the chart is the only illustration in the entire text that insists upon its primacy for readerly consumption.

18. The reason seems to have to do with an accusation of his flirting with a woman heavily implied to be white, which recalls the accusations against Emmett Till as well as the crime "reckless eyeballing," mentioned above.

19. For a more pointed discussion of the way *Roll of Thunder* intervenes in the teaching of history, see Martin as well Yoo, "Rewriting."

20. Several informational features of Taylor's text, such as Cassie's recounting of the material in Mrs. Logan's lesson, as well as Mr. Morrison's straightforward explanation of his parents being from "breeding stock" (149–50), liken her work to the fictional Mrs. Logan's.

21. *The Plot against America* is categorized as a "Roth" book by the author himself, meaning that it is one of several novels narrated by a character named "Philip Roth." This narrative choice "invites the reader to accept the internal narrator as Philip Roth himself and the events presented as part of his own life story" (Cooper 243).

22. While Berger's work can apply to any text in which a character sees in culturally saturated ways, his work is especially helpful for thinking through Roth's use of the gaze, as *Plot* overtly engages with deeply rooted, culturally specific modes of looking that become upended due to severe changes in national leadership. That is, the text makes a provocative statement about the frightening implications of the fact that environment shapes vision by way of the contrast it evokes.

23. For a discussion of the way the novel's depiction of child vulnerability supports a reading of the story as "trauma under the sign of realism," see Pozorski.

24. Roth himself encourages this comparison by including the text of the real-world speech and a citation for its source in his postscript under the heading "Some Documentation" (385–90).

25. That the Lincoln Memorial plays a central role in his experience is fitting. US popular memory casts Lincoln as preserver of the union and abolisher of slavery, but these roles also recall the long life of slavery in the United States, the racialized social hierarchy and economy that continue in its wake, and, of course, the factions of its citizenry whose sociopolitical orientations trend toward exclusionary national practices. The scene in *Plot against America* at the Lincoln Memorial is one of several moments in the novel that obliquely reference the inequitable and violent treatment of African American people in the United States.

26. For a similar scene in an autobiographical text with significant attention to the child gaze, see Audre Lorde's recounting of her childhood trip to Washington, DC, in *Zami: A New Spelling of my Name* 68ff.

27. See Shiffman.

28. In 2020, HBO released a well-received miniseries adaptation of the novel by the same name, written by David Simon when he was impressed by the relevance of the text after the 2016 election. See Bilmes.

29. See Towns 1818.

CHAPTER THREE: THE TRANSACTIONAL CHILD GAZE: WRESTLING WITH IDEOLOGY IN THE VISUAL SURROUND

1. This reading of child figures wielding the transactional gaze as never apart from but always a part of their social contexts in US literature is similar to Christine Wilkie-Stibbs's conclusion about "outsider" child figures in texts across geopolitical contexts, a reading that "unseat[s] the dualism of the insider-outsider discourses in which the child appears to have been inextricably located" (19).

2. Rosenblatt draws on Dewey's sense of "transaction" as an epistemological concept that entangles person and environment, as opposed to the distance between separately defined entities implied by "interaction" ("Aesthetic Transaction" 122).

3. See, for example, the foundational work of art critic John Berger and ecological psychologists Eleanor Gibson and James Gibson; consider, too, the works of philosopher Eugene Freeman, psychologists Robert Shaw and Michael McIntyre, and the visual theorists discussed in chapter two's consideration of countersurveillance and oppositional looking (e.g., Du Bois, hooks, Rogoff, Rony).

4. Blau and Capetta follow Kugler et al.'s formulation of the "World Line" and apply it to fiction: "The World Line is a collection of events and affordances that are meaningful to a specific person (or character), which collectively constitute the complete narrative of that person's life" (Blau and Capetta 4).

5. See, for instance, Sánchez-Eppler on the child's "mutability" (xxv) and Levander on the child's "protean" characteristics in US rhetorics (5).

6. It is not coincidental that foundational ecological psychologist Eleanor Gibson focused on children as subjects for her studies of visual perception; her famous visual cliff experiment with infant and toddler subjects, for instance, wrapped together questions about visual perception, experience, learning, and decision-making in relation to the rapidly developing child.

7. Those opportunities, it is important to note, are themselves limited in the early 1970s' United States, when Cisneros says her father urged her to become a weather girl, since that was the only job he saw Latinas occupy on American television ("House").

8. For works engaging this debate, see Manzanas Calvo (who employs Gloria Anzaldúa's concept of "mestiza consciousness"), Dubb (who also engages Anzaldúa via "*los intersticios*"), Olivares, Maycock, Saber, Carden, and Roszak. Still other critics seem to mention both possibilities as coexisting, as with Hartley-Kroeger, for instance, and Sonia Alejandra Rodríguez argues for the text's status as *conocimiento* narrative, wherein Esperanza finds healing through leaving as well as writing.

9. Rosenblatt, champion of the transactional theory, explicitly disagrees with the notion of the "spectator stance," which is the formulation of James Britton ("Viewpoints" 44).

10. Many critics, of course, have noted the window as a motif in *The House on Mango Street*, but none have attended to it as a visual object in Esperanza's gaze. See, among others, Eysturoy 101ff, Saber 82ff, Maycock 224ff.

11. It is worth noting that the narration dilates over Esperanza's gaze upon Mamacita's entrance into the story: "The taxi door opened like a waiter's arm. Out stepped a tiny pink

shoe, a foot soft as a rabbit's ear, then the thick ankle, the flutter of hips.... All at once she bloomed. Huge, enormous, beautiful to look at.... I couldn't take my eyes off her tiny shoes.... Then we didn't see her" (77). Esperanza notices her window sitting as a sad corollary to the beauty she initially witnessed: "I think she cries. I would" (77).

12. It is worth noting the significance of *The House on Mango Street* to, as Rodríguez puts it, "the development not just of Chicanx literature or Latinx literature but of American literature" (156). However, as Rodríguez also points out, the text must not be treated as representative of all Chicanx and Latinx experiences.

13. See Althea Tait's "The Harm in Beauty" for a discussion of the way Morrison "talk[s] back" (85) to the "cultural tutorials" about ideal white beauty that have "colonized [the] reason" of African American women and children (79).

14. See also Klotman, Ortega, Werrlein, and Roye.

15. Further evidence for this reading lies in the fact that "LOOKLOOKHERECOMESAFRIENDTHE/FRIENDWILLPLAYWITHJANETHEYW/LLPLAYAGOODGAMEPLAYJANEPLAY" (193) serves as the chapter heading above this conversation; Pecola has manifested, through her split psyche and in an echo of the primer mandates, her own "friend" who can admire her eyes. That friend's interrogation of Pecola about her eyes and her father also speaks to her tortured subjectivity, now seemingly locked away from the world but forever bearing its mark. Indeed, such chapter headings, in capital case to proclaim their no-room-for-deviation authority, only appear in the third-person chapters that examine Pecola and her family, not those narrated by Claudia; collectively, they might thus be read as a fourth instance of the prologue passages fractured over the course of Pecola's focalized story.

16. This scene, like the Dick and Jane primer and Shirley Temple references, is of analytical interest in much scholarship on *The Bluest Eye*. I emphasize here Claudia's visual quest for the doll's magic, but for other readings, see, for example, Vásquez, Ortega, and Yancy.

17. Though *The Bluest Eye* is not a novel written for young people, Nodelman's assessment of the role of alternate narration in young adult literature and my rejoinder regarding novels that do center the "what" apply to that text as well, where a third-person narrator delves into the intricacies of Pecola's transactional gaze as well as the historical and familial legacies that inform it, and Claudia narrates her own experiences. But while that text employs the transactional child gaze to indict racist ideologies in the United States by demonstrating the extent to which her characters are inured to them, Reynolds and Kiely employ their characters' transactional gazes by demonstrating the ways the child might be empowered to defeat them.

18. See Tait's "Empathy" for a rumination on the rhetorical use of the Black child's injured body and its implications for the continued subjugation and dismissal of the Black mind.

19. Angie Thomas's *The Hate U Give* is a similar text employing a transactional child gaze that also contributes to this different trend.

20. Gabrielle Owen argues that relationality, rather than rigidly benchmarked developmental notions of growth, is a liberating paradigm through which to consider children's participation in the world (*Queer*).

CHAPTER FOUR: COMICS FORM AND MATERIALIZATION OF THE CHILD GAZE

1. *Bass Reeves* is the first installment of his project to bring to the fore, in the medium of comics written for young people, life stories that should resonate alongside what he refers to as the "greatest hits" of African American history (NPR staff). To date, there are three volumes. The second is *Bessie Stringfield* (2016) and the third is *Robert Smalls* (2021).

2. The child on the comics page may also look in myriad other as-yet-to-be-theorized ways, as the epilogue of this book discusses.

3. Each of these gazes is theorized in earlier chapters as follows: appreciative in chapter one, countersurveillant in chapter two, and transactional in chapter three.

4. For an extended discussion of ethnic and racial stereotypes in Progressive Era US comics featuring child characters in relation to immigration trends and discriminatory racial practices of the late nineteenth and twentieth century, see the first two chapters of Saguisag's *Incorrigibles and Innocents*.

5. It is worth noting that *March* somewhat troubles the larger-than-life place Rev. Dr. Martin Luther King, Jr. holds in popular narratives of the civil rights movement by calling attention to some of the political tensions between various leaders within the movement and highlighting their accomplishments.

6. For discussions of other ways *March* knits together temporalities, see Chaney and Davis-McElligatt.

7. While I mention the direct gaze in my discussion of this text, I reserve full analysis of its narrative importance for *American Born Chinese* later in the chapter—though I do also make reference to these images as a preface to my remarks on that text.

8. See Wanzo for a discussion of the way Danny's storyline with Chink-Kee employs caricatures of white masculinity alongside those of Asian stereotypes.

9. In much of the academic work on *American Born Chinese*, scholars have paid significant attention to the ways Yang employs the figures of Chin-Kee and the Monkey King (see, for instance, Ma, Song, and Wanzo). I take up Jin's storyline, which is comparatively underexamined in its realism.

10. For a brief discussion of the impact of Asian stereotypes on Asian American young people, including Yang's own autobiographical reflections thereon, see Ma 65–66.

11. For a discussion of masculinity and the problematic treatment of women in the text, especially in the Danny storyline, see Yoo, "Reconstructing."

12. See Tilley, "Seducing the Innocent."

13. See, for instance, James Buckey Carter's edited collection aimed at K–12 teachers, *Building Literacy Connections with Graphic Novels: Page by Page, Panel by Panel*.

14. See, for example, Hansen, "In Defense of Graphic Novels."

EPILOGUE: ENVISIONING AVENUES FOR FURTHER STUDY

1. See Foucault's *The Birth of the Clinic: An Archaeology of Medical Perception* and Garland's *Staring: How We Look*. The April 2022 conference of the Center for Material Culture Studies at the University of Delaware is dedicated to "The Disability Gaze," "considering disabled people as subjects and the power of their gazes as they claim and assert their own performance, identity, and even citizenship" (Van Horn et al.).

WORKS CITED

Abate, Michelle Ann, and Gwen Athene Tarbox. "Introduction: The Varied Landscape of Contemporary Children's and YA Comics." *Graphic Novels for Children and Young Adults: A Collection of Critical Essays*, edited by Michelle Ann Abate and Gwen Athene Tarbox, UP of Mississippi, 2017, pp. 3–16.

Alban, Gillian M. *The Medusa Gaze in Contemporary Women's Fiction: Petrifying, Maternal and Redemptive*. Cambridge Scholars Press, 2017.

Aldama, Frederick Luis, editor. *Analyzing World Fiction: New Horizons in Narrative Theory*. U of TP, 2011.

Althusser, Louis. *Lenin and Philosophy and Other Essays*. Trans. Ben Brewster, Monthly Review Press, 2001.

Anzaldúa, Gloria E. *Borderlands/La Frontera: The New Mestiza*. 1987. Second edition, Aunt Lute Books, 1999.

Arzamarski, Ryan, et al. "Effects of Intention and Learning on Attention to Information in Dynamic Touch." *Attention, Perception, & Psychophysics*, vol. 72, no. 3, 2010, pp. 721–35.

Association of Jewish Libraries. The All-of-a-Kind Family Companion. *Association of Jewish Libraries*, 2004, https://jewishlibraries.org/images/downloads/Sydney_Taylor_Book_Award/companion.pdf. Accessed 10 September 2019.

Bakhtin, Mikhail. "Discourse in the Novel." *The Dialogic Imagination: Four Essays by Mikhail Bakhtin*, edited by Michael Holquist, translated by Caryl Emerson and Michael Holquist, U of Texas P, 1981.

Baldwin, James. "If Black English Isn't a Language, Then Tell Me, What Is?" *New York Times*, 29 July 1979, https://archive.nytimes.com/www.nytimes.com/books/98/03/29/specials/baldwin-english.html?source=post_page. Accessed 20 April 2021.

Baldwin, James. "A Talk to Teachers." *Black Sons to Mothers: Compliments, Critiques, and Challenges for Cultural Workers in Education*, edited by M. Christopher Brown and James Earl Davis, Peter Lang, 2000, pp. 123–31.

Baldwin, James, and Yoran Cazac. *Little Man, Little Man: A Story of Childhood*. Dial Press, 1976.

Barthes, Roland. *Camera Lucida: Reflections on Photography*. Translated by Richard Howard. Hill and Wang, 1981.

Beeck, Nathalie Op de. "On Comics-Style Picture Books and Picture-Bookish Comics." *Children's Literature Association Quarterly*, vol. 37, no. 4, 2012, pp. 468–76.

Berger, John. *Ways of Seeing*. Penguin, 1997.

Bernstein, Robin. *Racial Innocence: Performing American Childhood from Slavery to Civil Rights*. New York UP, 2011.

Bernstein, Robin. "'Too Realistic' and 'Too Distorted': The Attack on Louise Fitzhugh's Harriet the Spy and the Gaze of the Queer Child." *Critical Matrix: The Princeton Journal of Women, Gender, and Culture*, vol. 12, no. 1–2, 2000, pp. 2–47.

Berry, Mary Frances. "'Reckless Eyeballing': The Matt Ingram Case and the Denial of African American Sexual Freedom." *The Journal of African American History*, vol. 93, no. 2, 2008, pp. 223–34. *JSTOR*.

Bilmes, David Simon. "'There's Nothing to Do but Have the Fight': David Simon, the Creator of The Wire, on His New Philip Roth Adaptation, *The Plot against America*, plus Trump, TV, Twitter and the Most Important Election of His Life." *Esquire*, 11 July 2020, https://www.esquire.com/uk/culture/tv/a33274502/david-simon-plot-against-america/. Accessed 18 February 2024.

Bishop, Rudine Sims. *Free within Ourselves: The Development of African American Children's Literature*. Greenwood Press, 2007.

Blau, Julia J. C., and Emily Rose Capetta. "World Line and Narrative Realism." *Journal of Creative Writing Studies*, vol. 5, no. 1, art. 9, pp. 1–18.

Boggs, Nicholas. "Baldwin and Yoran Cazac's 'Child's Story for Adults.'" *The Cambridge Companion to James Baldwin*, edited by Michele Elam, Cambridge UP, 2015, pp. 118–32.

Boggs, Nicholas. "Of Mimicry and (*Little Man Little*) Man: Toward a Queersighted Theory of Black Childhood." *James Baldwin Now*, edited by Dwight A. McBride, New York UP, 1999, pp. 122–60.

Bonheim, Helmut. "Narration in the Second Person." *Recherches Anglaises et Américaines*, vol. 16, 1983, pp. 69–80. *EBSCOhost*.

Britton, James. "Viewpoints: The Distinction between Participant and Spectator Role Language in Research and Practice." *Research in the Teaching of English*, vol. 18, no. 3, 1984, pp. 320–30.

Browne, Simone. *Dark Matters: On the Surveillance of Blackness*. Duke UP, 2015.

Butler, Judith. *Gender Trouble: Feminism and the Subversion of Identity*. 1990. Routledge, 1999.

Cadden, Mike. *At Arm's Length: A Rhetoric of Character in Children's and Young Adult Literature*. UP of Mississippi, 2021.

Cadden, Mike, editor. *Telling Children's Stories: Narrative Theory and Children's Literature*. U of Nebraska P, 2010.

Capshaw, Katharine. *Civil Rights Childhood: Picturing Liberation in African American Photobooks*. U of Minnesota P, 2014.

Carden, Mary Paniccia. *Sons and Daughters of Self-Made Men: Improvising Gender, Place, Nation in American Literature*. Bucknell University Press, 2010. *ProQuest Ebook Central*.

Caron, Tim. "'Black and White and Read All Over': Representing Race in Mat Johnson and Warren Pleece's *Incognegro: A Graphic Mystery*. Comics in the U.S. South," edited by Brannon Costello and Qiana Whitted, UP of Mississippi, 2012, pp. 138–60.

Carter, James Bucky, editor. *Building Literacy Connections with Graphic Novels: Page by Page, Panel by Panel*. NCTE, 2007.

Chaney, Michael A. *Reading Lessons in Seeing: Mirrors, Masks, and Mazes in the Autobiographical Graphic Novel*. UP of Mississippi, 2016.

Chute, Hillary. "Comics Form and Narrating Lives." *Profession*, 2011, pp. 107–17.

Chute, Hillary. *Why Comics? From Underground to Everywhere*. Harper, 2017.
Chute, Hillary, and Patrick Jagoda. "Special Issue: Comics and Media [Introduction]." *Critical Inquiry*, vol. 40, no. 3, 2014, pp. 1–10.
Cisneros, Sandra. *The House on Mango Street*. Random House, 2009.
Clymer, Kenton. "The Ground Observer Corps: Public Relations and the Cold War in the 1950s." *Journal of Cold War Studies*, vol. 15, no. 1, 2013, pp. 34–52.
Cooper, Alan. "It Can Happen Here, or All in the Family Values: Surviving *The Plot against America*." *Philip Roth: New Perspectives on an American Author*, edited by Derek Parker Royal, Praeger-Greenwood, 2005, pp. 241–54.
Crawford-Garrett, Katherine. "Leaving Mango Street: Speech, Action and the Construction of Narrative in Britton's Spectator Stance." *Children's Literature in Education*, vol. 40, no. 2, 2009, pp. 95–108.
Cummins, June. "Becoming an 'All-of-a-Kind' American: Sydney Taylor and Strategies of Assimilation." *Lion and the Unicorn*, vol. 27, no. 3, 2003, pp. 324–43.
Cummins, June. "Leaning Left: Progressive Politics in Sydney Taylor's *All-of-a-Kind Family* Series." *Children's Literature Association Quarterly*, vol. 30, no. 4, 2005, pp. 386–408.
Davis-McElligatt, Joanna C. "'Walk Together, Children': The Function and Interplay of Comics, History, and Memory in Martin Luther King and the Montgomery Story and John Lewis's *March: Book One*." *Graphic Novels for Children and Young Adults: A Collection of Critical Essays*, edited by Michelle Ann Abate and Gwen Athene Tarbox, UP of Mississippi, 2017, pp. 298–311.
Dawkins, Laura. "Black Babies, White Hysteria: The Dark Baby in African-American Literature of the Harlem Renaissance." *The American Child: A Cultural Studies Reader*, edited by Caroline F. Levander and Carol J. Singley, Rutgers UP, 2003, pp. 167–83.
Day, Sara K. "Looking." *Children's Literature Association Quarterly*, vol. 45, no. 1, 2020, p. 103.
Day, Sara K. *Reading Like Girl: Narrative Intimacy in Contemporary American Young Adult Literature*. UP of Mississippi, 2013.
DeCoste, Kyle. "Music All Up and Down the Street: Listening to Childhood in James Baldwin's *Little Man, Little Man*." *Journal of Popular Music Studies*, vol. 31, no. 3, pp. 57–72.
Delgado, Richard. "Storytelling for Oppositionists and Others: A Plea for Narrative." *Michigan Law Review*, vol. 87, no. 8, 1989, pp. 2411–41.
Delmont, Matthew F. *Why Busing Failed: Race, Media, and the National Resistance to School Desegregation*. U of California P, 2016.
Duane, Anna Mae. "Introduction. The Children's Table: Childhood Studies and the Humanities." *The Children's Table: Childhood Studies and the Humanities*, edited by Anna Mae Duane, U of Georgia P, 2013, pp. 1–14.
Duane, Anna Mae. *Suffering Childhood in Early America: Violence, Race, and the Making of the Child Victim*. U of Georgia P, 2010.
Dubb, Christina Rose. "Adolescent Journeys: Finding Female Authority in *The Rain Catches* and *The House on Mango Street*." *Children's Literature in Education*, vol. 38, no. 3, 2007, pp. 219–32.
Du Bois, W. E. B. *The Souls of Black Folk*. 1903. Oxford UP, 2007. *ESBSCohost*.
Dudziak, Mary L. *Cold War Civil Rights: Race and the Image of American Democracy*. Princeton UP, 2011.
Eisner, Will. *Graphic Storytelling and Visual Narration*. Norton, 2008.

Elkins, James. *The Object Stares Back: On the Nature of Seeing*. Harvest, 1996.

El Refaie, Elisabeth. "Transnational Identity as Shape-Shifting: Metaphor and Cultural Resonance in Gene Luen Yang's *American Born Chinese*." *Transnational Perspectives on Graphic Narratives: Comics at the Crossroads*, edited by Shane Denson et al., Bloomsbury, 2013, pp. 33–48.

Epstein, Rebecca, et al. "Girlhood Interrupted: The Erasure of Black Girls' Childhood." Georgetown Law Center on Poverty and Inequality, 2020. https://genderjusticeand opportunity.georgetown.edu/wp-content/uploads/2020/06/girlhood-interrupted.pdf.

Eysturoy, Annie O. *Daughters of Self-Creation: The Contemporary Chicana Novel*. U of New Mexico P, 1996.

Fanon, Frantz. *Black Skin, White Masks*. Translated by Charles Lam Markmann, Grove Press, 1982.

Fish, Amy. "Baldwin's Children." Public Books, Children's and YA Literature, 15 April 2019, https://www.publicbooks.org/baldwins-children/. Accessed 20 April 2019.

Fludernik, Monika. "Second-Person Narrative as a Test Case for Narratology: The Limits of Realism." *Style: A Quarterly Journal of Aesthetics, Poetics, Stylistics, and Literary Criticism*, vol. 28, no. 3, 1994, pp. 445–79. *EBSCOhost*.

Foucault, Michel. *The Birth of the Clinic: An Archaeology of Medical Perception*. Vintage Books, 1975.

Foucault, Michel. *Discipline and Punish: The Birth of the Prison*. Translated by Alan Sheridan. Vintage Books, 1977.

Freeman, Eugene. "Objectivity and the Transactional Theory of Perception." *Philosophic Exchange*, vol. 1, no. 3, 1972, pp. 59–73.

Gardner, Jared. "Same Difference: Graphic Alterity in the Work of Gene Luen Yang, Adrian Tomine, and Derek Kirk Kim." *Multicultural Comics: From "Zap" to "Blue Beetle,"* edited by Frederick Luis Aldama and Derek Parker Royal, U of Texas P, 2010, pp. 132–47.

Garland-Thomson, Rosemarie. *Staring: How We Look*. Oxford UP, 2009.

Gateward, Frances, and John Jennings. "Introduction: The Sweeter the Christmas." *The Blacker the Ink: Constructions of Black Identity in Comics and Sequential Art*, edited by Frances Gateward and John Jennings, Rutgers UP, 2015, pp. 1–15.

Genette, Gerard. *Narrative Discourse: An Essay in Method*. Translated by Jane E. Lewin. Cornell UP, 1980.

Gibson, Eleanor J. *Principles of Perceptual Learning and Development*. Appleton, 1969.

Gibson, James. J. *The Ecological Approach to Visual Perception*. 1979. Erlbaum, 1986.

Gill, Joel Christian. *Bass Reeves: Tales of the Talented Tenth*, no. 1. Fulcrum, 2016.

Goff et al. "The Essence of Innocence: Consequences of Dehumanizing Black Children." *Journal of Personality and Social Psychology*, vol. 106, no. 4, 2014, pp. 526–45.

Goffman, Erving. *Forms of Talk*. U of Pennsylvania P, 1981.

Green, Lisa J. *African American English: A Linguistic Introduction*. Cambridge UP, 2002.

Greenwell, Amanda M. "Jesse Jackson's *Call Me Charley*: Protesting Segregated Recreation in Cold War America." *Children's Literature*, vol. 45, 2017, pp. 92–113.

Groensteen, Thierry. *The System of Comics*. Translated by Bart Beaty and Nick Nguyen, UP of Mississippi, 2007.

Gubar, Marah. "The Hermeneutics of Recuperation: What a Kinship-Model Approach to Children's Agency Could Do for Children's Literature and Childhood Studies." *Jeunesse: Young People, Texts, Cultures*, vol. 8, no. 1, 2016, pp. 291–310.

Hall, Jacqueline Dowd. "The Long Civil Rights Movement and the Political Uses of the Past." *The Journal of American History*, vol. 91, no. 4, 2005, pp. 1233–63.

Hansen, Kathryn Strong. "In Defense of Graphic Novels." *English Journal*, vol. 102, no. 2, 2012, pp. 57–63.

Hartley-Kroeger, Fiona. "Silent Speech: Narration, Gender and Intersubjectivity in Two Young Adult Novels." *Children's Literature in Education*, vol. 42, no. 4, 2011, pp. 276–88.

Hatfield, Charles. "Graphic Novel." *Keywords for Children's Literature*, edited by Philip Nel and Lissa Paul, New York UP, 2011, pp. 100–105.

Hattori, Tomo. "The Monkey and the Colonoscopy Machine: On the Destruction of Racism and Stereotype in Gene Luen Yang's American Born Chinese and Level Up." *Growing Up Asian American in Young Adult Fiction*, edited by Ymitri Mathison, UP of Mississippi, 2018, pp. 23–40.

Hayes, Emma. "The Secret Garden and the Gaze." *The Looking Glass: Perspectives on Children's Literature*, vol. 19, no. 1, 2016, https://ojs.latrobe.edu.au/ojs/index.php/tlg/issue/view/62. Accessed 29 January 2024.

Heer, Jeet. "Racism as a Stylistic Choice and other Notes." *Comics Journal*, 14 March 2011, http://www.tcj.com/racism-as-a-stylistic-choice-and-other-notes/. Accessed 1 December 2018.

Herman, David. "Textual You and Double Deixis in Edna O'Brien's *A Pagan Place*." *Style: A Quarterly Journal of Aesthetics, Poetics, Stylistics, and Literary Criticism*, vol. 28, no. 3, 1994, pp. 378–410. *EBSCOhost*.

Herman, David, et al. *Narrative Theory: Core Concepts and Critical Debates*. Ohio State UP, 2012.

Ho, Jennifer Ann. "Afterword: Intersections and Future Connections." *Narrative, Race, and Ethnicity in the United States*, edited by James J. Donahue et al., Ohio State UP, 2017, pp. 208–17.

Hogan, Patrick Colm. *Affective Narratology: The Emotional Structure of Stories*. U of Nebraska P, 2011.

hooks, bell. *Art on My Mind*. The New Press, 1995.

hooks, bell. *Black Looks: Race and Representation*. South End Press, 1992.

hooks, bell. "Representing Whiteness in the Black Imagination." *Displacing Whiteness: Essays in Social and Cultural Criticism*, edited by Ruth Frankenberg, Duke UP, 1997, pp. 165–79.

"'House on Mango Street' Celebrates 25 Years." NPR, 9 April 2009, https://www.npr.org/templates/story/story.php?storyId=102900929. Accessed 20 January 2020.

Hughes, Langston. "Red-Headed Baby." *The Ways of White Folks*. 1933. Vintage Books, 1962.

Jackson, Jesse. *Call Me Charley*. Harper & Row, 1945.

Keen, Suzanne. "Intersectional Narratology in the Study of Empathy." *Narrative Theory Unbound: Queer and Feminist Interventions*, edited by Robyn Warhol and Susan S. Lanser, Ohio State UP, 2015, pp. 123–46.

Kim, Sue J. "What Asian American Studies and Narrative Theory Can Do for Each Other." *Narrative, Race, and Ethnicity in the United States*, edited by James J. Donahue et al., Ohio State UP, 2017, pp. 13–26.

Klotman, Phyllis R. "Dick-and-Jane and the Shirley Temple Sensibility in *The Bluest Eye*." *Black American Literature Forum*, vol. 13, no. 4, 1979, pp. 123–25.

Kokkola, Lydia. "The Embodied Child: An Introduction." *The Embodied Child: Readings in Children's Literature and Culture*, edited by Roxanne Harde and Lydia Kokkola, Routledge, 2017, pp. 1–20.

Kugler, Peter N., et al. "The Physics of Controlled Collisions: A Reverie about Locomotion." *Persistence and Change: Proceedings of the First International Conference on Event Perception*, edited by William. H. Warren, Jr. and Robert E. Shaw, vol. 2, Psychology Press, 1985.

Leeming, David. *James Baldwin: A Biography*. Henry Holt, 1994.

Levander, Caroline F. *Cradle of Liberty: Race, the Child, and National Belonging from Thomas Jefferson to W. E. B. Du Bois*. Duke UP, 2006.

Levander, Caroline F., and Carol J. Singley, editors. *The American Child: A Cultural Studies Reader*. Rutgers UP, 2003.

Lewis, John, et al. *March: Book 1*. Top Shelf Productions, 2013.

Lindenmeyer, Kriste. "Children, the State, and the American Dream." *Reinventing Childhood after World War II*, edited by Paula S. Fass and Michael Grossberg, U of Pennsylvania P, 2012, pp. 84–109.

Lorde, Audre. *Zami: A New Spelling of My Name*. Crossing Press, 1982.

Lyon, David. *The Culture of Surveillance: Watching as a Way of Life*. Polity, 2018. *ProQuest Ebook Central*.

Ma, Ning. "Beyond Race: The Monkey King and Creative Polyculturalism in Gene Luen Yang's *American Born Chinese*." *Inks: The Journal of the Comics Studies Society*, vol. 5 no. 1, 2021, pp. 61–78.

Manzanas Calvo, Ana M. "The House on Mango Street and Chicano Space." *Revista de Estudios Norteamericanos*, vol. 7, 2000, pp. 17–26. *EBSCOhost*.

Marcus, Leonard C. *Minders of Make-Believe: Idealists, Entrepreneurs, and the Shaping of American Children's Literature*. Houghton Mifflin Harcourt, 2008.

Martin, Michelle H. "Let Freedom Ring: Land, Liberty, Literacy and Lore in Mildred Taylor's Logan Family Novels." *Oxford Handbook of Children's Literature*, edited by Julia L. Mickenberg and Lynne Vallone, Oxford UP, 2011, pp. 371–88.

Marx, Gary T. "Surveillance Studies." *International Encyclopedia of the Social & Behavioral Sciences*, 2nd edition, 2015, pp. 733–41.

Marx, Gary T. "A Tack in the Shoe: Neutralizing and Resisting the New Surveillance." *Journal of Social Issues*, vol. 59, no. 2, 2003, pp. 369–90.

Marx, Gary T. *Undercover: Police Surveillance in America*. U of California P, 1989.

Marx, Gary T., and Valerie Steeves. "From the Beginning: Children as Subjects and Agents of Surveillance." *Surveillance & Society*, vol. 7, no. 3/4, 2010, pp. 192–230.

May, Elaine Tyler. *Homeward Bound: American Families in the Cold War Era*. Basic Books, 1988.

Maycock, Ellen C. "The Bicultural Construction of Self in Cisneros, Álvarez, and Santiago." *Bilingual Review/La Revista Bilingüe*, vol. 23, no. 3, 1998, pp. 223-29.

Melamed, Jodi. *Represent and Destroy: Rationalizing Violence in the New Racial Capitalism*. Minneapolis: U of Minnesota P, 2011.

Mickenberg, Julia L. *Learning from the Left: Children's literature, the Cold War, and Radical Politics in the United States*. Oxford UP, 2005.

Mikkonen, Kai. "Focalisation in Comics: From the Specificities of the Medium to Conceptual Reformulation." *Scandinavian Journal of Comic Art*, vol. 1, no. 1, 2012, pp. 69-95. *EBSCOhost*.

Mildorf, Jarmila. "Reconsidering Second-Person Narration and Involvement." *Language and Literature: Journal of the Poetics and Linguistics Association*, vol. 25, no. 2, 2016, pp. 145-58.

Mintz, Steve. "The Changing Face of Children's Culture." *Reinventing Childhood after World War II*, edited by Paula S. Fass and Michael Grossberg, U of Pennsylvania P, 2012, pp. 38-50.

Mirzoeff, Nicholas. *The Right to Look: A Counterhistory of Visuality*. Duke UP, 2011.

Mitchell, W. J. T. *Picture Theory: Essays on Verbal and Visual Representation*. U of Chicago P, 1995.

Monahan, Torin. "Counter-Surveillance as Political Intervention?" *Social Semiotics*, vol. 16, no. 4, 2006, pp. 515-34.

Monahan, Torin. *Surveillance and Security: Technological Politics and Power in Everyday Life*, Routledge, 2006.

Morgan, Shaun. "Race as Interpretive Lens: Focalization and Critique of Globalization in Jhumpa Lahiri's *Sexy*." *Narrative, Race, and Ethnicity in the United States*, edited by James J. Donahue et al., Ohio State UP, 2017, pp. 149-61.

Morris, Monique. *Pushout: The Criminalization of Black Girls in Schools*. The New Press, 2016.

Morrison, Toni. *The Bluest Eye*. 1970. Vintage Books, 2007.

Mulvey, Laura. "Visual Pleasure and Narrative Cinema." *Screen*, vol. 16, no. 3, 1975, pp. 6-18.

Murphy, Emily A. *Growing Up with America: Youth, Myth, and National Identity, 1945 to Present*. U of Georgia P, 2020.

NCTE, with Laura M. Jiménez. "Diversity in Graphic Novels." *Blog: Literacy and NCTE*, 28 August 2018, https://ncte.org/blog/2018/08/diversity-graphic-novels/. Accessed 14 April 2020.

Newcomb, Erin Wyble. "Transformative Agency and the Pursuit of Justice in Mildred Taylor's Logan Family Series." *Children's Literature Association Quarterly*, vol. 46, no. 4, 2021, pp. 379-400.

"Niya Kenny." Represent Justice, https://www.representjustice.org/team/niya-kenny/. Accessed 15 October 2023.

Nodelman, Perry. *Alternating Narratives in Fiction for Young Readers: Twice upon a Time*. Palgrave Macmillan, 2017.

NPR Staff. "'Strange Fruit' Shares Uncelebrated, Quintessentially American Stories." *All Things Considered*, 14 February 2015, http://www.npr.org/sections/codeswitch/2015/02/14/384947485/strange-fruit-shares- uncelebrated-quintessentially-american-stories. Accessed 22 February 2017.

Olivares, Julián. "Sandra Cisneros' *The House on Mango Street*, and the Poetics of Space." *Chicana Creativity and Criticism: Charting New Frontiers in American Literature*, edited by Maria Herrera-Sobek and Helena Maria Viramontes, Arte Publico, 1988, pp. 160–69.

Ortega, Gema. "The First of Many Heroines: Claudia's Dialogic Escape in Toni Morrison's *The Bluest Eye*." *South Atlantic Review*, vol. 83, no. 2, 2018, pp. 126–44.

Owen, Gabrielle. "Adolescence, Blackness, and the Politics of Respectability in *Monster* and *The Hate U Give*. *Lion and the Unicorn*, vol. 43, no. 2, 2019, pp. 236–60.

Owen, Gabrielle. *A Queer History of Adolescence: Developmental Pasts, Relational Futures*. U of Georgia P, 2020.

Park, Hyesu. *Alterity and Empathy in Post-1945 Asian American Narratives: Narrating Other Minds*. Routledge, 2022.

Paxton, Alexandra, et al. "The Case for Intersectionality in Ecological Psychology," *PsyArXiv*, 13 June 2019, https://osf.io/preprints/psyarxiv/jtmea. Accessed 29 January 2024.

Pérez, Roy. "Homo-Narrative Capture, Racial Proximity, and the Queer Latino Child." *Narrative, Race, and Ethnicity in the United States*, edited by James J. Donahue et al., Ohio State UP, 2017, pp. 193–207.

Phelan, James. *Experiencing Fiction: Judgments, Progressions, and the Rhetorical Theory of Narrative*. Ohio State UP, 2007.

Pozorski, Aimee. *Roth and Trauma: The Problem of History in the Later Works (1995–2010)*. Bloomsbury Academic, 2011.

Rabinowitz, Peter J. *Before Reading: Narrative Conventions and the Politics of Interpretation*. Cornell UP, 1987.

Rembowska-Płuciennik, Magdalena. "Second-Person Narration as a Joint Action." *Language and Literature: Journal of the Poetics and Linguistics Association*, vol. 27, no. 3, 2018, pp. 159–75.

Reynolds, Jason, and Brendan Kiely. *All American Boys*. Atheneum, 2015.

Rickford, Russell. *We Are an African People: Independent Education, Black Power, and the Radical Imagination*. Oxford UP, 2016.

Rifas, Leonard. "Race and Comix." *Multicultural Comics: From "Zap" to "Blue Beetle,"* edited by Frederick Luis Aldama and Derek Parker Royal, U of Texas P, 2010, pp. 27–38.

Rimmon-Kenan, Shlomith. *Narrative Fiction: Contemporary Poetics*. 1983. Routledge, 2002.

Rodríguez, Sonia Alejandra. "More than Esperanza: Revisiting Sandra Cisneros's *The House on Mango Street*." *Critical Explorations of Young Adult Literature: Identifying and Critiquing the Canon*, edited by Victor Malo-Juvera and Crag Hill, Routledge, 2020, pp. 152–67.

Rogoff, Irit. "Studying Visual Culture." *The Visual Culture Reader*, edited by Nicholas Mirzoeff, Routledge, 1998, pp. 14–26.

Romagnolo, Catherine. "Narrative Disidentification: Beginnings in Toni Morrison's *Song of Solomon*." *Narrative, Race, and Ethnicity in the United States*, edited by James J. Donahue, et al., Ohio State UP, 2017, pp. 43–56.

Rony, Fatimah Tobing. *The Third Eye: Race, Cinema, and Ethnographic Spectacle*. Duke UP, 1996.

Rosenblatt, Louise. "The Aesthetic Transaction." *The Journal of Aesthetic Education*, vol. 20, no. 4, 1986, pp. 122–28.

Rosenblatt, Louise. "The Transactional Theory of Reading and Writing." *Making Meanings with Texts: Selected Essays*. Heinemann, 2005, 1–37.

Rosenblatt, Louise. "Viewpoints: Transaction Versus Interaction—A Terminological Rescue Operation." *Making Meanings with Texts: Selected Essays*. Heinemann, 2005, 38–49.

Roszak, Suzanne. "Coming of Age in a Divided City: Cultural Hybridity and Ethnic Injustice in Sandra Cisneros and Veronica Roth." *Children's Literature*, vol. 44, 2016, pp. 61–77.

Roth, Philip. *The Plot against America*. Vintage International, 2004.

Royal, Derek Parker. "Introduction: Coloring America: Multi-Ethnic Engagements with Graphic Narrative." *MELUS*, vol. 32, no. 3, 2007, pp. 7–22.

Roye, Susmita. "Toni Morrison's Disrupted Girls and Their Disturbed Girlhoods: *The Bluest Eye* and *A Mercy*." *Callaloo: A Journal of African Diaspora Arts and Letters*, vol. 35, no. 1, 2012, pp. 212–27.

Saber, Yomna. "The Charged Strolls of the Brown Flâneuse in Sandra Cisneros's 'The House on Mango Street.'" *Pacific Coast Philology*, vol. 48, no. 1, 2013, pp. 69–87.

Saguisag, Lara. *Incorrigibles and Innocents: Constructing Childhood and Citizenship in Progressive Era Comics*. Rutgers UP, 2018.

Said, Edward W. *Orientalism*. Vintage Books, 1979.

Sánchez-Eppler, Karen. *Dependent States: The Child's Part in Nineteenth-Century American Culture*. U Chicago P, 2005.

Sartre, Jean-Paul. *Being and Nothingness*. Translated by Hazel E. Barnes. Washington Square Press, 1956.

Schieble, Melissa. "Reading Images in American Born Chinese through Critical Visual Literacy." *English Journal*, vol. 103, no. 5, 2014, pp. 47–52.

Schmid, Johannes C. P. "Graphic Nonviolence: Framing 'Good Trouble' in John Lewis' March." *European Journal of American Studies*, vol. 13, no. 4, 2018, https://journals.openedition.org/ejas/13922. Accessed 29 January 2024.

Schmidt, Gary D. *Making Americans: Children's Literature from 1930 to 1960*. U of Iowa P, 2013.

Schwebel, Sara L. *Child-Sized History: Fictions of the Past in U.S. Classrooms*. Vanderbilt UP, 2011.

Selig, Diana. *Americans All: The Cultural Gifts Movement*. Harvard UP, 2008.

Shaw, Robert, and Michael McIntyre. "Algoristic Foundations to Cognitive Psychology." *Cognition and the Symbolic Processes*, edited by W. B. Weimer and D. S. Palermo, Lawrence Erlbaum Associates, 1974, pp. 305–62.

Shaw, Robert, et al. "The Role of Symmetry in Event Perception." *Perception: Essays in Honor of James J. Gibson*, edited by Robert Brodie Macleod and Herbert L. Pick, Jr., Cornell UP, 1974, pp. 276–310.

Shiffman, Dan. "*The Plot against America* and History Post-9/11." *Philip Roth Studies*, vol. 5, no. 1, 2009, pp. 61–73.

Siegel, Jason. "*The Plot against America*: Philip Roth's Counter-Plot to American History." *MELUS*, vol. 37, no. 1, 2012, pp. 131–54.

Slivka, Jennifer A. "History and the 'I' Trapped in the Middle: Negotiating the Past in Roth's *The Ghost Writer* and *The Plot against America*." *Philip Roth Studies*, vol. 8, no. 2, 2012, pp. 127–44.

Smith, Betty. *A Tree Grows in Brooklyn*. 1943. Harper, 2005.

Smith, Judith E. *Visions of Belonging: Family Stories, Popular Culture, and Postwar Democracy, 1940–1960*. Columbia UP, 2004.

Smith, Shawn Michelle. "Guest Editor's Introduction: Visual Culture and Race." *Melus*, vol. 39, no. 2, 2014, pp. 1–11.

Smith, Shawn Michelle. *Photography on the Color Line: W. E. B. Du Bois, Race, and Visual Culture*. Duke UP, 2004.

Song, Min Hyoung. "'How Good It Is to Be a Monkey': Comics, Racial Formation, and *American Born Chinese*." *Mosaic: An Interdisciplinary Critical Journal*, vol. 43, no. 1, 2010, pp. 73–92.

Sorkin, Amy Davidson. "What Niya Kenny Saw." *New Yorker*, 10 October 2015, https://www.newyorker.com/news/amy-davidson/what-niya-kenny-saw. Accessed 15 October 2023.

Steedman, Carolyn. *Strange Dislocations: Childhood and the Idea of Human Interiority, 1780–1930*. Harvard UP, 1995.

Stelloh, Tim, and Tracy Connor. "Video Shows Cop Body-Slamming High School Girl in S.C. Classroom." *NBC News*, 26 October 2015, https://www.nbcnews.com/news/us-news/video-appears-show-cop-body-slamming-student-s-c-classroom-n451896. Accessed 10 April 2020.

Sweeney, Meghan M. "Checking Out America: Libraries as Agents of Acculturation in Three Mid-Century Girls' Books." *Children's Literature*, vol. 33, 2005, pp. 41–65.

Tait, Althea. "Empathy: 'The [Probing] Problem We All Live With.'" *Lion and the Unicorn*, vol. 43 no. 2, 2019, pp. 215–35.

Tait, Althea. "The Harm in Beauty: Toni Morrison's Revisions of Racialized Traditional Theories of Aesthetics in *The Bluest Eye*." *Globalizing Beauty: Consumerism and Body Aesthetics in the Twentieth Century*, edited by Hartmut Berghoff and Thomas Kühne, Palgrave Macmillan, 2013, pp. 75–89.

Taylor, Mildred D. *Roll of Thunder, Hear My Cry*. Puffin, 1991.

Taylor, Sydney. *All-of-a-Kind Family*. 1951. Yearling, 1984.

Thomas, Angie. *The Hate U Give*. Walker, 2017.

Tilley, Carol. "Seducing the Innocent: Fredric Wertham and the Falsifications That Helped Condemn Comics." *Information & Culture: A Journal of History*, vol. 47, no. 4, 2012, pp. 383–413.

Towns, Armond R. "Gamifying Blackness: From Slave Records to *Playing History: Slave Trade*." *Information, Communication, & Society*, vol. 24, no. 12, 2021, pp. 1814–28.

Tribunella, Eric L. "Benjamin, Benson, and the Child's Gaze: Childhood Desire and Pleasure in the David Blaize Books." *Pedagogy, Culture & Society*, vol. 24, no. 4, 2016, pp. 505–15.

Tribunella, Eric L. "Children's Literature and the Child Flâneur." *Children's Literature*, vol. 38, 2010, pp. 64–91.

Trites, Roberta S. *Disturbing the Universe: Power and Repression in Adolescent Literature*. U of Iowa P, 2000.

"United States Flag Code." *American Legion*, 2019, www.legion.org/flag/code. Accessed 29 January 2024.

Van Horn, Jennifer, et al. The Disability Gaze: Material and Visual Approaches. https://disabilitygaze2022.squarespace.com/. Accessed 26 November 2022.

Vásquez, Sam. "In Her Own Image: Literary and Visual Representations of Girlhood in Toni Morrison's *The Bluest Eye* and Jamaica Kincaid's *Annie John*." *Meridians: feminism, race, transnationalism*, vol. 12, no. 1, 2014, pp. 58–87.
Wall, Anthony. "Characters in Bakhtin's Theory." *Studies in 20th Century Literature*, Special Issue on Mikhail Bakhtin, vol. 9, no. 1, 1984, pp. 1–16.
Wanzo, Rebecca. "Identity Temporalities and *American Born Chinese*." *Inks: The Journal of the Comics Studies Society*, vol. 4, no. 1, 2020, pp. 82–100.
Werrlein, Debra T. "Not So Fast, Dick and Jane: Reimagining Childhood and Nation in *The Bluest Eye*." *MELUS*, vol. 30, no. 4, 2005, pp. 53–72.
Whitted, Qiana. "'And the Negro Thinks in Hieroglyphs': Comics, Visual Metonymy, and the Spectacle of Blackness." *Journal of Graphic Novels and Comics*, vol. 5, no. 1, pp. 75–100. Tandfonline.com.
Wilkie-Stibbs, Christine. *The Outside Child In and Out of the Book*. Routledge, 2008.
Wondra, Janet. "A Gaze Unbecoming: Schooling the Child for Femininity in Days of Heaven." *Wide Angle*, vol. 16, no. 4, 1994, pp. 4–23.
Wright, Nazera Sadiq. *Black Girlhood in the Nineteenth Century*. U of Illinois P, 2016.
Yancy, George. *Black Bodies, White Gazes: The Continuing Significance of Race*. Rowman and Littlefield, 2008.
Yang, Gene Luen. *American Born Chinese*. First Second, 2006.
Yoo, Hyun-Joo. "Reconstructing Asian American Male Masculinity in *American Born Chinese*." *Journal of Narrative Theory*, vol. 52, no. 2, 2022, pp. 160–80.
Yoo, Hyun-Joo. "Rewriting American History in *Roll of Thunder, Hear My Cry*: Metahistoricity, the Postcolonial Subject, and the Return of the Repressed." *Children's Literature in Education*, vol. 50, no. 3, pp. 333–46.
Zelinzer, Viviana A. *Pricing the Priceless Child: The Changing Social Value of Children*. Princeton UP, 1994.

INDEX

Abate, Michelle Ann, 138, 169
activism, 121; in *All American Boys*, 19, 122, 130; antiracist, 101, 143; and appreciative child gaze, 23; in *Call Me Charley*, 80; civil rights, 141, 146; and cultural gifts movement, 27, 176n5; in *March*, 142, 146; in *Roll of Thunder, Hear My Cry*, 78, 98; and World War II, 28
adult gaze, 7
adultification, 55
agency, 178n13; in *Bass Reeves*, 135, 137, 148, 152, 153; in *The Bluest Eye*, 116; of children, 12, 14, 17, 18, 55, 106; and countersurveillant child gaze, 59; in *The House on Mango Street*, 113, 114; and Mildred D. Taylor, 70; oppositional, 98; personal, 8, 18, 60, 61; in "Red-Headed Baby," 92; and transactional child gaze, 18, 53
All American Boys (Reynolds and Kiely): belonging in, 16; dual narration in, 19; and transactional child gaze, 101, 107, 121–31
All-of-a-Kind Family (Taylor), 176n5; and appreciative child gaze, 17, 30–35, 41, 52, 53, 99; belonging in, 16; genre of, 24
allohistory, 3, 15, 57, 81–83, 86–88, 94, 172
Althusser, Louis, 98, 105
America/American: canon, 169; child, 4, 23, 25, 26, 29, 54, 88, 133; childhood, 28, 65, 70, 85, 115; flag, 68, 72, 178n16; heroism, 83; identity, 30, 33, 84, 86, 129; literature, 16, 61, 181n12; paradise, 87; revolution, 5. *See also* United States

American Born Chinese (Yang), 3, 158, 172, 182n9; and direct child gaze, 158, 159, 162, 164, 165; and transactional child gaze, 19, 136, 137, 141, 167, 168
antiracism, 42, 52; antiracist, 42, 98, 101, 121, 130, 136, 137, 143, 145, 153, 155, 162, 169
anti-Semitism, 81, 84, 87, 88, 94
Anzaldúa, Gloria, 110, 111, 113, 180n8
approximation, 56
attensity, 104, 106, 115; in *All American Boys*, 122, 126, 127; in *The Bluest Eye*, 132; in *The House on Mango Street*, 110; and transactional child gaze, 132
attunement, 106, 128. *See also* education of attention
autobiography, 15, 137, 162
Aydin, Andrew, 19, 136, 137, 141, 147

Bakhtin, Mikhail, 11, 103
Baldwin, James, 59, 177n7, 177n12; and *Little Man, Little Man*, 16, 17, 19, 21, 24, 22, 25, 42–52, 97, 176n6; and *Go Tell It on the Mountain*, 172; and "A Talk to Teachers," 43, 48
Barthes, Roland, 18, 104, 110
Bass Reeves, 19, 182n1; and comics, 134–36; and countersurveillant child gaze, 133, 136, 137, 141, 148–60; as nonfiction, 172
Beeck, Nathalie op de, 140
Being and Nothingness (Sartre), 13
Berger, John, 83, 84, 179n22, 180n3
Bernstein, Robin, 5, 15, 55, 69, 80
biography, 15, 51, 169; biographers, 133

195

Birchbark House, The (Erdrich), 52
Black Bodies, White Gazes (Yancy), 59
Black Lives Matter, 16
Black Looks (hooks), 7–9
Black Power movement, 71, 78
Black studies, 71, 78
Blau, Julia J. C., 67, 180n4
Blume, Judy, 17
Boggs, Nicholas, 44, 176n6, 177n7, 177n10
Boulley, Angeline, 171
Boy Meets Boy (Levithan), 52
Brink, Carol Ryrie, 171
Brooklyn, New York, 3, 17, 24, 25, 36–41, 132
Browne, Simone, 17, 59, 76
Brown Girl Dreaming (Woodson), 171
Brown v. Board of Education, 66, 70
Bush, George W., 88
busing crisis, 71, 178n14
Bluest Eye, The (Morrison), 19, 98, 101, 107, 114, 115–21, 181nn16–17

Cadden, Mike, 14
Caddie Woodlawn (Brink), 171
California, 3, 158
Call Me Charley (Jackson), 16, 18, 84, 105, 132; and appreciative child gaze, 40; and countersurveillant child gaze, 56, 63–70, 79, 80, 93; and focalization, 11; and historical context, 14; and surveillant child gaze, 171; and transactional child gaze, 132
Capetta, Emily Rose, 104, 180n4
Capshaw, Katharine, 5
caricature, 91, 124, 139, 140, 145, 150
Caron, Tim, 139
Cazac, Yoran: and appreciative child gaze, 42, 43, 45–52; and *Little Man, Little Man*, 21, 22, 24, 25, 42, 43, 45–52, 97, 177n12
Chaney, Michael, 138, 139, 182n6; and graphic narrative, 135, 138; and *March*, 145, 146, 148
character rhetoric, 11–14; mimetic, 12, 23, 53, 57, 66, 69, 82, 93, 114; synthetic, 12, 23, 53, 57, 66, 69, 82, 89, 93; thematic, 12, 23, 53, 57, 66, 69, 78, 89, 93, 172

Chicago, Illinois, 19, 108, 113
childhood studies, 15
children's literature, 14–17, 28, 30, 69, 79
Children's Table, The (Duane), 8
Christianity, 6, 9, 170; in *All-of-a-Kind Family*, 25, 30, 33; and appreciative child gaze, 17, 23; and countersurveillant child gaze, 88, 95–96; in *The Plot against America*, 4, 83; in *A Tree Grows in Brooklyn*, 36, 37, 39
Chute, Hillary, 138, 140
Cisneros, Sandra, 180n7; and exceptional child, 120; and *The House on Mango Street*, 16, 19, 101, 107–11, 113, 114, 131, 132
Civil Rights Act of 1964, 70
civil rights movement, 56, 79, 137, 145, 182n5
Cold War, 16, 26, 28, 176n5; and boyhood, 64; in *Call Me Charley*, 63, 68, 70; and children's literature, 28, 177n5; and defense initiatives, 29; and Jesse Jackson, 63; and Sydney Taylor, 30
Communism, 30; Communist Party, 28
counterstory, 62; counternarrative, 44, 83
Crawford-Garrett, Katherine, 109
critical race narratology, 13. *See also* narrative theory
critical race studies, 13
critical race theory, 13, 15, 62
cultural gifts movement, 17, 25–29, 176n5. *See also* Selig, Diana
Cummins, June, 30, 34, 176n5

Dark Matters (Browne), 59
Davis, Angela, 59
Davis-McElligatt, Joanna C., 142
Dawkins, Laura, 93
Day, Sara K., 6, 14
Days of Heaven (Malick film), 15
Dewey, John, 18, 100, 103, 180n2
Diawara, Manthia, 150
dilation, 4, 32, 40, 65, 68, 72, 86, 118, 180n11
direct gaze: in *American Born Chinese*, 4, 136, 137, 141, 158–62, 164–68; in *Bass Reeves*, 150, 154, 155, 159; and comics, 160. *See also* fourth wall

disability studies, 19, 172, 182n1
Discipline and Punish (Foucault), 58
discourse, 5, 11, 19, 20, 27, 60, 98, 104, 140, 170, 176n6; American, 33, 86; in *Bass Reeves*, 136, 152; in *Call Me Charley*, 63; and radical liberalism, 28; and transactional child gaze, 99, 131, 180n1; verbal-visual, 136
Donahue, James J., 13
double consciousness, 59, 60, 153
Douglas, Aaron, 124, 125
drama, 19, 173
dramatic irony, 77, 118, 120
Duane, Anna Mae, 5, 8
Du Bois, W. E. B., 17, 59, 60

ecological perception theory, 15, 18, 67, 100, 104, 119; and visual perception, 67, 102, 106, 180n6
education of attention, 106, 127. *See also* attunement
ekphrasis, 43, 50, 86, 94, 96, 135
Ellison, Ralph, 59
Elkins, James, 18, 103, 104, 123
embodiment, 8–10, 12–15, 104, 172; and adult gaze, 7, 59, 109, 172; in *All-of-a-Kind Family*, 31; in *Bass Reeves*, 151; in *Black Bodies, White Gazes*, 59, 91; and comics, 135, 148; in *The House on Mango Street*, 108; in *Roll of Thunder, Hear My Cry*, 74
Emezi, Akwaeke, 172
Erdrich, Louise, 52
ethnocentrism, 41, 78, 139, 140, 162
ethos, 108, 113, 125, 138
exceptionality: in *All-of-a-Kind Family*, 34; in *The Bluest Eye*, 115; in *The House on Mango Street*, 101, 108, 114, 120, 131
Eysturoy, Annie O., 108

Fanon, Frantz, 59
Fields, Ben, 54
film, 7, 59, 60, 177n4; and advertising, 16; critics, 146; *Days of Heaven*, 15; and drama, 19, 173; and point-of-view, 160
Firekeeper's Daughter, The (Boulley), 171

Fitzhugh, Louise, 15
Flake, Sharon, 107
Fludernik, Monika, 159
focalization, 13, 20, 40, 69, 122, 177n7; in *The Bluest Eye*, 118, 181n15; in *Call Me Charley*, 11, 12, 64; in *Little Man, Little Man*, 44; in *The Plot against America*, 57, 81, 84; in "Red-Headed Baby," 12, 89, 92; in *A Tree Grows in Brooklyn*, 38; in *The Ways of White Folks*, 81
foil, 115, 118
Foucault, Michel, 17, 58, 60, 172
Fourth of July, 34, 35, 83
free indirect discourse, 15, 177n7; in *All-of-a-Kind Family*, 31; in *The Bluest Eye*, 116; in *Little Man, Little Man*, 47; in "Red-Headed Baby," 57, 81, 89–91; in *A Tree Grows in Brooklyn*, 37
Freeman, Eugene, 102
Freud, Sigmund, 59; post-Freudian, 16
Forever (Blume), 172
fourth wall, 137, 159, 161; in *American Born Chinese*, 158, 168; in *Bass Reeves*, 155; and second-person narration, 136. *See also* direct gaze
futurity, 96

Garland-Thomson, Rosemary, 172
Gateward, Frances, 139
Gibson, Eleanor, 180n6
Gibson, James J., 67
Gill, Joel Christian, 19, 134, 136, 137, 148–58; as a comics artist, 133
Giver, The (Lowry), 172
Goffman, Erving, 165
Go Tell It on the Mountain (Baldwin), 172
graphic narrative, 19, 135, 136, 138–40, 145, 169; graphic memoir, 141, 145; graphic novel, 3, 19, 169
Great Depression, 16, 71, 94
Groensteen, Theirry, 139
Gubar, Marah, 82, 106, 175n3

Hall, Jacqueline Dowd, 56
Harlem Renaissance, 93, 124

Harriet the Spy (Fitzhugh), 15
Hartley-Kroeger, Fiona, 180n8
Hattori, Tomo, 158, 167
Hayes, Emma, 15
Heer, Jeet, 139
hierarchy, 4, 8, 10, 24, 26, 54, 111, 170, 173; in *American Born Chinese*, 168; and appreciative child gaze, 29, 35, 52; in *The Bluest Eye*, 117; and countersurveillant child gaze, 55, 59, 61, 75; and Foucault, 58; in *The House on Mango Street*, 110, 113, 131; racial, 3, 66, 72, 162, 179n25; in "Red-Headed Baby," 89; social, 79; and transactional child gaze, 99; in *A Tree Grows in Brooklyn*, 36, 41
historical fiction, 3, 15, 56, 71, 169
Hitler, Adolf, 85, 86, 139
Ho, Jennifer Ann, 13, 171
Hogan, Patrick Colm, 13
Homestead 24, 85, 88
hooks, bell, 17, 175n4, 177n3, 180n3; and *Art on the Mind*, 146; and *Black Looks*, 7–9, 60, 61, 120, 173; and photographs, 145; and "Representing Whiteness in the Black Imagination," 61, 157
House on Mango Street, The (Cisneros), 16, 19, 101, 107, 181n12; and transactional child gaze, 108–14; and window motif, 180n10
How I Became a Ghost (Tingle), 171
Hughes, Langston: and countersurveillant child gaze, 89, 90, 92–94; and "Red-Headed Baby" 12, 18, 57, 81, 89, 90, 92–94, 96; and transactional child gaze, 97; and *The Ways of White Folks*, 18

ICE, 16
iconography, 140
ideological surround, 9, 19, 98–101, 109, 115, 116, 119, 121, 123–25, 131, 132, 135, 136, 141, 143, 146, 148, 158, 161, 172
illocutionary force, 135, 157
immigration, 16; immigrant, 16, 27, 35–37, 41
innocence, 5, 6, 95–96; in *The Bluest Eye*, 115; in *Call Me Charley*, 69; child, 56; and countersurveillant child gaze, 54, 95–96; and experience, 57, 63; in *The Plot against America*, 84; racial, 5, 55; in "Red-Headed Baby," 92, in *Roll of Thunder, Hear My Cry*, 70, 76, 77, 80
interlocutor, 41, 135, 136, 142, 152, 165, 167
interpellation, 98, 99, 101, 105, 106; in *American Born Chinese*, 167; in *The Bluest Eye*, 114–16, 119–21, 131. See also Althusser, Louis

Jackson, Jesse, 178n7; and *Call Me Charley*, 11, 16, 18, 40, 64, 68, 79, 80, 93, 176n9; and countersurveillant child gaze, 56, 63, 65, 67; and *Roll of Thunder, Hear My Cry*, 70; and transactional child gaze, 132
Jagoda, Patrick, 140
Jennings, John, 139
Jim Crow, 61, 70, 89, 91, 155
Jones, Claudia, 59

Keen, Susan, 13
Kennedy, John F., 145
Kiely, Brendan, 16, 19, 101, 107, 121, 122, 124, 125, 128, 130, 181n17
Kim, Sue J., 13
King, Martin Luther, Jr., 143, 145, 148, 182n5
kinship model of child-adult relations, 82, 94
Kokkola, Lydia, 7

Last Night at the Telegraph Club (Lo), 172
Last Stop on Market Street (Peña), 52, 173
Leeming, David, 51
L'Engle, Madeline, 172
Levander, Caroline F., 5, 6
Levithan, David, 52
Lewis, John, 19, 136, 137, 141–48
Lindbergh, Charles, 81, 83–85, 87
Little House on the Prairie (Ingalls), 171
Little Man, Little Man (Baldwin and Cazac), 17, 176n6; and appreciative child gaze, 21–26, 42–52; Harlem, 17, 21, 22, 24, 25, 42–44, 48, 51, 177n10; as a picture book, 16
Lo, Melinda, 172

logos, 96, 114, 125
Lowry, Lois, 172

Ma, Ning, 158
Mann, Steve, 55
March (Aydin, Lewis, Powell), 19, 137, 182n5; and appreciative child gaze, 136, 141–48; as nonfiction, 172
Marx, Gary T., 7, 58, 61, 62
May, Elaine Tyler, 26
McIntyre, Michael, 104, 127
Melamed, Jodi, 29, 42, 48, 51
metacommentary, 39, 86, 152
metonymy, 93, 135, 146, 148
Mickenberg, Julia, 5, 17, 28, 176n3, 176n5
Mikkonen, Kai, 159, 165
Mildorf, Jarmila, 161
minstrel, 133, 135, 137, 139, 149, 150–53, 155, 157, 158
Mintz, Steve, 64
mise-en-page, 138, 150
Mitchell, W. J. T., 87
Monahan, Torin, 58, 62
Morgan, Shaun, 13, 14
Morris, Monique, 54
Morrison, Toni, 19, 98, 101, 107, 114, 116, 118–20, 181n13; and transactional child gaze, 115, 120
Murphy, Emily A., 5
museum silence, 63, 64, 68, 69, 132, 176n9

Nakamura, Suzy, 163
narration: dual, 15, 19, 130; first-person, 15, 20, 36, 70, 78, 98, 108, 112, 115, 118, 141, 160, 177n7; second-person, 15, 20, 36, 136, 137, 159–62, 165–68; third person, 11, 15, 20, 36, 37, 44, 63, 64, 69, 90, 97, 114, 118, 159, 181n15, 181n17; verbal narration, 45, 51, 164; verbal-visual, 19, 133, 136, 137, 148, 155, 159, 173
narrative levels: diegetic, 4, 12, 18, 23, 24, 29, 52, 56, 57, 62, 63, 68, 80, 88, 91, 96, 101, 107, 114, 115, 121, 131, 135, 136, 143, 147, 152, 158, 166, 168, 175n6; extradiegetic, 4, 12, 56, 57, 63, 70, 91, 101, 107, 114, 131, 136, 152, 175n6; extratextual, 4, 12, 24, 121, 131, 136, 175n6
narrative theory, 4, 10, 13–15, 19. *See also* critical race narratology; rhetorical narrative theory
Nash, Diane, 145
national belonging, 4–6, 11, 15, 20, 100, 106, 136, 141, 168, 170, 171; in *All American Boys*, 16, 29; in *All-of-a-Kind Family*, 25; in *American Born Chinese*, 168; and appreciative child gaze, 23; in *Call Me Charley*, 70; and countersurveillant child gaze, 55, 56; in *The Plot against America*, 16, 83, 87, 88; in "Red-Headed Baby," 93; in *Roll of Thunder, Hear My Cry*, 79
neoliberalism, 100
Nodelman, Perry, 122, 129, 181n17

Obama, Barack, 141
ontological position, 59, 160, 161, 168
Orientalism, 40
Ortega, Gema, 116
Owen, Gabrielle, 107, 181n20

Passover, 34, 35
pathos, 32, 39, 57, 70, 76, 80, 81, 86, 96, 125
patriotism, 26–28, 37, 64, 83, 87
Paxton, Alexandra, 67
Peña, Matt de la, 52, 173
Pérez, Roy, 14, 56
perlocutionary, 157
Pet (Emezi), 172
Phelan, Jim, 13, 178n11
photographs: and bell hooks, 145, 146; and James Elkins, 124; in *March*, 143, 145, 146; and Roland Barthes, 104
picture book, 16, 21, 22, 24, 25, 42, 43, 51, 52, 173, 177n7, 177n11
Plot against America, The (Roth), 16, 18, 57, 105, 179n21, 179n25; and allohistory, 3; and countersurveillant child gaze, 81–89; and kinship model of adult-child relations, 94; and transactional child gaze, 132
police brutality, 16, 107, 122–24, 128, 130

postmodern metatextuality, 161
Powell, Nathan, 19, 136, 137, 141
punctum, 104, 110, 116, 119
purity, 55, 94–95

queer theory, 13, 15, 19, 172

Rabinowitz, Peter J., 11
racism: anti-Asian, 136, 141, 159, 162, 167; anti-Black, 42, 63, 66, 93, 94, 101, 114, 121, 128, 130, 131, 136, 139, 141, 149, 150, 152, 157, 158; anti-Blackness, 94, 114
Raisin in the Sun, A, 173
reader-viewer, 139, 146, 148, 155, 158, 160–63, 168, 169
realistic fiction, 15, 19, 81
"Red-Headed Baby" (Hughes), 12, 57, 81; and countersurveillant child gaze, 89–97; from *The Ways of White Folks*, 18, 57
Red Scare, 28
Refaie, Elisabeth El, 158
relationality, 10, 109, 131, 181n20
Rembowska-Płuciennik, Magdalena, 159
Reynolds, Jason, 16, 19, 101, 107, 121, 122, 124, 128, 130, 181n17
rhetorical narrative theory, 10, 178n11. *See also* character rhetoric
Rimmon-Kenan, Shlomith, 11, 69
Robinson, Christian, 52
Rogoff, Irit, 9, 17, 18, 58–60, 106
Roll of Thunder, Hear My Cry (Taylor), 3, 18, 56, 105, 178n12; and countersurveillant child gaze, 70–81, 84, 93, 94; and transactional child gaze, 98
Romagnolo, Catherine, 13
Romantic Child, 18, 38, 55, 85, 94
Rony, Fatimah Tobing, 9, 17, 60
Rosenbergs, 30
Rosenblatt, Louise, 18, 100, 102, 104, 180n2, 180n9. *See also* transaction
Roth, Philip, 3, 16, 18, 57, 81, 82, 85–89, 94, 105, 132, 179nn21–22, 179n24
Royal, Derek Parker, 135, 140
Rustin, Bayard, 145

Sabbath, 32
Saber, Yomna, 109
Saguisag, Lara, 5, 140, 141
Sánchez-Eppler, Karen, 5, 105
Sartre, Jean Paul, 13, 91–93
Schieble, Melissa, 167
Schmid, Johannes C. P., 142
scripts, 5, 13, 41, 51, 88, 99, 131
Secret Garden, The (Burnett), 15
segregation: de facto, 16, 66, 71; de jure, 16, 66, 71
selective attention, 104
Selig, Diana, 17, 26–28
semiautobiographical novel, 3, 24, 25, 162
Shaw, Robert, 104, 106, 127
Shawl, Nisi, 172
side-eye, 134, 135, 155
Siegel, Jason, 83
Singley, Carol J., 5, 6
Skin I'm In, The (Flake), 107
Slivka, Jennifer A., 83
Smith, Betty, 3, 16, 17, 41, 171; and appreciative child gaze, 24, 25, 36–39; and transactional child gaze, 132
Smith, Judith, 36–37
Smith, Shawn Michelle, 9, 59
social cognition theory, 159
sociopolitical environment, 3, 13–15, 171, 173; and appreciative child gaze, 29; in *Call Me Charley*, 74; and the Cold War, 63; and countersurveillant child gaze, 18, 55, 80, 95–96; in *The Plot against America*, 84, 87, 179n25
Song, Min Hyoung, 139, 158
Speculation (Shawl), 172
Steeves, Valerie, 7
storyworld, 8–10, 12, 13, 42, 70, 79, 101, 114, 159, 160, 174, 175n6
subjectivity, 16, 101, 102; in *All American Boys*, 122, 125, 126, 130; in *All-of-a-Kind Family*, 99; in *American Born Chinese*, 162, 167, 168; and appreciative child gaze, 44; in *Being and Nothingness*, 13; in *The Bluest Eye*, 115–18, 131, 181n15; child, 60, 81; and countersurveillant child gaze,

93; in *The House on Mango Street*, 110, 112, 113; in "Red-Headed Baby," 91; and transactional child gaze, 10, 18, 98–100, 105, 172; in *A Tree Grows in Brooklyn*, 38
surveillance, 17, 18, 55, 56, 58–62, 64–66, 68, 70, 72, 75, 76, 78, 85, 88, 95–96, 178n7; and children, 7; contemporary surveillance studies, 58, 177n2; and social sorting, 57; and sousveillance, 54, 61; top-down surveillance, 55, 95
systemic inequities, 30, 55, 108; in *All American Boys*, 129; and appreciative child gaze, 30; and systemic racism, 63, 67, 131, 168

Tait, Althea, 94
"Talk to Teachers, A" (Baldwin), 43, 48
Tarbox, Gwen Athene, 138
Taylor, Mildred D., 3, 17, 19, 56, 57, 70, 71, 73, 78, 79, 93, 94, 97, 178nn12–13, 178n16, 179n20
Taylor, Sydney, 16, 17, 24, 30–34, 41, 97, 176n5
tenement, 3, 17, 24, 25, 30, 33, 35, 36, 38, 39, 41
Till, Emmett, 61, 179n18
Tingle, Tim, 171
transaction: aesthetic, 100; visual, 100, 110, 114, 117, 118, 122, 123, 125, 127, 129, 131, 162. *See also* Rosenblatt, Louise
Tribunella, Eric L., 15
Trites, Roberta Seelinger, 105, 130
Tree Grows in Brooklyn, A (Smith), 16, 17, 106, 171; and appreciative child gaze, 25, 36–42, 52, 132; as a semiautobiographical novel, 3, 24

United States: childhood, 55; culture, 5–7, 17, 26; identity, 5, 88; ideologies, 12, 82, 131, 158, 180n1; imaginary, 9, 20; imagination, 14; 52; literature, 4, 5, 14, 19, 25, 30, 52, 98, 170, 173. *See also* America/American

visual culture studies, 4, 9, 15, 17, 100, 103
visual discourse, 63, 98, 131, 140, 152; visual narrative, 135, 145, 160; visual rhyme, 159
visual pedagogy, 137–40, 152, 155, 167

Wall, Anthony, 103
Wanzo, Rebecca, 140
Ways of White Folks, The (Hughes), 18, 57, 81
Western ideology, 9, 14, 105, 107
Weston, Mikayla L., 67
white gaze, 9, 58, 59, 91, 145; in *All American Boys*, 125; in *All-of-a-Kind Family*, 33; in *Roll of Thunder, Hear My Cry*, 72; and George Yancy, 9
whiteness, 27, 37, 106, 157; in *American Born Chinese*, 137; in *The Bluest Eye*, 117–19, 121; Christian, 36; in *The House on Mango Street*, 112; in *A Tree Grows in Brooklyn*, 41
Whitted, Qiana, 139, 140
Wilder, Laura Ingalls, 171
witness, 60; in *All American Boys*, 122, 124, 126–30; in *American Born Chinese*, 141; in *All-of-a-Kind Family*, 32; and appreciative child gaze, 24, 44; in *Bass Reeves*, 158; in *Call Me Charley*, 63, 68; and countersurveillant child gaze, 55, 56, 89; in *The House on Mango Street*, 181n11; in *Little Man, Little Man*, 25, 41, 44, 49–51; in *March*, 145; in *Roll of Thunder, Hear My Cry*, 71, 72, 75, 78; and transactional child gaze, 131; in *A Tree Grows in Brooklyn*, 38, 40, 41
Wrinkle in Time, A (L'Engle), 172
Wondra, Janet, 15
world line, 104, 180n4
World War II, 16, 27–29, 37, 139
Woodson, Jacqueline, 171

Yancy, George, 9, 17, 59–61, 72, 91, 119
Yang, Gene Luen, 3, 19, 136, 137, 158–68, 182n9
Yiddish, 33, 40
young adult literature, 6, 15, 181n17

Zelinzer, Viviana, 17, 26, 29

ABOUT THE AUTHOR

Amanda M. Greenwell is associate professor of English at Central Connecticut State University. Her work has appeared in journals such as *African American Review*; *Children's Literature*; *Jeunesse: Young People, Texts, Cultures*; *Lion and the Unicorn*; *Studies in the Novel*; *Studies in the American Short Story*; and other publications.

www.ingramcontent.com/pod-product-compliance
Lightning Source LLC
Chambersburg PA
CBHW022019220426
43663CB00007B/1144